INSIDE

Letters from the World's Largest Prison System

Edited by Chuck Brown

PublishingWorks, Inc.
2008

PublishingWorks, Inc.,
60 Winter Street
Exeter, NH 03833
603-778-9883
For Sales and Orders:
1-800-738-6603 or 603-772-7200

Designed by:
LCCN: 2007936921
ISBN: 1-933002-64-6
ISBN-13: 978-1-933002-64-4

To Lee, my devoted wife of forty-five wonderful years, who has provided indisputable and continued encouragement to begin and complete this venture. You have inspired me to achieve limitless goals. Your devotion, love, and friendship, along with your caring and thoughtful spirit, have made our days together an enormous gift. You have been my pillar of support; without you, I would not be who I am today.

I love you, I have always respected you, and I look forward to spending the rest of our days together.

ACKNOWLEDGMENTS

There is a definite process by which one makes people into friends, and it involves talking to them and listening to them for perhaps hours at a time. To be a good friend depends not upon fancy, imagination, or sentiment, but upon character.

When you come to understand a person and the burdens he may bear, and you're aware of the fight he is making and the trouble he faces, and you come to learn that he is different than you thought him to be, somehow you begin to realize that whatever his faults may be, they are trivial when compared to his character. As you grow to understand him, you begin to see the texture of his good side, and your prejudice and prejudgment start to disappear. You will begin to find his virtues and overlook his shortcomings. We must always be conscious that dignity is our birthright, and as human beings, we are all entitled to human rights regardless of what we've done in the past.

It is true that we are a nation of many religions, and yet we seem to lean toward warehousing offenders versus rehabilitating them so they may be accepted as they reenter our society. This book is dedicated to all the men (my friends) who have contributed to making this book possible, and to all other men and women who are serving time in the world's largest prison system. Please take the time to listen to their words. You may be surprised at what they have to say.

Abelardo
Adam
Anthony
Arnold
Augustine

Bill
Billy (2)
Bob
Bruce

Carlos
Charles (2)
Charlie
Christopher (3)
Curtis

Dan
Daniel
David
Dennis
Doug
Dutch

Ed
Edward
Ernie

Garnet
Gary
Gene
George
Gil

Hank
Harry
Henry

Jackson
James
Jason
Jeff
Jessi
Jim
Joe
Joel
John
Johnathan

Keith
Kent
Ken

Lou

Marcos
Mark (3)
Martin
Mat
Mike

Nelson
Nick

Oscar

Patrick (2)
Paul
Peter
Philip

Reil
Rob
Robert (2)
Robin
Russ

Smitty
Stephen
Steven (2)

Thomas
Tomas
Tony
Ty

Wayne
Will
Wilson

TABLE OF CONTENTS

FOREWORD

For many, the word *prison* alone is unnerving, but imagine asking, "How would you like to visit a prison with me?" This often results in dead silence. When most people think of prison, they envision confrontation with dangerous people, or a condemned killer walking to the electric chair. Most individuals would be surprised to learn that there are many good, spiritual men and women in prison.

Ironically, I began my professional career with the Federal Bureau of Investigation in New York City, and as a member of the FBI, I actively participated in the apprehension, prosecution, and imprisonment of criminal offenders. During my tenure, I entered a Special Employee program designed and implemented to recruit individuals who met the FBI's qualification standards, and who were enthusiastic about becoming Special Agents. The Special Employee program involved three years of intensive training in all aspects of the Bureau's province, which at the time was comprised of Criminal, Subversive, Espionage, and Administration divisions. Upon successful completion of a college degree, the Bureau's three-year curriculum, and superior proficiency reports, the candidate was entitled to enter the FBI Academy at Quantico, Virginia.

My career extended into the private sector when I was recruited by Coopers and Lybrand's management consulting practice (now known as PricewaterhouseCoopers (or PwC), where I was responsible for managing numerous multifaceted and multimillion-dollar contracts, both in the private and public sectors.

Today, as a retiree, I am a member of the Catholic Diocese of Richmond Prison Ministry Advisory Committee, and I care for and visit offenders in prison. I believe that every human being has an inviolable dignity, value, and worth, regardless of race, gender, class, or any other characteristic. Each of us is born with free will that must be nurtured and informed by spiritual, emotional, intellectual, and physical disciplines. It follows that we must respect the life and dignity of every human being, even the perpetrators of terrible acts. This is not to say that offenders should not be punished—by all means, they should be—but the punishment should be consistent with the demands of justice and with respect for human life and dignity.

Regrettably, our society seems to prefer punishment to rehabilitation failing to recognize prisoners as human beings. Building new prisons to warehouse offenders without adequate treatment programs is not the answer. It creates an injustice for the victims as well as the offender because it often leads the offender to recidivism. From a broken home in an inner-city housing project to the troubled neighborhood on the wrong side of the tracks, or the hollow walls of drug dens and back-street clusters, the environment from which a convict comes is often that to which he returns. Divesting prisoners of their human rights, including adequate treatment for their illness while imprisoned, results in building more resentment and adds to recidivism rates once the prisoners are released or paroled. Any system of justice should provide whatever is necessary to enable inmates to live with dignity as they reenter society. To be excluded or neglected by friends and family only serves to further isolate victims and damage their self-respect. One of the most significant changes in the criminal justice system over the last few decades has been the increase in the number of those incarcerated. Twenty-five to thirty years ago, there were approximately 250,000 people in prisons in the United States. Today, there are well over two million people serving time behind the razor-wire fence, a tenfold increase in the prison population. The rate of recidivism among the incarcerated is staggering. It has been estimated that two-thirds of inmates will be rearrested within three years of their release. When you combine those numbers with all the public policy changes over the last thirty years or so, it is no wonder we have an inflated prison population. The U.S. Bureau of Justice Statistics projection estimate for state and federal prisons reveals that the system is expected to grow by 13 percent in the next four years (2008–2011), at an additional cost of $27.5 billion. By 2011, the number of women prisoners will have grown by 16 percent.

The male prison population will have increased by 12 percent. These numbers are at least twice the projected growth rate for the overall U.S. population by 2011.

For many years, society has taken a hard line about restoring felons' rights—even to the extent of saying it should be difficult for felons to regain their franchise. Depriving people of their rights while imprisoned is an important part of punishment. But after an individual has done his time, finished his probation or parole, and proven himself ready to be reintegrated into society, he should be welcomed back, not shunned. Everyone is entitled to a second chance.

There is evidence in the last four years that state agencies, local government, and private religious organizations are at last paying attention to prisoner reentry needs. The growing cost of prisons in America have politicians and policy makers in Washington and in state houses across the nation focusing more attention on how to keep inmates from returning to prison after they are released. In November 2007, a bill was passed in Congress called "The Second Chance Act," which had bipartisan support. And, in March 2008, after the bill was introduced to the Senate, it was passed unanimously. On April 9, 2008, the President of the United States signed the bill into law. The intent of the act is to reduce the number of repeat offenders by helping prisoners successfully reenter their communities.

There is a growing movement to introduce faith-based programs into prison. It's been shown that these programs can reduce recidivism, resulting in less violence. If we ignore the introduction of faith-based programs, we are losing out on their potential benefits for prisoners, and for society as a whole.

Many of the prisoners I visit suffer from extreme loneliness. They have been deserted by family and friends, and often consider volunteers their only family. And while many people may be intolerant of those who have committed crimes, I think of some of those I visit as sons, some as brothers, and all as companions. Some will never see the outside of their prison walls again, yet some will; as a volunteer, I am hopeful that in some small way, I will make a difference in their lives, and in what they will become once they are back on the outside.

One inmate recently wrote to me: *"Volunteers will see the man or woman, the child of God, the forgotten or abandoned by family and friends, come together in the spirit of fellowship and faith to worship and praise God."* He further states,

To many of us, this is the only "visit" we get behind this razor wire . . . Our faith is strengthened by such people who see the pain, suffering, brokenness, and humanity that exists in prison. God bless these volunteers. I challenge churches to take up Jesus's instruction to visit the imprisoned. You may be surprised at what you find there.

And, now as you turn the pages of this book, you will come to know some of these men who are trying to turn their lives around. In my two-plus years as a volunteer, I have written and received over fifteen hundred letters from inmates. This book is a compilation of some of those letters. Some of the letter writers admit they have received justice for the crimes they committed; others are convinced of injustices handed down to them through the bureaucracy of the criminal justice system. Many of the men write of how faith-based programs in prison have changed their lives.

In these letters from the inside, you will read about some who are still searching for God's forgiveness, and others who cannot forgive themselves. You will hear from those who will never see outside their prison walls, and who have accepted their place in the world, and from those who look forward to a new life for themselves on the outside. You will read about those who seek the same love and forgiveness that we all seek in our own lives. I hope you will be enriched by their words, and find hope in these pages.

SOCIAL JUSTIFICATION

Our history tells us that the prison system was in some ways built on a moral vision of how humans should behave in society—that the prison system combined spiritual rekindling with punishment and correction. However, sexual and physical behavior among inmates and corrections officers, gang violence, racial division, the absence of adequate treatment programs, the increasing use of isolation units, and society's willingness to sentence children to adult prisons are all contributing factors that add to a high rate of recidivism. We are all sinners, and our response to sin and failure should not be abandonment and despair, but rather justice, contrition, reparation, and integration of everyone in our community.

In some ways, an approach to criminal justice is a paradox. We cannot and will not tolerate behavior that threatens lives and violates the rights of others. Those who harm others or damage property must be held accountable for the hurt they have caused. The community has the right to establish and enforce laws to protect people and to advance the common good.

At the same time, we believe that both victims and offenders are children of God. Despite their very different claims on society, their lives—and their personal dignity—should be protected and respected. We seek justice, not vengeance. Punishment should have clear purpose: protecting society and rehabilitating those who violate the law.

Today, the criminal justice system is a social enigma that perpetuates justice but exudes a social aroma of distrust. Excluding the incarcerated, many of those with whom I have consulted during the last few years of volunteering agree on one main issue: *The status quo is not working*. Victims are often ignored, offenders are not always rehabilitated, and many communities have lost their sense of security. All of these committed people I've spoken with, including occupational professionals and nonprofessionals alike, believe passionately and urgently that the system is broken in many ways. It is true that the wheels of justice grind slowly; hence, those individuals who are convicted and incarcerated are warehoused and returned to the community void of any traces of rehabilitation.

Over 98 percent of the incarcerated offenders will return to society to live next door to us. We must ask ourselves: In what condition do we want them to return? If we take the position that the policies and tough legislative laws of the Department of Corrections will foster rehabilitation, then we are ignoring reality. Antisocial breakdowns occur when humanity deviates from social norms. Whenever human behavior transcends the boundaries of what is deemed "socially acceptable," crime and civil disobedience prevails. When this happens, certain segments of our society will often be ostracized, leading to hopelessness, despair, and gloom.

The challenge of curbing crime and reshaping the criminal justice system is not just a matter of public policy, but also a commitment that should be undertaken by all of society. A good starting point is to create volunteer ministries that can encourage victims to redirect their anger from vengeance to true justice and real healing. We should offer victims of crime the opportunity to participate more fully in the criminal justice process. We should also reach out to offenders, advocate more (and better) treatment, and provide for their spiritual needs. We should advocate policies that help reduce violence, protect the innocent, and offer real alternatives to crime. We should resist policies that simply call for more prisons and harsher sentences. Rather, we should promote policies that put more resources into restoration, education, and substance abuse programs. And we should build community by forming partnerships among all churches, law enforcement, and mental health agencies to help address crime in neighborhoods.

Here are some examples that support these assertions:

A DAY IN THE LIFE OF AN AMERICAN CHILD

(from "Prison Ministry Guidelines—Elements of the Criminal Justice System")

- 9 children are murdered
- 30 children are wounded from child abuse
- 3 children die from child abuse
- 27 children die from poverty
- 2,350 children are in adult jails
- 307 children are arrested for firearms or violence
- 5,703 teenagers are victims of violent crimes
- 2,255 teenagers drop out of school
- 2,868 babies are born into poverty daily

U.S. PRISON STATISTICS, AS OF DECEMBER 31, 2006

(provided by Bureau of Justice Statistics)

- 2,258,983 prisoners were held in federal or state prisons or in local jails, which amounts to an increase of 2.9 percent from mid-year 2005, less than the average annual growth of 3.4 percent since year end, 1995.
- 1,502,179 sentenced prisoners were under state or federal jurisdiction.
- There were an estimated 501 prison inmates per 100,000 U.S. residents, which is up from 411 at year end, 1995.
- The number of women under the jurisdiction of state and federal prison authorities increased 4.5 percent from mid-year 2005, reaching 112,498, and the number of men rose 2.7 percent, totaling 1,458,363.
- At year end, 2006, there were 3,042 black male sentenced prison inmates per 100,000 black males in the U.S., compared to 1,261 Hispanic male inmates per 100,000 Hispanic males and 487 white male inmates per 100,000 white males.
- In 2004, there were an estimated 633,700 state prisoners serving time for a violent offense. State prisons also held an estimated 265,600 property offenders and 249,400 drug offenders.

Percentage of Sentenced State Inmates

Most Serious	1995	2004
Total	100%	100%
Violent	47	52
Property	23	21
Drug	22	20
Public Order	9	7

Correction Center Statistics as reported by the Bureau of Justice Statistics indicates an increase from 1980 to 2006. In 2006, over 7.2 million people were on probation, in jail or prison, or on parole at year end, 2006, amounting to 3.2 percent of all U.S. adult residents, or 1 in every 31 adults. State and federal prison authorities had custody of 1,570,861 inmates at year end, 2006: 1,377,815 in state custody and 193,046 in federal custody. And, local jails held 766,010 persons awaiting trial or serving a sentence at mid-year 2006. An additional 60,222 persons under jail supervision were serving their sentence in the community.

After sharp increases in the 1980s and 1990s, the incarceration rate has recently grown, but at a slower pace. Population growth during the twelve-month period ending December 31, 2006, was higher in state prisons (up 3.2%) than in federal prison (up 2.4%) and local jails (up 2.5%).

Number of Persons under Correctional Supervision

Year	Probation	Jail	Prison	Parole	Total
1980	1,118,097	183,988	319,598	220,438	1,842,100
2006	4,237,023	766,010	1,492,973	798,202	7,211,400

Expenditure and Employment Statistics

Local governments spend more on criminal justice than state governments.

By level of government:

2005 Federal	State	Local
$35,415,000,000	$64,947,744,000	$103,773,271,000

By criminal justice function:

2005 Police	Judicial	Corrections
$94,437,440,000	$44,607,363,000	$65,091,212,000

In fiscal 2005, federal, state, and local governments spent an estimated $204 billion for police protection, corrections, and judicial and legal activities, a 5.5 percent increase over the previous year. Per capita expenditure across the three government types and criminal justice functions was approximately $660 billion.

In fiscal 2005, state and local governments spent a combined 83 percent of all direct justice dollars; the federal government spent the rest.

Federal government spent more than $35 billion on direct expenditures for criminal and civil justice in fiscal year 2005. State governments spent over $65 billion, and local governments spent over $104 billion.

Another study by the Bureau of Justice Statistics, "Research on the Prison Complex," shows that on December 31, 2005, there were 2,193,798 people in U.S. prisons and jails. The United States incarcerates a greater share of its population—737 per 100,000 residents—than any other country on the planet. But when you break down the statistics, you see that incarceration is not an equal-opportunity punishment. Just look at the numbers:

U.S. incarceration rates by race, as of December 31, 2006:

Whites:	487 per 100,000
Hispanics:	1,261 per 100,000
Blacks:	3,042 per 100,000

Gender is also an important "filter" on who goes to prison or jail.

U.S. incarceration rates by gender, as of June 30, 2006:

Females:	134 per 100,000
Males:	1,384 per 100,000

Look at just the males by race, and the incarceration rates become even more frightening.

U.S. incarceration rates of males by race, as of June 30, 2006:

White males:	736 per 100,000
Hispanics:	1,862 per 100,000
Black males:	4,789 per 100,000

If you look at males by both race and age, focusing on males between the ages of 25 and 29, you can clearly see what is going on.

U.S. incarceration rates of males by race and age, as of June 30, 2006:

White males, ages 25 to 29:	1,685 per 100,000
Hispanic males, ages 25 to 29:	3,912 per 100,000
Black males, ages 25 to 29:	11,695 per 100,000

(that's 11.7% of black men in their 20s)

Or you can make some international comparisons:

South Africa under apartheid was internationally condemned as a racist society.

South Africa under apartheid (1993)

Black males: 851 per 100,000

U.S. under George Bush (2006)

Black males: 4,789 per 100,000.

What does it mean that the leader of the "free world" locks up its black males at a rate 5.8 times higher than the most openly racist country in the world? It doesn't mean equal opportunity punishment.

Here are some statistics using just one state as an example:

PRISONER REENTRY IN VIRGINIA

(taken from the Urban Institute—www.urban.org)

Incarceration and release trends

Virginia's incarceration and reentry trends are similar to those observed at the national level. Between 1980 and 2003, the Virginia prison population more than quadrupled, increasing from 8,521 to 35,429 people. The per capita rate of imprisonment in Virginia rose from 159 to 471 per 100,000 residents in the state between 1980 and 2002, an increase of almost 200 percent. Virginia's release patterns reflect admission and population trends: 10,635 prisoners were released from Virginia prisons in 2003, nearly three times the number released in 1980 (3,582).

Crime Rate for Virginia vs. National Average (2005)

Rates	Virginia	National Average *(per 100,000)*
Crime Rate	2,921	3,751
Incarceration Rate	464	400
Probation Rate	788	1,542
Parolees Rate	78	243
2001 Taxpayer Cost per Inmate	$22,942	$24,052

Characteristics of prisoners released in 2002

Of those released in 2002, the majority were male (89%) and black (63%). The average age of released inmates was thirty-five. One-half had been serving time for a violent offense; one-quarter had been serving time for a nonviolent offense; and the remaining quarter had been serving time for a drug offense. The average time served was 3.6 years.

In terms of admission type, 10 percent of those released in 2002 were incarcerated for a parole violation. Almost one-quarter of individuals released in 2002 were released from a local jail facility. Educational levels among released prisoners were severely limited; over half had not graduated from high school. A majority had a history of drug or alcohol abuse, and almost one in five had been diagnosed with a physical health condition. Almost half of released prisoners had participated in vocational or educational programs provided by the Virginia Department of Correctional Education. More than two in every five releases had participated in substance abuse programming while in prison.

Release and supervision policies and practices

The vast majority of the state's prisoners are released through a mandatory process, and most—81 percent—are released to a period of supervision. Since parole was abolished in Virginia in 1995, the number of individuals supervised on parole has decreased. However, more than half of Virginia's exiting prisoners are released to probation supervision. The average caseload for supervision officers is seventy-seven cases per officer. In recent years, about 45 percent of admissions to prison were the result of violations of probation or parole.

Geographic distribution of released prisoners

Prisoners released in Virginia return to most counties in the state, but distribution is not even. The jurisdictions with the highest number of returning prisoners are the cities of Richmond and Norfolk. Fifteen percent of the prisoners released in 2002 came from two jurisdictions—Richmond City and Norfolk City—that together house but 6 percent of the state's population. These two cities face greater social and economic disadvantages than many other jurisdictions throughout the state. The number of individuals living in poverty is more than twice as high in Richmond and Norfolk cities than in the state as a whole. Unemployment rates are higher, and the share of families that are headed by a single female is significantly higher than the state as a whole. Within the cities, releases are most heavily concentrated in a small number of the cities' block groups. High levels of disadvantage and crime also characterize some of these neighborhoods.

One of Virginia's largest employers is the Department of Corrections, with over 13,000 employees.

As of 2008, the cost to build a prison is $100 million, and to operate it is $25 million per year. The value of rehabilitation programs that reduce recidivism rates and populations of inmates is enormous.

DIGNITY IS OUR BIRTHRIGHT

Dear Brothers in Christ,

I am writing to let you know that people outside your facility care about your well-being and the cross you carry while serving out your term. It would be foolish for me to say that I understand the limitations imposed on you while incarcerated, but I do have compassion, and I try to understand the best I can.

Each of you has different worries and problems to deal with, no different from folks on the outside. The situations are unique for each person, of course, but it is true that none of us can escape them. Worries and problems are part of life, and for some of us, they can often seem insurmountable. As grown men, we like to be in control, to exercise influence and authority over our conditions, and to have the power to choose what is going to happen, and when.

One thing I've learned is that we cannot always escape bad situations. We have to accept them in the best way we can. And, despite our faults and weaknesses, no matter how horrific, God still loves us. He created all of us with personal dignity. This means we are worthy of respect—that as human beings, we possess a value. Our dignity is our birthright as Christians. You know better than I that prison life can destroy any small bit of dignity that you possess. Crowded, impersonal conditions, rude remarks, people trying to gain power over others and to use them for their own purposes—it adds up to an overall lack of control over personal decisions. To one degree or another, you know the loss of personal dignity.

I have often thought about what you can do to live in dignity and promote self-worth while you are in prison. One way may be to respect the dignity of others. Depending on your own maturity in Christ, you may need to avoid those people and situations that are destructive to your own self-esteem. But even more, you should embrace the grace of God. Let it change you and make you strong. You are not alone. He is with you and he is your hope. Try to seek out other like-minded people and support one another. If you believe it, you will become more and more who you were created to be. You have dignity—believe it, live it.

I am also writing to let you know that if any of you have a need or desire to talk or discuss anything with me, please feel free to drop me a line. Know that I am here to listen. No medicine is more valuable, none more efficacious, none better suited to the cure of all our temporal ills than a friend to whom we may turn for consolation in time of trouble, and with whom we may share our happiness in time of joy.

God love ya,

Chuck

PART I

COMPASSION

Dear Brothers,

A long time ago, I read a book entitled *Dead Man Walking*, written by Sr. Helen Prejean. In it she tells a story of Patrick, a death row inmate. No one had ever told Patrick that God loved him. If Patrick had known God's love, it would probably have changed his life. It also may have changed the lives of his victims and their families and friends too.

We often think of love in terms of emotion or special need. We say that we are *in love* when we desperately need another person—when we consider him or her indispensable to our happiness, even our life. But such love is only a form of self-love, mainly concerned with our own needs and happiness. True love or mature love is not based on emotion or need, but on our willingness to go outside of ourselves and to be truly present to another, regaining our original nature, becoming what we were created to be—"You shall love your neighbor as yourself." This kind of love is also called *compassion*.

When we go to church, if we listen carefully, we will hear God's love proclaimed in many ways. Listen and let his love change you, for God *is* love. God is compassion. In sending the Holy Spirit, God's love is intimately present with us. His love guides and teaches, heals and restores. His compassion is like a fire; it ignites and burns, it sears and warms. Compassion incinerates denial; it warms and melts cold hearts, frozen minds, and self-satisfied lifestyles.

When we love God and our neighbors, the Spirit changes us. We turn from mortality, impurity, jealousy, anger, and the like. Instead, we experience the fruit of the Holy Spirit: "love, joy, peace, kindness, generosity, faithfulness, gentleness, self-control."

Let God love you, brothers. And love God and your neighbor in return.

Chuck

Dear Chuck,

After reading your letter, where you talk about one of your neighbors dropping a fork at the dinner table, and her husband dropping his jaw and losing his upper dentures at the same time—after they were told you visit the incarcerated—I burst out laughing. And now they turn their heads when they see you passing the house? Just unbelievable! I thought about it and just shook my head. Some people just believe that the criminal justice system is infallible and anyone who has anything to do with the incarcerated is bizarre, strange, or out of the ordinary. I came across this in one of my books. It fits very well with the situation with your unfriendly neighbors from the dinner party:

A man found an eagle's egg and put it in the nest of a backyard hen. The eagle hatched with the brood of chickens and grew up with them. All through his life, the eagle did what the backyard chickens did, thinking he was also a backyard chicken. He scratched the earth for worms and insects. He clucked and cackled. And, he would thrash his wings and fly a few feet into the air like the chickens. After all, that is how a chicken is supposed to fly, isn't it?

Years passed and the eagle grew old. One day he saw a magnificent bird far above him in the cloudless sky. It floated in graceful majesty among the powerful wind currents, with scarcely a beat of its strong golden wings. The old eagle looked up in awe. "Who's that?" he said to his neighbor.

"That's the king of the birds," said his neighbor, "but don't give it another thought. You and I are different from him."

So the eagle never gave it another thought. He died thinking he was a backyard chicken.

My friend Chuck, God is the graceful eagle flying majestically above. You saw this eagle and realized that you could aspire to be like him, and you're well on your way. Your neighbors, on the other hand, may or may not have seen this eagle. In either case, whether they claim to be Christians or not, they chose not to give it another thought. Instead, they chose to close their minds and follow the rest of the chickens.

Jesus said in John 8:31–32, "If you remain in my word, you will truly be my disciples, and you will know the truth, and the truth will set you free." So, what are these truths? We both know that there are many, but one, which is a favorite and kinda sums it all up, is the judgment of nations found in Matthew 25:31–46.

Your neighbors either do not know these truths or have chosen to disregard these truths. The latter is more damning. In either case, they are in bondage. They are not free to fly. They are clipping their own wings and allowing others to think for them. Unfortunately, this is much of the world. The path into the Kingdom is narrow, but this is not a problem, because fortunately, it is not crowded. Most are not freethinkers but instead bond themselves to the world.

Well, Chuck, I thought I would just remind you that you are indeed an eagle. I'll close for now and will be in touch again soon. Have a good week, and God bless you.

Dear Chuck,

Thanks for your letters. Always good to hear from you. Wish we had more time for that as well, but we deal with what we are dealt. I enjoy any time that we have as a gift from God. It may be short, but it is always enjoyable.

I wrote to the director of the Office of Justice and Peace at the Diocese about the Dismas/Magdalene Project—the "Catholic Kairos"—and that I wanted to get it started here, and could we get support from the Diocese? Also, would the committee look at the organization as an option for prison ministry in Virginia? I have not heard back from him; maybe he will write after your meeting.

One of the ways we can change the image of prisoners is to change us prisoners so that we do not have relapses and get rearrested. Dismas, or any prison ministry, helps us to reorient our lives. Books about the system are good and needed, but we also need to be responsible for ourselves and to commit to becoming better men and women when we are released, and that starts RIGHT NOW, while we are here. We need both in order for it to be objective.

Mark is still in jail in northern Virginia. Talked to one of the Kairos brothers this weekend. Mark is spiritually and mentally in good shape. The appeal is on the 21st of March at 1300 hours. By that time he will have served the time he was sentenced to. This is about getting his conviction overturned and to get the system off his back. We need to continue to pray for him. The date is Good Friday, so let's hope another innocent man does not have to suffer. I'll keep you up-to-date.

My take on the letters (and this is just my take on it): Most of the men like and appreciate your letters each month. But most are not public writers in return. I have heard this more than once from different men: "Who wants to read about my life in here? I'd rather hear about what goes on 'out there,' because this is the same thing, day in and day out." Many just do not know what to say. You do a great job of giving us spiritual things to think about. Some things we need to think over and meditate on.

Others—they also like the letters, and since they see you once a month, they feel that is enough. There is no need to write you. You give a good message, you visit, so they say, "I will save the stamp and not write. I will write to those who don't visit."

Lastly, a number of the men who write you regularly are no longer here because they have transferred. Guys are also dealing with their own issues and don't write anyway.

Basically, Chuck, we all love you—your writing and your visiting. You are loved and valued by us—even if that is not always spoken, we like you and your visits.

I also think that many of us have been abandoned so much in the past, we get to feel that if we get too close, it makes the pain all the worse when you leave, or they think that you will leave, just like the rest of our family and friends have, so best not to get too involved. I think this is closer to the truth now that I write it. But, no one would admit to it. We do love you; that is the bottom line, Chuck.

I think it is great that you are getting mail from all over the system. It means you are touching more and more men. *That* is a good thing and something Jesus did—touch more and more lives—he didn't meet all who believed. You are doing good work, Chuck!

I'm out of the cooking class. I was a victim of reverse discrimination in that class—black to white. I prepped the last meal but was not invited to eat it, and I was not asking to be allowed to—Momma taught us that was not polite. So, I got the boot. I'm actually glad, it frees up time—especially to write—like now!

Here is a new one: They no longer sell us mirrors—the plastic, handheld ones. There was a "security issue" at another prison—and *no*, it was not made into a weapon—but they won't say what the issue was, so it won't be repeated. But, no more mirrors at any prison, just like the sewing kits. Who knows? Crazy.

I saw an article in the Farmville paper about prisoners in Iowa who run an inmate hospice for life. They and a nurse got it started, and it is funded entirely by families, friends, grants, and other donations. Iowa Department of Corrections pays for it and the men love it. I need to get cracking on this idea here, in our system. I could do this; I need some help and contacts, but I pray it would work.

Here is another interesting observation: They sent us movies on the weekend, one for Friday, Saturday, and Sunday. They are now showing R-rated movies. We have seen some pretty violent, gory, bloody movies. They have all that gore with a little sex and nudity. But, they won't show comedies or romantic-type movies where sex may be the subject or the main theme. I'm not talking about X-rated movies here, but popular movies that have been out. Our assistant warden is our movie "censor," and he won't allow them in here. So, we can't see sex, but we can see people get killed, maimed, gored, etc. Something is amiss here.

And, we have noticed that movies on TBS, TNT, WGN, and BET have been showing male bare behinds, but if a female has a bare behind or a thong, it is blocked out. Even VH1 does this. So, it is okay to show nude male behinds but not a female's? What is up with that? Yes, we have too much time on our hands in here!

Okay, Chuck, I've gone on long enough. God bless you and God love you, Chuck! Hang in there. You and Lee are in my prayers. You are a good man, doing good work.

Dear Chuck,

Thank you for your letter. It was good to hear from you.

I have learned that there are men who like to receive mail, but they are not good at writing back. I suspect many are shy about a learning disability, or some can't afford the items needed to write. All I know is that I like to get mail, and I do and will write back.

I agree that it is too bad that we never really have the time to sit and talk. We are always so rushed during services. Oh well, it is good we get to see each other at all sometimes. We take what we get.

Thanks for the encouragement about my own therapy issues. Actually, this past week's readings—26th Sunday in ordinary time—really hit home. I learned *a lot* from these readings. They helped me put many things into perspective and gave me insight into myself and what was going on inside of me, to get me in here. So I am going to focus more on God and let him work in me. The rest will come.

I think I am figuring out the group and how it operates and what is going on. So for now I'm going to calm down and pray and meditate on things and see where it all shakes out.

Yes, I have twenty-two years left to do if I have to do 85 percent of my time—the Virginia law. If I have to do 100 percent, it is twenty-six years. Since there is no more parole thanks to a former governor, I have no hope for an earlier release unless I find a legal loophole in my case, or if the law changes (allowing earlier release), or parole comes back. I may have found a legal loophole from a case in Maryland, but that would not affect Virginia law. It *is* worth a shot, but it seems cheap since I really was guilty of my crimes and should be here. How is that for self-flagellation!

Thanks for your prayers, Chuck. Know that I appreciate them very much. I need all the help I can get. I pray for you, too. I appreciate your willingness to come here and visit us.

Well, Chuck, take care for now, and be safe. See ya in a couple of weeks.

Dear Chuck,

How have you been, my friend? Family doing okay? I hope this letter finds you doing well and in good spirits. I received both of your letters and want to apologize for responding a little late; I have been preoccupied with my mother's health issues. She's pretty much all I have, and since I love her very much, I tend to worry a lot about her.

Chuck, if you have family concerns, I understand that my problems may seem bigger to you, yet in my life I learned that we all are affected differently by different situations. What brings me down, someone else can just shrug off. What I mean is that we all have different problems and we all react to them differently. It does not change the fact that we all feel the pain of our situation. I wish I could help you, Chuck; I hope this holiday season will bring you some good news. I will keep you and yours in my prayers, and if I can do anything to help, please do not hesitate to ask; I honestly mean that, Chuck—just say the word.

Chuck, I believe God would forgive me; problem is, I can't forgive myself. I know I am not a bad person, and I did some good deeds and helped many people in my life. I just can't forgive myself for committing the crime I committed. All the good I've done, all the good in me, is now tainted by that. Nothing I did matters but that. I feel . . . tarnished.

Perhaps out there is a woman who is meant for me. How can I explain to her what I've done? Is there really a woman alive who can love me regardless of my past? I have yet to find her.

Now I believe it is time for me to stop speaking in riddles and attempt to tell you why I am in prison. I will understand if you decide to stop writing to me, and I know you will probably look at me differently. After I tell you, you will understand why I feel how I feel. Whatever you decide, I will not blame you.

There is no easy way to say this, so I will just say it. I am a convicted sex offender; I inappropriately touched my sister when I was sixteen or seventeen, and she was ten. I make no excuses; I don't know how that could have happened or why I did it. I never had such a problem with anyone else; that is not who I am. God is my witness; God knows I tell the truth. Anyone who knew me could tell you, that person is not who I am! Now maybe you understand better; now you know why I loathe myself.

And now I have to close this letter. I cannot keep writing because I am not feeling up to it anymore. Sorry, Chuck; perhaps I'll write more later. God bless.

Dear Chuck,

Hello, my friend! Just a short note to let you know I am thinking of you, and to send you many blessings. As always, I hope and pray that you and the family are doing well, and that all else is just great!

Again, I am truly sorry for my past transgressions, and I pray that you will forgive me! I assure you that my past actions and conduct are not the true person I am! The demeanor I described was indeed an aberration from my natural self!

I have been wanting to send you the enclosed "Prisoner to Prisoner" daily devotional booklet (Kairos). I am not sure if you are familiar with it, but I wanted to be sure that you have a copy, as I find the writings from various prisoners very touching and enlightening. I am certain that you will agree, and find them very personal from within, as they are reflections of feelings and experiences from different people and backgrounds, and various walks of life. I reflect on these writings—testimonies—quite often, and find them very helpful in dealing with my own personal grief and feelings of serious guilt and dismay.

I hope and pray that some of them will also touch you personally, as they define sincere inner feelings of others, and bring solace to many by staying close to God by trusting in HIS everlasting love and promises! True and sincere faith can and has changed many good people in miraculous and most spiritual ways—personal will, desire, and love is all that is necessary to walk with God! God will right all wrongs, love all people, guide those that are astray, heal the sick, and bless the poor and lonely in heart! He is our strength, energy, light, and direction in life; through his love and grace we are drawn and shaped according to God's purpose, and do not walk alone, regardless of our sinful desires.

Being led by the Holy Spirit, I have experienced many changes within myself since my incarceration. Life has taken on a new and different meaning now; although still physically the same, my inner being and spiritual self has taken on a new challenge. My ways of thinking and my natural senses have been transfigured and oriented away from the usual worldly aspirations and personal values of materialism, selfishness, greed, lust, and personification! Love itself has taken on a completely different meaning, as I have discovered a new sensation of God's love and love for others. I have conquered and broken through the shell of deceptive and worldly love—it is more important to love God and others first, before one can find love, peace, contentment, and true righteousness within oneself.

Well, Chuck, my friend, I suppose I have surrendered enough of myself for now, so I guess I will stop rambling on, and get this into the mail. I am doing fine myself, and will enjoy the rest of this beautiful day!

Again, please forgive me, and keep me in your prayers. So for now and always, take good care of yourselves, stay well, and be safe. May God's love, grace, peace, and many blessings otherwise, be yours this day and always.

Dear Chuck,

Hi! I was finally able to get this letter off to you. Being poor at remembering names anyway, I couldn't remember your last name—sorry! And I had to check to find out how to get a letter to you, for I forgot to get your address.

I hope this letter finds you doing well. As I mentioned briefly to you, I've been staying busy building a model ship—the HMS *Victory*. It was Lord Nelson's ship at the Battle of Trafalgar in 1805. It should be completed by the end of August. I'm trying to figure a way to have it picked up here and transported to the Scranton, Pennsylvania, area so the family can pick it up there and give it to my son for Christmas. Right now, though, my drawback is finding any detailed pictures of the ship so I can complete all the rigging and sails. Everything else is finished. The ship is just two feet long by ten inches wide by just over two feet high.

Well, now the personal stuff. I'm serving a sentence of life plus eighty years for rape and breaking and entering and abduction. I don't mean to say that matter-of-factly, because I don't take the matter lightly at all! I'm currently working on year fifteen, and as of 1996, I have confronted my demons and have overcome them. I decided back then I didn't want to continue to be that person any longer, and after several good hard looks in the mirror, and being asked if I've forgiven myself, I decided to deal with the problems I faced and that have haunted me for most of my life!

In the late eighties I became addicted to pornography and sex. This, in addition to my continued struggle with depression and anxiety attacks, was a lethal combination—and I fell.

I've been up for parole once already for the first time, and I received a three-year deferment—or—a three-year hit. So I won't go up again until about November '06. I imagine I'll get turned down yet again—hopefully with just a one-year hit. I believe they want me to do about twenty years on this sentence. The fact that I've completely turned myself around and am not a threat to society and can be a contributing member, etc., is of no consequence. It's all about politics. So I've completely surrendered myself back to God and am now at peace with it all.

I enjoyed speaking with you when you were here, and I look forward to seeing you once more. I also would like to hear from you when you get a chance.

Your brother in Christ.

Dear Brother Chuck,

Thanks for being here for us. I realize coming here takes time and money; this is the reason why not many volunteers show up, until now. Thanks, again.

When I set up for service on Tuesday night, I really enjoy it very much. I'm trying to pick up spirits at the same time. When I start off with my notes after the readings, I'm trying to get the mind working and also to break the ice, so to speak. I can really see a big difference in the way the guys are getting into it, because you are here for us. Amen.

Brother Chuck, I really think that what you are doing with your artwork—to help others out because they are poor, and just to give a helping hand—is a very good thing. God is smiling on his son. Keep it up.

Dear Chuck,

Good to have gotten your letter a couple of weeks ago. I've just gotten off lockdown for shakedowns. They did not shake our pod down. They have already done enough random shakedowns. We did not need a full going-over. Go figure. Well, I got to lay in the bed for three days and read a good book I got from the library here.

I am glad the surgery went well on the prostate. I was praying for you extra that day.

I want to share two stories one of my Kairos friends sent to me.

1) Here is one woman's response to her husband's end-of-life request: My wife and I were sitting in the living room and I said to her, "Just so you know, I never want to live in a vegetative state, dependent on some machine and fluids from a bottle. If that ever happens, just pull the plug." She got up, unplugged the TV, and threw out all of my beer!

2) "I Wish You Enough," by Bob Perks. Recently I overheard a father and daughter in their last moments together. They had announced her flight departure, and standing near the security gate, they hugged. He said, "I love you. I wish you enough."

She in turn said, "Daddy, our life together has been more than enough. Your love is all I ever needed. I wish you enough, too, Daddy." They kissed and she left. He walked over toward the window where I was seated. Standing there I could see he wanted and needed to cry. I tried not to intrude on his privacy, but he welcomed me in by asking, "Did you ever say good-bye to someone knowing it would be forever?"

"Yes, I have," I replied. Saying that brought back memories of expressing my love and appreciation for all my dad had done for me. Recognizing that his days were limited, I took the time to tell him face-to-face how much he meant to me. So I knew what this man was experiencing.

"Forgive me for asking, but why is this a forever good-bye?" I asked.

"I am old and she lives much too far away. I have challenges ahead, and the reality is, the next trip back will be for my funeral," he said.

"When you were saying good-bye, I heard you say, 'I wish you enough.' May I ask what that means?"

He began to smile. "That's a wish that has been handed down from other generations. My parents used to say it to everyone."

He paused for a moment and looked up as if trying to remember it in detail. He smiled even more. "When we said, I wish you enough, we were wanting the other person to have a life filled with just enough good things to sustain them," he continued. Then, turning toward me, he shared the following as if he were reciting it from memory:

"I wish you enough sun to keep your attitude bright. I wish you enough rain to appreciate the sun more. I wish you enough happiness to keep your spirit alive. I wish you enough pain so that the smallest joys in life appear much bigger. I wish you enough gain to satisfy your wanting. I wish you enough loss to appreciate all that you possess. I wish you enough hellos to get you through the final good-bye."

He then began to walk away, saying, "I wish you enough."

Chuck, I wish you enough.

This story is bittersweet for the two of us because of our family situations, but it is a good reminder to focus on what we have, and let God take care of the rest. I have to remind myself that God works for our good in all things, even the pain. We both have enough pain, so we should be getting some good soon.

Dear Chuck,

Thanks for your recent letter. What an incredible story you wrote about! I have heard of this crash and the need to eat human flesh, but never from this perspective. The men had great insight into the true meaning of the Eucharist.

The following is from Chuck's letter:

On October 12, 1972, a Fairchild F-227 took off from the airport of Montevideo, Uruguay, for Santiago, Chile. It never arrived. Somewhere in the upper reaches of the Andes, the plane crashed, plunging its crew and passengers into one of those fierce and elemental experiences that befall human beings from time to time.

For ten solid weeks, sixteen survivors struggled to stay alive by munching on a few bars of chocolate and drinking from a few bottles of wine that had been brought along for occasional refreshment, for what they believed would be a short trip of a few hours' duration. But as the days dragged into weeks, their pathetically small supply of food became exhausted, and a terrifying realization took hold of them. If they were to survive, they would have to partake of the only nourishment now available to them: the flesh of the dead bodies of their friends.

As it happened, most of the survivors were young men, graduates of Catholic colleges, who had enough theological sophistication to understand that this course of action would be entirely compatible with their Christian commitment. And, yet, they could not master the ferocious revulsion they felt at the thought of consuming human flesh. Until, that is, one of their number was inspired to say: "We should do this; it will be like Holy Communion. When Christ died, he gave his body to us so that we could have spiritual life. My friend has given us his body so that we can have physical life."

An insight into the Eucharist that is as true as it is touching.

I agree with you that death is *not* morbid. It is a part of life. We will all go through it. As one of my friends always says, we only die once. The experience should be the full culmination and celebration of the life of the person. I so much wanted to do my PhD work on ICU death, but I was sidetracked. A new plan needs to be made. But yes, death is a BEGINNING and an end. Sadness and joy together—like Jesus on the Cross. Amen!

Thanks for your help with Father. The letter went out that I am okay with the annulment investigation proceeding. So I now wait to see what will happen. It will take a while to get all the questions and responses in and out. I will take it as it comes. I can't control anything but my responses.

My ex's letter to me was *very* telling. She *never once* mentioned my mom's death and how it must have affected me being in here. It was all about the "wrongs" committed against her at the funeral. I still do not know what to make of that. It kind of blows me away.

I am honoring her request to have no further contact with me. I do not think her remarriage will last, not when she is clearly still angry with me and not over me, but I can't and won't tell her that. I'll pray for her that it *does* work. She has always been an "out of sight, out of mind" principled person. So in all fairness to her marriage, I will not write anymore.

What a heck of a mess families are! Oh well, we'll both get through our trials with God's help. Thanks for you support, Chuck. Thanks for your prayers for my mom. God bless ya, God love ya!

Dear Brother,

I pray that you and yours and all our brothers and sisters are doing well. Brother, I want to thank you from the bottom of my heart for all your letters and all your prayers. You are a blessing to all of us, and for that I ask the Lord to bless you and yours.

Also, I was transferred about two and a half months ago. They moved me to a different correctional center to be closer to home and better recreation, but I keep all my brothers and sisters deep inside my heart. You guys are forever going to be my family.

My brother, I'm getting real short on my time—five more months, maybe less. And so, for thanks to our Lord and the prayers from my families, the one in Christ, and my family on the outside, everything appears to be going well. Also, when you write to the men, please let them know that that I'm doing fine, and I say "hello" to everybody and I miss everybody.

Take good care of yourself and may the Lord bless you always.

Sinceramente—

To Chuck:

I was very glad to get your letters. I was also happy to hear how excited you and your wife are in sponsoring a child through Christian Children's Fund. Years ago, back when my daughter was between the ages of eight and ten, we sponsored a little boy from Guatemala. He was nine years old. He had no mom. She passed away. He had an older dad of sixty-two, and eight brothers and sisters. We were blessed to help this young boy out, and we sent extra money for his birthday and holidays. His name was Francisco. He was part of our lives for eight years. He has grown up and moved on. What a joy it was for our family.

Now in prison, I am still sending money to help a poor family in the Philippines. I am sure we will also get great joy with this child.

They have a Catholic service here twice a month. I joined a group of twenty-five to thirty good men.

Hello, my brother,

I pray that you and yours are doing well. I got your beautiful letter, and, like always, was glad to hear from you. I'm happy for the new member of the family. The Lord has chosen a good family to take care of this beautiful angel.

Now, according to your letter, two more brothers have transferred to new places. I'm happy for them, and let's keep them in our prayers. I miss everybody, and when you visit again, let them know that I miss them as well as you. You and the brothers are forever going to be my family. I love you guys and I thank you for staying in touch. I always look forward to your letters. I love the message in the story about the Fairchild F-227 Andes plane crash, because it's true.

Chuck, I thank you, and at the same time, I want to let you know that I'm doing okay. My family has been coming to see me smile and I'm staying strong always. When you see everybody, please let them know I said hello and God bless. And tell Superman that I said hello, and to keep saying things to you, like "stop over and have a beer with me," because things like that make us smile for a long time. Tell them I miss them all.

Well, my brother, once again, thank you for your beautiful letter and for being one of a kind. You are a special person, and I ask our Lord to bless you and yours always.

Sinceramente, Brother.

P.S. Say hello to your wife, and I wish you guys the best of everything.

Dear Brother Chuck,

I received your letter yesterday and was especially pleased to read that my family of strong brothers and sisters are doing well and are staying strong in the Word. Chuck, I thank you from the bottom of my heart for your friendship. I'm proud to call you my brother for life. I want you to know that I'm doing well. Forty-two more days and I'm done with my time in this place. I'm happy and ready because I have our Lord to guide me and to keep me safe. I will write you until I go, and after that I might give you a call. For now, I'm going to end this letter. I just wanted to say hello, and to let you know that I'm doing okay.

Take good care of yourself and yours. Also, say hello to all my brothers and sisters.

God bless, Brother.

Dear Chuck,

Hi! I'm a little late in getting this off to you. It was my intention to get all my cards out by the 1st, but there are many things that are said about good intentions. By the way, I'm reminded about a saying I heard once while in training with the service. It goes, "A man who has to be convinced to act is not a man of action. You must act as you breathe."—Unknown.

So, I finally got a chance to read the article about you in the *News and Advance*. Impressive! It was also very kind of you to mention your work with us in here. The term "upstanding gentleman" doesn't carry enough weight when it comes to describing the good man you are! Began your career with the FBI, huh? Well, that's out now! My wife and I were visiting her brother who worked up at the Pentagon back around '88, and we ran into a representative of the Secret Service. He tried to recruit me, and I may have jumped at the offer. He slipped up, though, and mentioned the strain it would have on married life, especially if I had kids. I was getting ready to part with the navy then because I was away from home too much. So I didn't take the offer. On a number of occasions I've regretted doing that. If I were single—man, I would have had it made doing that kind of work!

From the picture in the paper, the stained-glass piece of the "eagle" looks great! That kind of work is something I always had a passionate interest in—that, along with doing work in a bicycle shop. So my shipbuilding, and now lighthouses, also, will be a means of extra income for me, and as you mentioned, it'll keep me busy!

By the way, I noticed that your sons were quoted in the article. With all due respect to them, it would be my opinion that the things you've accomplished in your life, and now, pursuing a passion you have that obviously makes you happy and content, is not "crazy," it's certainly admirable! Some people get stuck doing just one or two things in their lives and never really experience life, pursue their dreams, or venture out after a passion. Too many people live their lives to please others, and they are miserable people. I'm proud and honored to know a person who has accomplished as much as you have in your life, and . . . has been able to retain a good heart from the whole experience. From Special Operations to fire/rescue work, I know about sacrifice and love of country. And now having lost it *all*, I've come to learn about contentment.

It seems as though I do have a couple of months at least to come up with a few solutions with residence and employment. Plus, this is only my second time up for parole and I feel it would be almost foolish to think I could get released. But then, with God, anything's possible, right?

I understand from the chaplain that the sanctuary bells are in his vehicle, and that he's waiting for official notification for them to be permitted into the facility. I hope you didn't spend too much money on those bells.

Well, we'll speak more on Tuesday, and I very much look forward to seeing you. It seems as if it's been forever since we last gathered.

Till then, please take care!

Dear Chuck,

Hi—how are you doing, brother? I hope you are well, and your family, too. I want you to know how pleased I was when I received the letters that you have been writing me.

I really feel very happy, because each one of your letters shows me how God takes care of each one of us, and I feel very grateful that I made the decision to belong to the community of Jesus Christ, and to share His Holy Word every Tuesday with each one of the good brothers that you already know.

It is wonderful how God shows each one of us that we are never alone, because He is always beside us. We only have to trust in him.

Well, I want to apologize that I haven't written to you all this time. But I think that you understand why. However, I want you to know that it is time for me to try to write English. I hope to see you soon.

God love ya, and God bless ya too, my brother.

Dear Chuck,

How are you? I'm okay. I like the letter you sent to *Catholic Virginian*. I hope some good comes out of it. I know the state officials don't want to hear any of it. One day they will.

I want to thank you for the hobby address. I had a problem with it. Can you look for another? Thanks.

Also I am enclosing another poem in this letter. Could you again do me the favor of putting it in a computer-written format for me, and also, share it with the "good men" where I used to be?

I am reading the Bible with my cellmate each morning. We take turns reading.

My parents are planning to see me May 20. They're coming from Maine. It has been five years since I have seen them.

Well, take care, my friend, and God bless.

'Twas the Night Jesus Came

Twas the night Jesus came and all through the house,
Not a person was praying—no one in the house . . .

The Bible was left on the shelf without care,
For no one thought Jesus would come there . . .

The children were dressing to crawl into their beds,
Not once ever kneeling or bowing their heads.

The wife in her rocking chair with the baby on her lap;
She was watching a movie while I took a nap.

Away to the window I flew like a flash.
I tore off the shutters and lifted the sash . . .

When what to my wondering eyes should appear?
Angels proclaiming that Jesus was here.

The light of his face made me cover his head.
It was Jesus returning, just like He said.

And though I possessed worldly wisdom and wealth,
I cried when I saw Him in spite of myself.

In the book of life which He held in His hands,
Was written the name of every saved woman and man.

He spoke not a word as He searched for my name,
When He said "It's not here," I hung my head in shame.

The people whose names were written with love,
He gathered them all to take to His Father above . . .

With those that were ready He rose without a sound,
While all of the others were left standing around.

I fell to my knees but it was too late.
I waited too long and I sealed my own fate.

I stood and I cried as they rose out of sight.
Oh! If only I'd known that this was the night . . .

In the words of this poem the meaning is clear:
The coming of Jesus is now drawing near . . .

There's only one life and when comes the last call,
We'll find out the Bible was true after all!

Dear Chuck,

Got your letter. Thanks for responding. If I can offer to you some words of encouragement—you know this, as you said, there are some who will disagree with your position; actually, many will. Don't get caught up in the negative responses. Some do have valid points about being victims of crime or know someone who is a victim of a crime. If your loved one or a friend is raped, murdered, beaten, etc., it will be difficult to forgive, to see the humanity in the criminal. Restorative justice does not enter into their equations. They are blinded by their revenge so they are mad at the world. You won't reach these people, and a letter like yours, especially about sex offenders, will be sure to ruffle a few feathers. I'm curious to see what the responses will be.

To humanize us, especially us sex offenders, is a very threatening thing to some. It is much easier to point to us and blame us for their woes in life. To come to prison and listen to us, to sit in the same room with us, to see and hear us as humans—Whoa! Very threatening! Can't do that. As long as I am a "that" or an "it," I can be treated any way they see fit. I get what I deserve, as an animal or a monster. To see me as human would upset their world. Right or not, that is how it is.

I got a response from my letter to the Office of Justice and Peace about prison ministry. They thanked me for my letter. They understand the challenges we face, but it was a short letter and did not say much. At least they read it and acknowledged what I said. I hope that you will be named to the Prison Ministry Advisory Board. We need some advocates in there.

Peace and love.

Dear Chuck:

Hello. I received your letter; thank you for your reply. I hope this finds you well. And thank you for your prayers, and for passing my letter on to the director of Citizens United for Rehabilitation of Errants (CURE). Or, I should say, my girlfriend's letter. I have since rewritten what she wrote. She was a very spunky, high-spirited lady. She wanted, and needed me to be out there with her, and was rather disgusted with the parole board. So I have toned her letter down a bit, added a couple things, and sent it to a family member in hopes that they will mail it to some delegates. The parole board is a tough nut to crack. They are almost all powerful in their discretion and beyond reproach. But I do not believe anyone ever intended for them to be able to override a judge. I think it's going to take someone of stature, such as a state legislator, to be able to even make a wave in their pond. The words of ordinary folks seem to have no impact upon them.

Anyway, thank you for your help. I realized, as you humbly put it, you are but a mere volunteer. But also, Esther was a slave, Joseph a convicted sex offender, Paul a murderer, Rachael a thief, Rahab a prostitute, etc. I don't believe there are any "meres" with God, for with God all things are possible. God can bring great results from small acts. A boy's bag lunch can feed 5,000 people. A small little creek stone can fell a mighty, giant warrior. So never underestimate what a mere volunteer can accomplish, with God's help. Sometimes, God's just waiting on the volunteer! Thank you for your prayers and efforts. Even if you don't see it, you're making a difference. God bless . . .

Dear Chuck,

Praise the Lord!

There once was a man who hitchhiked from Virginia to Alabama. The Good Lord blessed the man to find a job in ten days. A month later God blessed him to have two jobs and an apartment of his own! God blessed him to meet the right people at the right time and to be at the right place. Praise God! The Lord led the man to find a church home, and was very blessed! God blessed him to meet a lovely sister in Christ called Margey. They met in church while a revival was going on. They talked, dated, and fell in love. The man was very happy. He felt he had found his soul mate. Margey was also blessed, saved, sanctified, and filled with the precious Holy Ghost! They prayed together, studied the Word together, went to church and ministered the Word and power of salvation together. They were a tag team for God.

On February 14, the man proposed to Margey and she accepted, and both cried. Two days later the man went by Margey's apartment to pick her up and take her to town to handle some business. They left, went to a park first, stood outside in the cold and held each other while praying to Father God. They left the park, and went to the bank and paid bills. Afterwards the man suggested going to his church for noon prayer (the place where they first met), and Margey agreed. They met other believers at church, fell on their knees, and prayed.

About 12:35 P.M., they left church and decided to go get something to eat at Dairy Queen. It was on the way to Margey's place. The man turned in at the Dairy Queen, went to get in line at the drive-through, when all of a sudden, a red car ran into the back of them. The man looked in the rearview mirror to see what was going on, and it happened again. The man attempted to move out of the drive-through line to pull over into the parking lane and see who this fool was. What was his problem? Margey looked back and hollered, "No, just take me home. That's my ex."

As the man went to leave the parking lot, the traffic light turned red, and all traffic came to a stop. The ex got out of his car, ran up to them while holding a Taurus 9mm gun in his hand. Kids and adults were all over the parking lot; the inside of Dairy Queen was packed. The man made an attempt to go out into traffic, but when he hit the gas pedal, the car stalled and cut off. The man tried to restart the car when the ex started shooting. The man pulled Margey to him, pushing her down and laying over her, trying to protect her. The man watched the ex as he ran back to his red car and left. The man rose up looking at the rearview mirror, saw that his face had been split open. He reached down to lift Margey up when he felt the pain in his chest. He had been shot in the chest also.

Margey looked fine, no blood anywhere, and she was calm. The man turned to get someone's attention to call 911. People had run up to the car in total shock and disbelief. When the man looked back, Margey had fallen back over. He lifted her back up and inside his heart begged God that she would be okay. She was gasping for air. He signaled for someone to help and to call 911 again. Margey fell over again, gasping for air. She took a deep breath and looked at the man and said, "I love you." The man replied, "I love you too. Don't talk. Just breathe slow and hold on. The ambulance is on the way."

She looked into his eyes and said, "Jesus, Jesus, Je—" and died.

The man stared into Margey's beautiful eyes, hoping she was just in shock, but in his heart he knew God had called her home. The man pleaded with God but she was gone. He reached up and closed her eyes while saying good-bye to his fiancée of two days. He held her until the rescue squad came and they took her out of his arms. The man never saw her again.

The following year the man got into trouble, went to jail, then to prison. A few months later, the ex ended up at the same prison with the man. The Lord spoke to the man one day while he was lying on his bunk and said: "Your testimony for me is not complete." The man answered, "But I've forgiven him and sent word to him that God loves him and so do I." God said to the man, "Your testimony won't be complete until you go yourself and tell him." The man pondered things in his heart and said to God, "Your will be done, Amen!"

The Lord had already blessed the man to be on the prison ministry team as a minister of the Word, and they had access to the lockdown area for those serving life without parole and those on death row. The ex was in the lockdown area, so the man went to him and reached through the prison bars to shake his hands. The man told the ex what God had told him to say: "God loves you and so do I. I forgive you. God wants you to get your life right with Him." The ex broke down in tears and repented and recommitted his life back to Jesus, praise God! The man and the ex joined hands and the man prayed for both of them.

The man came back home to Virginia in '03. God blessed him to meet another woman of his dreams. He married the beautiful lady on February 15th, two years later.

God bless you,

The man

Dear Mr. Chuck, I thank you for your letter and reply, I was blessed to hear from you, and yes, I would like you to include my name on your mailing list. When I wrote about me marrying a sister in Christ, it was not Margey's sister. I met my wife here in Virginia in '03 and we got married in '05.

I pray that God is well with you and your family. God is truly good to us, and I hope you will keep me in prayer. I'm to be released from here in September, and I need all the prayers I can get. I'm sorry I didn't respond sooner, but I didn't have any stamps. God bless you, and you continue to stay on the battlefield for the Lord!

In Christ,

Brother

Dear Chuck and Lee,

I wanted to write this letter to tell you both how much I appreciate the love and caring that you have brought into my life, and how grateful I am to know you. I am currently going through a Kairos weekend here at the correction center. If you don't know what Kairos is, it is very similar to a Crisillo weekend [Christian retreat].

Lee, I don't know how much Chuck has told you about me, but I feel I need to tell you what I have gone through during the last year so that this letter will make a little more sense. I lost my twenty-five-month-old baby on March 17 of this year, in an automobile accident. I have been blaming myself for the accident. During this weekend I was able to talk to a priest and through his help, I was able to see that I can let go of the guilt to start the healing process without forgetting my son and without dishonoring his memory.

Along with losing my son, I also lost my home to the wildfires in Georgia this summer. I don't say this looking for pity, but for prayer. I don't get a lot of mail here and I haven't had a visit since I left the jail, but I am not upset. I am a very understanding young man, and so your letters that I get every month are very important to me. I know I haven't known you for all that long, but I view you and all of the Catholic community, both outside volunteers and inmate members, as a part of my extended family. I have to say that for me, it is a great joy, and the highlight of my month is to see Chuck and the other volunteers and to get your letters each month. I am just sorry that this letter was not written sooner and that it is so short, but I have got to get some sleep because this weekend has been very emotionally draining and it's not over yet.

Dear Chuck, and, of course, Lee,

Well, it's been a good year on the whole, I think! I sit here writing this to you while listening to Bruce Springsteen sing about the old days. It's comforting music.

As I've said before, I admire you a great deal. Your passion, compassion, love, and wisdom have been a great inspiration for me. It gives me hope and strength. I pray we can get together upon my release so we can sit and just talk.

Till then, my friend and brother, I wish for you and yours, a wonderful Christmas filled with peace and joy.

Dear Chuck,

Thank you so much for your letters. They always offer us words of encouragement and leave us with a smile at your sign-off. I miss our "face-to-face" interaction, but I continue to benefit from your wit and wisdom in your letters. Thank you for sharing those qualities with me.

Our Catholic community here is growing, "little by slowly." New inmates come and others leave, but we've had as many as thirty-five in attendance when Father came to say Mass. We started with one volunteer. He arranged for Father to come once a month, and he, in turn, encouraged Catholic volunteers to join him in visiting us. He succeeded in bringing in seven new people. They vary in attendance due to outside obligations.

Currently, Father is on sabbatical in Rome, but he'll be back with us in December. Meanwhile, our volunteers are joining us twice a month, once to bring us the Eucharist and once for a group study. The other weeks are on me, our Catholic community facilitator. It's the same role I had before being transferred, and I am truly blessed to serve in this capacity. I used to think that to be a missionary, one had to be on the outside and off in some remote corner of the world. I think, here I am learning what missionary services is meant to be.

We have members of our community in wheelchairs, one with no legs at all. Then, there is one friend who lives in the infirmary but is wheeled over for services. He is in the advanced stages of Lou Gehrig's disease—ALS. He can only smile, blink his eyes, and slur out a bit of conversation, usually something about what a blessing it is to wake up every morning. He humbles all of us. When we have no one coming from the outside, I usually have from ten to twelve attendees. I guess I'm not as exciting as people from the outside. Outside visitors are so special to all of us. We see each other all the time, so we relish our time with our volunteers.

So, I can understand the attendance drop on our off weeks. On those weeks, I use the exact same format used before my transfer. Some weeks, we add a Rosary; others, we watch an inspirational DVD together. We just got through with *Becket* (the life of St. Thomas Becket), with Richard Burton in the role—an oldie but a goodie. We meet for two hours from 6:00 to 8:00 P.M. on Tuesdays. We remember in intercessory prayer our brothers in prison communities around the state, especially our brothers who are meeting during the same time period. So tell these guys they're in our prayers.

I continue to stay busy. I am enjoying my job as an aide in the electrical class, and I volunteer as a facilitator for Breaking Barriers to Change on Thursday afternoons. We are allowed to attend other services in addition to our primary faith, so I have been sitting in and learning the traditions and tenets of the Messianic Jewish Community. I have managed to get some of them to attend our Catholic services. Being able to have this ecumenical experience really affirms my Catholicism. I also very much respect and endorse the men who are in the Messianic community.

They had a big banquet here on this past Tuesday put on by Virginia Chaplain Services to honor all the volunteers of all the religions. Four of our volunteers were at the banquet, and each group's inmate facilitator was encouraged to attend. I felt a little guilty eating that good food while my fellow inmates had fish squares for supper. But, when I saw how much our visitors were enjoying the program, the food issue became insignificant.

Thank you again for your love and devotion to us.

Dear Chuck,

How are you doing? I hope well as I write this short letter to you.

First, I want to thank you for coming to our correction center for a visitation. It is not the ideal place to make new acquaintances. This place can be quite intimidating to some, including us, but we try and do the best we can with what we have.

Chuck, I just want you to know that you are an important link to the outside world for us. Some of us have minimal contact with the outside world. Families desert us; friends forget you ever existed; spouses divorce us and forget entirely about our past together.

To know that good people like you are willing to come into this environment and listen to us is truly a miracle and a blessing only God can bestow on us. Many of us recognize where we went wrong and want to change, and are truly repentant for our crimes and sins.

I just wanted to let you know that I and the others here wish to thank you for taking the time out of your schedule to come and be with us.

God bless you, Chuck.

Dear Chuck,

I thank you again for remembering me; I know how life can keep us busy, so we don't have time for the small things (or we don't make the time), but you seem to make the time, and I can tell you, I very much appreciate it and definitely respect that. I am sure all the guys that you remember and take the time to drop them a line also appreciate it. You, sir, are making a difference!

I had told you that I started saying the Rosary. I have not missed a day since I started. I have made it my every-morning regular routine.

I am now interested in learning about novenas. You mentioned about someone saying them. Although my mother is a devout Catholic, I am not familiar with novenas. I asked a few guys from church services, but no luck yet. I will inquire next church service.

I will now end this by saying thank you again.

Bless God!

Dear Chuck,

Your message was very timely for me—as are many readings I have been through this week on hope and trust in God. I have been depressed this holiday season, more so than the others I have spent in here. I found out that my ex and her new husband are moving to a new house, but presumably closer to their jobs. My daughter is applying to the University of Delaware and my son is doing well. An uncle died, my dad got a new car, and other family members are getting ready for the Christmas season. I want to be happy for all of these people. I know my ex and children are better off now with me moving on, but I feel stuck in here. I know God will work for me and does all for his good, but I still get down. Then I was hit with all these messages of love and I realized I am not alone; I have people who care. I need to put the energy of missing my ex and children into loving God, building my relationship with God, and letting go of all I can't control and leave them to God. This is not an easy road, but it will build me.

So, thank you for your message, Chuck, to remind me of all of these things and to let God work. I can be happy for all of them and be happy myself when I let go of the attachment I have for them, and work on God and me.

Dear Pop (Chuck),

Just for the record, I get my work ethics from you. A chip off the old block—no pun intended. Before I dig my own grave, I better move on.

Over the weekend, I got a little Mother's Day card put together for Mom (aka, your wife, Lee). I had planned to mail it Tuesday, but for some reason, Tuesday came and went without me opening my calendar. Yes, it has been that kind of week. I almost forgot to mail it.

Mother's Day Card for Lee:

Dear Lee,

Chuck might have told you about my adoption—or was it I who adopted Chuck? My mind is cloudy on the details. Chuck could even be my biological father had he strayed forty-six years ago (years you and he have been married), but I really don't want to go into the details of my conception. I just want to wish you a very nice Mother's Day. You are in my prayers.

Happy Mother's Day! God bless—with love.

At dinner this evening, I chose a bean tray over the mystery meat tray, but I only received four ounces of beans rather than twelve. I showed the lieutenant, and she told me to put it on paper. In other words, submit a complaint. She could have saved some headaches by telling the server to give me a cup of beans (just one of many episodes that rank in the stupidity category). I went back to my room and made a bowl of noodles. I did submit the complaint, though.

I appreciate the offer to give me all the sponsor names for the Second Chance Act [On April 9, 2008, the President of the United States signed into law legislation that will reduce recidivism rates and give ex-offenders a second chance at life], but there is no need. I wrote them down when I first read about it. My transfer shouldn't be much longer. I'm almost at eleven months in waiting. I figure I could be told to pack up anytime now. In fact, about six months ago, I had a funny feeling about May 14. I don't know why, so I marked the day on my calendar with a big question mark. God is speaking to me . . . maybe. Just another day . . . maybe. Whatever the case, God has taught me to listen to my intuition. I'll be sure to share with you what happens on that day.

Last Thursday, I was sent to the doctor's office. Neither she nor I knew why. Go figure that one out. Also on Thursday, I exchanged my underclothing for new. Then Friday my outer-clothes laundry bag was lost by the laundry facility. I seem to have enough stolen from me. Remember my money orders—two of them for $100 each?

I told my sister about your wanting to adopt her and her daughter in my last letter. I know that she will get a kick out of that, but will be very moved by the gesture. I haven't heard back yet. She'll probably write me while she is camping again this coming weekend. Then they leave again for the Memorial Day weekend. Their cats enjoy the mobile home so much that they refuse to leave it upon returning home without putting up a fuss. The youngest one darts to get under the couch.

Well, my friend, I'm sitting here looking at May 14 in my journal, wondering what life holds for me in a week. Until then, I remain,

The prodigy [sic] son

Please give my best to Lee for Mother's Day. You're both in my thoughts, prayers, and heart.

PART II

HOPE

Dear Brothers,

Faith, hope, and love. These three are called *the theological virtues*, the qualities that make us most like God. We hear much about faith and love, but when is the last time you heard a story on hope? Why is hope important? And what is it, precisely?

"I **hope** it doesn't rain the day of the picnic." You and I have no control over the weather. Hoping it doesn't rain is nothing more than wishful thinking. Is Christian hope wishful thinking in the face of all that we can't control?

"I **hope** to catch a world-record tuna this coming season." I might; it's possible to be sure, even though it's extremely unlikely. Is Christian hope a hankering after what is extremely unlikely?

"I **hope** we'll soon learn to get along together, and class hostility, social conflict, racial prejudice, and financial exploitation will soon be a thing of the past." Anyone who speaks this way is most naive concerning human nature, and utterly ignorant of human history. Is Christian hope merely a childlike naiveté with respect to our human nature, and inexcusable ignorance with respect to our history?

You may have often wondered what hope there is for you and your situation in prison. Even in the best of circumstances, people can lose hope. But when facing time in prison, holding on to hope can be even more difficult.

Here is a short story I read recently about an ordained

brother. I pray it might give you some encouragement going forward. This brother is a professional brother in the Capuchin-Franciscan order, and has been for over thirty years. You may wonder what a religious brother has in common with you; after all, he lives such a different life. This is how the story is told.

He lives a tough life. He is a convicted felon. He received a sentence of life imprisonment at age twenty in 1948 for murdering his wife. As a child, his life had been hard; his family struggled through poverty during the Depression of the 1930s. His mother died while he was still a young boy. Only six months into his marriage, he snapped.

Grief and guilt overcame him as he was sent off to prison. He lived in a black hole of depression. He felt his only hope was to escape prison and disappear . . . and he began to plan for it. After several years, he was moved to another prison with lower security. His plan was to work his way up to a prison job where he would drive unaccompanied in a truck through the prison gates, never to return.

He played a game to get where he needed to be. He got a job cleaning the chapel, went to confession to try to impress the chaplain, and all the while, he was *stone cold* toward God. But something began to happen. Slowly his heart opened to God, and his life and attitudes began to change—without him noticing at first. The Scripture he read, the religious services he attended, and the words the chaplain spoke, all began to sink in—and change him. God never gave up on the brother, nor did the chaplain.

The result was slow and steady growth. He made a conscious decision to turn to God and to change his life. He trusted that God could and would work with him. He began to take prayer and religious services seriously. His reading of Scripture and fellowship with other like-minded prisoners made a difference.

Eventually, the chaplain gave him greater responsibility in the fellowship group. As he took that responsibility, he came to see God working in the lives of other prisoners as well. This further deepened his trust in God. It convinced him that God is real and loves people . . . including himself!

After his release from prison in 1967, he experienced further healing as he began to trust people and realize that he wasn't as worthless and unlovable as he thought. Steady and determined growth in the knowledge of God's life and love now sustains him.

This good brother's life shows that there is reason for hope. God never abandons his people. He pours out His love freely and generously. God gives hope to those struggling with life, who may believe that there is no life for them. The brother's life shows that there is. It shows, too, that God has great surprises in store for those that open their lives to Him.

I hope and pray that the story of this good brother gives each of you hope for your life and will serve as an example and inspiration to you. He is only one example of someone who has risen from darkness to walk in the light of Christ. Keep in mind that God is generous with us.

In the spiritual life, you'll never do great things for God unless you have your eye on the long-term goal—indescribable joy in his presence forever. The ecstasy of gazing upon Him whose beauty eternally awes the hosts of heaven, the exhilarating company of friends, family, and fascinating people from all ages—purified, glorified, finished masterpieces of divine love—this is what God will usher in, for those who are ready. May that truth strengthen you each day of your life.

God bless ya and God love ya too!

Chuck

Dear Chuck,

I have been trying to complete this to get it out to you. The truth is, I have been occupied with my case, although I have my attorney working on a habeas corpus petition. I am also putting together a habeas, because I had started to prepare one prior to my family retaining him, so I just continued on with it, with my friend helping me.

I wanted to continue it for a couple of reasons: to see how strong of a claim I have, and also, how good the case is that I would use to substantiate it. I also wanted to prepare one to make sure all the claims were covered with nothing at all left out. I again hope everything is well with you and yours. I hope to see you soon.

Chuck, I want you to have some record of my case, so I have attached a synopsis for you.

Synopsis:

I was driving to work on the morning of July 11, 2005, after a weekend of heavy drinking. I saw a girl I had been dating until a few days prior. I will quote the Virginia State Police report, as it is accurate. "An eyewitness observed a white Ford truck (me) ram a red Chevrolet truck (girl)." After the initial contact with the vehicles, police indicated that "the two vehicles were traveling in separate lanes, in the same direction. The witness reported that the white truck began moving left and the wreck happened." This version is from the Virginia State Police report given by an eyewitness on the morning of the accident. However, this version was never disclosed at trial or any other court proceedings. I was charged, tried, convicted, and subsequently sentenced to eighteen years for two attempted murders in the first degree because the girl had a passenger with her.

At trial the eyewitness testified to a completely different version as to what occurred, a version that suggests that I intentionally pushed the red truck into the opposite lane and oncoming traffic. The Commonwealth Attorney's theory was that my motivation to kill the driver and her passenger was because "she left me for her passenger and I became angry." At trial, while the prosecutor was putting on his witnesses and his evidence, my retained attorney never objected to any of the prosecutor's leading questions and didn't cross-examine the witnesses or question the totally different version of the statement already given to police.

My only witness was the driver of the red truck (girl); she was in court to testify on my behalf. I was thinking that when we called her to the stand, she was going to not only contradict the Commonwealth Attorney, but most importantly, she would prove wrong this theory that I was angry about her leaving me for her passenger, because she was, in fact, seeing someone else that I was fully aware of. The passenger even stated this fact at trial, but again, my attorney failed to bring this to the court's attention. Hired to represent me, it was my attorney's job to protect my constitutional rights. The Commonwealth Attorney's duty is to uphold the law and seek justice—not to fabricate or manipulate evidence to assure a conviction.

It was now the defense's turn to present witnesses and evidence, if any. I had been anticipating this moment, when we would call my witness, the driver of the red truck. My attorney called a recess and went to speak with my witness. It is an attorney's obligation to discuss strategies with clients, but here my attorney was telling me he wasn't calling my witness to the stand. Although I was insisting he call her, he ignored me and told the judge that he wasn't calling her, as he had stated in his opening statement before the court, "My witness will testify that he did not try to kill her, that it was an accident." I was dating the girl for about a year, and in that time I had stopped taking medication for a mental disorder, and I'd started drinking heavily, self-medicating myself. This is what caused us to break up.

Prior to my trial, my attorney motioned the court to have me psychologically evaluated to determine whether I was "suffering from mental diseases or defect." This was strongly urged by my mother and sister. I was evaluated by two state psychiatrists by order of the court to see if in fact I was competent to stand trial and determine my mental status at the time of the alleged offenses. I was never made aware of the results, so I assumed that there was nothing of any use in the evaluation. It wasn't until two years later—when I received my entire case that had been filed by my appeal attorney—that I discovered the report of the psychological evaluation, among other things that I did not know existed. The doctors who had examined me also interviewed the girl and learned that my condition had deteriorated over the length of time that she had known me, and that I wasn't trying to kill her. It was further concluded in the report that I was "exhibiting symptoms" of mental illness on the morning of the alleged offenses.

I thought my original attorney had been working in my best interest, even though he refused to call my witness, the driver of the red truck, the one I am accused of trying to kill. I now discovered this evaluation (by the two very reputable state psychologists) which states that I was affected by a mental disorder on the morning of the accident. Why would my attorney withhold this information from the court, and from me? Why would he not use this in my defense at my trial? Why would he not call my only witness to testify, the driver that I am accused of trying to kill, when she already testified at a preliminary hearing prior to the trial that it was an accident?

I have retained an attorney who is working on a habeas corpus petition, claiming violations of my constitutional rights. This all started in July 2005, and I don't know when it will end. The truth is, once the courts convict and sentence you, it is very difficult to get your conviction overturned. To get a habeas corpus petition granted on constitutional violations is even more difficult, even when trial errors are obvious or when the trial attorney made prejudicial errors, as mine did.

The driver of the red truck, who I was charged and convicted of attempting to murder, was in court to testify on my behalf, stating that the incident was an accident. She had already testified to this at my preliminary hearing. In fact, the local newspaper printed an article that stated she had testified that the incident was an accident. But they wanted to try me for attempted murder of two people because she had a passenger in the truck. My attorney refused to call on her in court, against my insisting, and because of this, I had no defense.

It is my personal belief that my attorney intentionally didn't call her to the stand. The reason I believe this is that my truck collided with another car, a Ford, whose driver's family name is associated with a judgeship. In all honesty, I was negligent and caused this accident. I am in NO WAY guilty of attempted murder, but with no defense, no witness, the Commonwealth had a field day.

The Commonwealth presented an eyewitness who testified to my pushing and ramming the red truck until it swerved over into oncoming traffic. I have a partial copy of a police report where the same eyewitness gives a completely different version.

I forgot to say that the driver of the Ford automobile also had a two-year-old with her. Thank God he was uninjured.

Here is another issue: The most severe injury was a concussion that my witness sustained. At trial the red truck passenger traveling with my witness (the driver of the truck) claimed a long list of major injuries. But my attorney failed to object or ask for proof of injuries. I know what the passenger said was false because my witness told me his worst injury was when the EMTs were removing him from the vehicle. My witness would not only have testified it was an accident, but she also would have discredited a lot that was testified to by the Commonwealth.

I hope this clarifies the situation. I am enclosing the eyewitness testimony I refer to above, and the police report statement that was given nine months apart. I also want to clarify that in the eyewitness testimony, he is saying that I was bumping and pushing, and then backed off and kept pushing it. It shows intent. However, in the police report, it doesn't show intent! My attorney had this information and never presented it or argued the conflicting testimony.

Dear Chuck,

I'm grateful that you took the time to search for info for me regarding my project. I've asked several other people on the outside for assistance, and they either seem too busy or feel I should be doing something else with my time. That attitude tells me they truly don't know anything about me and are judgmental.

In the mail we are permitted to receive five pieces of paper (per envelope) on any combination of paper/photos. I'm not suggesting anything, of course, but in the mail we are only permitted to receive letters, photos, money orders, and newspaper clippings. That's it! No stamps, unsigned greeting cards, etc.

Anyone can receive a letter from anyone on the outside . . . generally speaking. You should have no trouble writing to anyone in here from the group. I will, however, (tonight) obtain a paper with names and send it with this letter, if possible.

In a number of ways I can certainly empathize with the situation regarding those who are forgotten in nursing homes. I was in a Catholic orphanage up in Jersey until the eighth grade. There were four of us boys and eight girls in our class. For a field trip once, we were taken to a mental hospital in Philly for a tour. It was to enlighten us further on a human condition that is typically shut out from our society. I also worked in a hospital as a registered nursing student and had the chance to work with elderly patients who seemed to me to have no one. Working in the rescue business, I also have visited homes where elderly people were living alone. I'm well aware of this human condition—and it is sad. Lastly, I'll never forget the movie *The Trouble with Angels*, starring Hayley Mills. Her character had a hard time understanding why the people she loved had to die because she loved them so. She was referring to an elderly person. Somehow that struck me back then in the sixties, and it helped me form my compassion for this transition in life.

I don't know if I mentioned it much in my last letter, but I do my best to manage my depression. At one time I suffered greatly from it. I now know what the triggers are, and I deal with them as they come up. The elderly in nursing homes is one of them. I could not be in such an environment. It's too hard for me!

We in here do suffer some. Many are forgotten and have absolutely no one. In spite of what you may have heard otherwise, the people who work in this system don't care about the people in here. Granted we have many amenities that many people on the street don't even have, but opportunities to grow and change for the better, moral support, self-respect, hope, etc., for the most part do not exist. It has to come from the inside of an individual. Very few have the ability to do that. And so, in essence, we are warehoused like dogs in a kennel. This is the reality of our situation. The difference between us and the elderly in nursing homes is the fact that as younger individuals, we have the ability to better ourselves.

The support that is needed for these guys is hope. Maybe from time to time, obtaining info from the Internet—for things they need, like an address to get their TV fixed, or watch repaired. Maybe help in finding a book that is otherwise unavailable. These are the things that help keep the spirits up in addition to hope and urging someone to turn to God. Many in here are lost, confused, and broken spiritually. They are not academically inclined, so each individual must be addressed delicately.

I didn't mean to go on and on—sorry! I get that way from time to time. I hope my handwriting isn't too out of whack for you to read. I don't write much anymore.

Hello, Brother Chuck,

I'm sorry I have not answered your last letters. Just so much going on with my moving and all. I miss you and the brotherhood we shared. I don't know what happened, but I pray God will make a way to solve the hurt you must feel. This place is all right, but it is not private here. I share a dorm with ninety-three other people. In some ways it is a blessing, and at times it can be crazy. But all things considered, God wants me here. So who am I to deny his will?

I don't know what's going on with my family. None of my letters are being answered. All I can do is talk to God and ask him to find out how I can get in touch with them. The hardest part I have to deal with is being alone—forgotten, locked up, and unwanted by my old girlfriend because of the crime that I committed. I can't blame her for not wanting me anymore, or taking everything that I ever owned. I pray that God will send me a helpmate like he did for Adam. It's hard for me to go through this sentence without a soul mate, someone to call and write to. So all I can do is trust in God to find me somebody that loves God more than me. Because all of the other loves I had did not. And I did not live for God the way I should have.

Anyway, please pray for me, Chuck. Thanks, and God bless you.

Your brother in Christ.

Chuck,

Hello! Received your letter today. Thank you. Actually, it lifted my spirits. It is rather depressing here. In a way I miss the old place. I do miss services there. I don't get that experience here. The group is basically nonexistent. Only two of us inmates show up, and then it is only us, so there is no structure. I've made suggestions about it, but to date, no response. We do have a volunteer, though. He comes from Virginia Beach. He brings the Eucharist. Still no priest yet.

I'm still trying to get confirmed. I did receive a letter from the bishop informing me that he asked Father to do it, but now I'm not sure where he is, so that setback depresses me more, because I've been trying to have it done since '04. The chaplain here has done all he can do to help. Hopefully soon!

Good news! Two weeks ago I saw my daughter. It was all I could do not to cry. She is almost seven, and going on sixteen. Smart as a whip! That day was beautiful. I was able to get a picture of her and I just got it back last Thursday. I can't believe how big she is and how beautiful she is. I have been praying for a long time to see her. Goes to show how praying works!

Please pray that we get a priest here soon and that will motivate the Catholic men here to attend services. Please pray for me and healing, and for my daughter. I'll send you my photo if you'll send it back. Then you can see a little angel.

Bye for now.

Dear Chuck,

It was good to see you again. I wish we had time to talk more, but I take what I can get.

You are correct. My ex-wife moving on is the best alternative; at least, for her it is. I feel better after I wrote what I did and sent it off. We are living very different lives, and I have to accept that which I cannot change and move on myself.

I have decided to write the book. Even if it never gets published, at least it will be written down. Before my TV burned out, I did watch some of those *Dateline* reports. And you are correct: I was caught in a sting by the county police department. I have a difficult time with the label "predator." Not all of those men are predators. They are making poor choices; some are sex addicts, some *are* pedophiles, and some are predator pedophiles. Mine was part of my addiction and an opportunity that presented itself. I also think some of those men are trapped into doing it. And their decoy looks like she is having too much fun on a very serious matter. One of my friends in my pod had a great analogy for this: What do you do if your child is playing in traffic? You remove the child from traffic. Now these stings and laws reduce the traffic, but there is still traffic. So if they don't monitor their children's online activity and who and where they are online, then they are still in the traffic. They need education and what to do to be safe online. I like this analogy. It makes sense.

I found some info on Liberty University in the pod, and it looks like the MBA is the best option from them.

One of our Kairos outside team members is very into the rule of St. Benedict. My friend and I have looked at my incarceration as a monastic-style living metaphor. My Kairos friend has an idea to have a loose, monastic rule for us here and base it on the rule of St. Benedict, a "Ten Commandments for Prisoners" and other "rules" that pertain to the prison environment specifically. We want to be as inclusive as we can. It would be Christian but not denominationally tied. As we work it out, we eventually want to go to the outside with it and do sort of what the Dismas/Magdalene project does with housing and employment. So we have more going on. This will take years to come to fruition, but this would be a great thing to do while in here, and to take it to the outside upon my release. And the men, we could help, and the community we could build from the *inside* out, rather than trying to impose from the *outside* in. I am very excited about this.

Well, Chuck, I need to get going. God bless ya and God love ya, Chuck. See you soon.

Peace and Love

Ten Commandments for Prisoners of All Kinds:

I lay in the Hole in pitch blackness. The cell was six by eight feet, with a toilet and a washbasin. It was August. I'd been there naked, sweating, and stinking for eleven days. I knew that it was Hell and that I deserved to be there.

For months I had cursed the guards, screeched at my fellow inmates, thrown trays of food, hurled obscenities at God. Willing myself to die, I refused to take a bite of food for eighteen days. At the end of my ordeal, I was little more than a skeleton. But I found strength to rant and rave at anyone who came near me.

This was death row and I was exploding with hate. More than anything or anyone else in the universe, it was myself who I loathed. And with cause. In a homicidal rage I had shot a man. I admitted to myself—in June 1974—that I was a murderer, an adulterer, a coward, and a weakling. I was all these things and more, bur for the years of my manhood I had never been in jail and had been smug in my conviction that I was compassionate, valuable, intelligent, useful. Facing my own evil was a shock.

It is only God who can ease human suffering. I am an ignorant man, but I have learned one truth: God's grace is the paramount blessing of life. We grasp in a frenzy for baubles and disdain a treasure more valuable by far than diamonds or rubies.

It was this truth that I perceived there in the Hole. I came out of the bleak place and returned to my cell on death row, which was only less hopeful and stark. But then miraculously as I now feel, there was a light. Suddenly serenity flooded over me. I don't know where it came from, but I know it was not there before.

I sat at my tiny desk and tried to put on paper the thoughts, the emotions, the revelation, call it whatever you wish. I devised ten rules. In my vanity (for I am certainly a vain and ego-burdened man), I call them my "Ten Commandments for Prisoners of All Kinds."

I believe these precepts will bring peace to any person who tries to practice them. I stress that word because I know perhaps more than many that ideals are impossible to achieve in any kind of totality. But I know something else. I have been at peace during these past months. Despite the starkness of my position, and despite the fact that unless my sentence is changed by a higher court, I shall die reviled and dishonored in the gas chamber.

Please let me offer these commandments with some little measure of explanation. With them I give my sincere prayers that they will content some other friendly person, and give him peace and hope in this troubled and turbulent universe.

I. **I shall remember that I made my own troubles.** This memory will help me keep from whimpering. For many months I lay abed at night and whined. It was God, I said, who brought me this disaster. For surely I was innocent! I was not a felon but a good man. It is self-deception which is the worst kind of folly. For I was guilty as sin, and my soul was black.

II. **I will put away stereotypes and refuse to think in terms of "them" and "me."** In my frenzied dreams I was a powerful, omnipotent being. "They" were the judges, the prosecutors, the doctors, the jurors.

III. **I shall not vegetate. I will work gladly with my hands and my back, and try to create beauty with my words.** Since then I have written two novels and fifteen articles. Here on death row I can't work with my hands and my back. But if I should ever be free, I will try to be useful with my hands. Labor of a manual kind, I think, is perhaps one of the noble aspects of grace.

IV. **I will try each day to do at least one positive deed of which a free man might be proud.** One must never recount or even try to remember these acts. They must be done quietly, with no thought for gain of any kind. Yet the reward is vast. I, reviled at one time by all these friendless and hopeless boys on death row, am now cherished and loved by these, my comrades. If I have been able in some way to lessen their awful burdens, then I give sincere thanks to God.

V. **I will stay away from filth in language, thought, or deed.** This commandment, for me, is now impossible to keep. I am lustful and profane. But I can, and do, ask God's forgiveness, and strive continually to improve.

VI. **I will not be swayed by the scum which is to be found in all kinds of prisons.** And indeed, dear friends, those inmates of this and other prisons are no "scummier" than their comrades who enjoy "freedom." No person is free if he or she be evil and unrepentant. There is no liberty for any human except in the citadel of his secret heart.

VII. **I will embrace laughter and be determinedly cheerful.** For how could any gift be richer or more utterly free? When we smile, laugh, and joke, do we not escape for that moment from the delusion that we are paramount among God's creatures? And do we not refrain from the serious blunder of taking ourselves too seriously?

VIII. **I will try always to lessen these burdens that I have created for my loved ones.** I will kiss the tears that spill from my mate's faithful and beautiful eyes when we sing to each other on Saturday morning. I'll caress and comfort as best I can my beautiful children. I'll tell them that if it's God's will, we will be together one day in freedom. And if not, then in eternity.

IX. **No matter how I lived, I shall die with honor.** Trying to follow these commandments will free any of us from the

prisons we foolishly make for ourselves. My hope is that you find the peace of God.

—By Charles Doss, written while in prison in Florence, Arizona

To my friend, Brother Chuck,

How are you doing? I understand that your wife is not doing well in health. The golden years are not so golden. I talked with my dad this past Sunday evening. I always try to call them at a regular time (8:00 p.m.) on Sundays. I always called them each Sunday, even when I was not in prison. My dad tried to talk but got short-winded because of his health (bad heart). I called to talk to my mother but she was not home yet. She had her second knee replacement done on the 11th. My dad said she was in pain and walking with a walker, but still in rehab. So my mind is never here. I'm always thinking of my wife and daughters and my parents.

I want to ask you a question, and tell me if you are comfortable with it or not. I know you can't do anything that will jeopardize your status as a visitor. I wrote a poem entitled "My Lady of The Sea." I can share it with you, and I'd like to know if you can type it for me. I do not have access to a typewriter or a word processor. So please let me know.

I love woodworking, carpentry, fishing, going to flea markets, and collecting guns and target shooting. I did all of that outside. I had a job as a building engineer running a building. I was a contractor for the agency. I did this type of work in Virginia for twenty years. Oh, yes—I also restored my '53 Chevy pickup. I used to go to truck shows all the time. Now I have nothing.

My Lady of the Sea

When I was young, I was told that there are as many
women in the world as there are fish in the sea.
I have looked long into the sea, as far as I could see

for the lady of my dreams.
I've looked when the waters have been so rough
and at times with the slightest breeze.
Then one day, before my eyes, sitting on a rock
was the most beautiful creature I have ever seen.
She had long dark hair that blew with the slightest breeze.
When I looked into her eyes, I knew she was in need.
Her skin was so smooth and with a light tan;
I knew she must have traveled from over the sea.
At last I have found
my lady of my dreams.
Now the waters are so rough
which kind of pulled us apart.
I do hope no harm comes to her
or she gets caught in some fisherman's net.
One day when the waters become calm
I will go out and find
my lady of my dreams.

Dear Chuck,

I've finally been able to keep myself busy with a number of different projects. As I may have mentioned earlier, I'm now building a lighthouse, and I gotta say, it looks pretty good. I've got lights inside the living area, and one big one on the top. What I'm working on this week is attempting to rig the base of the big light with a rotating cover assembly. Tough, tough, very tough job, and if I can, I'm going to try and get it finished in time to bring over on visitation day. No promises though.

I'm also taking this month to prepare my lessons for a five-day session on anger management. I'm co-facilitating along with one of the counselors here. Then, starting in January, we'll begin a twelve-week course one night a week. It's all good for me because it gets me back into the classroom. I was a navy instructor for a while, and on the outside I was also a CPR instructor. I was also the training officer for our rescue squad. I like to teach, obviously, or maybe I just like to hear myself talk—ha ha!

I'm also still writing up my story on paper for the sex offender support group I'm in. It's hard doing that because it now seems so long ago; fifteen-plus years, and I'm certainly not the same person who came in here. But I guess it'll be good for me to tell it all, just to see how strong I am in still facing what I've done; and what perspective I take on it all.

I still have my electrical studies that I now keep up with.

I had forgotten to mention to you, and I'm sure you had been wondering, what I've been using for tools in building the ships and this lighthouse. Believe it or not, there are only a few. Several pairs of fingernail clippers . . . one main pair and several backups; a paperclip used for a small hooking tool and to apply glue-gel glue or white Elmer's school glue. And I use it for making and burning holes. Also, of course, a lighter for soldering. Small razor blades from the Bic razors, several large and small black clamping paper clips to help hold the glued wood and paper together, etc. And that's pretty much it! Amazing what one can do to improvise in a crunch!

Well, I was able to finally get everything paid off (my TV, CD player, CDs) and purchase some long johns and a knit cap for the upcoming winter. It was the attorney who is representing me before the parole board, and who is a friend of a friend of my foster family, who was kind enough to treat me with the loan to finally get up-to-date with my electronics. My TV had been out for a year and a half, and I was still nursing my old cassette player and cassettes . . . yikes! Never again. I was in the process of paying $25 a month for about at least the next two years, that is, until I was blessed by a dear friend.

Already, it seems, I go up for parole again next month. Or at least I should. I don't have any kind of parole release plan in place because I don't expect them to release me yet. It's only my second time up, and I believe they'll want me to be in here yet for another five to seven years. In other words, I received a sentence of life plus eighty years for a first-time rape conviction, and an offense which is very probably not going to recur. And, although I was eligible for parole in twelve and a half years, they'll want me to do about twenty to twenty-two instead. Maybe, just maybe, it's unfair, but it is what it is, and it also wasn't just my victim that was affected by what I'd done. There was my wife and son, and all of the rest of my family, and my coworkers and friends, and everyone else I've hurt because of my betrayal and illness. So, to put it all in perspective, twenty to twenty-two may, just may, be fair!

I don't really know of the cause about the above, it's not for me to judge. And so I am left to continue to work on myself day by day.

You should know, though, that it's people such as yourself and others who make it all just a little more bearable, and allows some kind of hope to stay alive.

Dear Chuck,

Well, I'm writing in part because a situation has come up with me. I was expecting to go up for parole later this month, only to find out that I'll be going up be this Thursday.

I also wasn't expecting my attorney in D.C. to be active during this round of parole hearings because it is only my second time up. Also, because of the fact that it is the second time, I'm not bothered to network any prospects for a place to stay—or employment.

Given, though, that we have a good case to present to the board, and the fact that the attorney representing me is intelligent, efficient, thorough, and from a huge law firm, my chances are significantly enhanced when it comes to possibly making parole—even this time around. I'm still not optimistic—but considerably more hopeful this time around.

My problem is this: If they were to release me, I need first to give them information about where I would stay and work before they did, and it would be better, of course, if I did this before they made their decision, because it would reflect better on my being proficient.

I'm trying to seek out all possible avenues to effect resolving this problem. My aunt and uncle, who are now in their late seventies and early eighties respectively, were going to help me three years ago, and hire me on as a handyman and caretaker for a number of months, until I could seek out and establish a more permanent form of residence and employment. But now they are thinking of selling their home and moving into a condo. So the former arrangement will not be possible.

As you can imagine, I'm a person of good skills when it comes to working with my hands. I'm good at general building maintenance and management. I spent ten years in the navy in operations intelligence, and seventeen as a volunteer firefighter—six of which I was an EMT. I also have registered nursing training and ER experience. We also spoke of my experience in the horse farm. I'm a quick learner and hard worker, and am in reasonably good health at fifty. I have about three years of college under my belt as well.

I am also not the same person who came into the system fifteen years ago. I've matured significantly and educated myself with regard to the factors that brought me in here, and I've faced my demons straight in the eyes and stared them down. I'm loyal and am a person of deep conviction, and I can be trusted.

I'm confident that my release would be contingent also to meeting restrictions placed on me by the parole/probation office. These restrictions would include but not be limited to an ankle bracelet or some form of monitoring system for a period of time, personal visits by the parole officer, maybe a polygraph for me every month or so, and my being involved in some sort of support group for sex offenders.

I don't struggle with sex-addiction problems any longer, and I know how and where to turn for help and support for strength should and when I would need such help. And I'm not afraid to ask for help—or ashamed, for that matter—any longer.

I do struggle with depression still, but mainly now because I don't have a good support network in place here. It's simply not possible. Close friends, acquaintances, and support professionals are whom I would count on, on the outside. My faith in God and staying healthy are key to my staying strong with regard to dealing with and keeping my depression in check.

So you see, I have what I feel is a good potential plan in place and have attempted to attain all the tools necessary to effect succeeding at implementing that plan.

I'm sending this to you now because I'll be seeing my attorney next Saturday. He'll probably meet with me for about an hour. He is also working on having the parole board defer on making a decision regarding my release until he's had time to discuss it with the chairperson. I imagine that may be a month from now.

Chuck,

Thank you for you recent letter. It was nice to hear from you. Yes, Father did come on October 24. I am so glad to have finally completed the confirmation! I am also very thankful that Father was willing to drive for eight hours to do it (four here/four back). The sad thing is that of the approximate fifteen listed Catholics, only three showed up. At this point there are only three of us that come to the weekly services regularly. I have made suggestions to the chaplain to try to reach out to the other men who are not coming. We will see how that turns out. We still do not have a priest that comes. Father was the *first* in over a year. A sad thing it is! I feel that something should be done. Our chaplain is in constant contact with the bishop's office, and he has been for months. Nothing yet. I truly miss our services every week before my transfer. Please tell the men there that they truly have something special!

Ask that they pray for our group, so that the men who don't come have a change of heart and start to come so we will be ready for the soon-to-arrive new inmates. We are expanding by approximately 600 real soon.

Thank you again, and hope to hear from you soon!

Dear Chuck,

I received all your letters, Chuck; I am sorry for taking so long to write back, but November and December are the hardest months of the year for me, and my mind is never in the right place during those months. The reason the Chaplain has not seen me lately is because I have missed the services on Tuesday for nearly a month now. I asked to be placed on the list once again, so I hope I can be there next week.

As for my mother, she lives in Washington State on the West Coast with her boyfriend. She is doing okay but could be better if she could let go of the past.

In regards to my sister now; last I heard from her was during my trial in 1997. I'd love to speak to her and seek forgiveness, Chuck, but I would have to deal with Social Services to find and contact her, and after the way they portrayed me during my trial, I want nothing to do with them at all. If I could speak to her and know she forgave me and see she was okay, maybe then I would be capable of forgiving myself, but until then. . . .

I really appreciate your words of encouragement and your discretion regarding my situation, Chuck. I am okay; a bit depressed, because next week I will be twenty-eight years old and on the same day I will begin my ninth year in prison.

The main purpose of me writing is to wish you and your family a Merry Christmas and a Happy New Year! I hope you all have a good one!

I will close for now, but I will write again soon.

God bless you.

Dear Chuck,

Hi there, brother. I got your Christmas letter. I felt I owed you one since I only had time to send a card. While the sentiment rang true, I wanted to relate a few more things than a warm holiday greeting. Hopefully, your Christmas went well and provided you and your lovely wife with joy.

Life here continues to offer challenges. Nevertheless, our Lord has been ever beside me and all is well to some degree. In truth, there really is no place one may go in prison to escape the injustices. Tell my friends that they really have it good by comparison to *this* place. It's funny what "blessings" we may count when we know not the truth of each condition in our lives.

Other volunteers told me they might come to visit me. Tell 'em I can't wait to see them the next time you do. I told them as much in my last letter, but extra positive thoughts sent are always a good thing. In truth, I miss you all very much. It's not that I don't have friends and brothers in the faith here. It's just that you were, and are, very special to me, and will always have a special place in my heart.

As to my biological mother, she hasn't responded since her first and apparently only letter. I'm not sure what to make of this. She mentioned in that letter that she was on disability, but didn't clarify. I hope and pray she's doing all right. A letter from my (before this unknown to me) brother was also enclosed. I wonder if he would write if she were fallen ill? Perhaps she simply needs time to process that fact that I am where I am . . . ? I'll simply trust that the Lord will work out the details.

How are the stained-glass projects coming along? Glad to hear you still visit my brothers at my former facility. Wish them well for me. Hope your holidays are going well. Let me know what all you've been up to besides your ministry to the sick, poor, elderly, and imprisoned. Jump out of any good airplanes lately? That's something I've always wanted to do. Maybe one day we can go together? Wheee! (Three more years barring an early release.)

My folks went to see my sister up north for Christmas. My nieces are overjoyed. Sadly, my sister switched phone carriers, so I've been unable to call because of some technical difficulties that still need to be worked out. Thus, save for my aunts whom I still *can* call, it's been a lonely week. Ah, well, I'll always have Jesus with me as we celebrate his birthday. Thank you for helping to keep me mindful of the season with your letter. It gets tempting to be a Scrooge as a form of emotional self-preservation.

Well, my brother, I shall leave you to your merrymaking, with a fond wish for a Happy New Year. Take care of yourself. May God bless and keep you and your family.

Love, in Christ.

Dear Chuck,

Thanks for your last letter; it was good to see you last week! Never enough time to talk.

You have seen the fallout from the increase in inmates here; some of us possibly going, and yes, some in the group have had to give up, or will be giving up, single cells as this happens. You are correct about it not being fair, but nothing in prison and in life is fair. So far, the honor pod will not be affected. Last week, I was #11 on that list.

Dorms are cheaper to build. All they have to do is secure a building, not a building and a cell. So they became more popular for lower-security prisons as a money saver. These are overcrowded as well, but there is a limit to what they can do, and things are more "open" so you are not on top of each other—so I am told.

We were told we could choose cell partners, so I am looking for one. No takers yet. If I can't find one, I will get someone off the bus. I am praying for guidance; let God give me what and whom *He* feels is best for me.

Ah, spreading some more time to us through the program with kids and incarcerated fathers. I know of this program vaguely. It does meet at night—I think every two weeks, or monthly. I don't know anyone in it. I don't attend. I can't have contact with my kids, so it is moot for me. It is supposed to be a good program. I hope it works out for you to participate.

There is a mess going on with the lockdowns they did last week. One man from my pod is now in jail, and may not be returning, and possibly may be transferred. Two of the roof construction men (inmates) were fired and put into jail. The construction crew inmates were moved to another prison on Thursday. Three shanks (knives of some sort) were found—supposedly.

Tearing my cell apart, they found nothing, as I knew they would. But it took me forty-five minutes to put my cell back together—not fun.

I won't say I'm not displeased that the man is no longer in my pod, but I won't gloat over it. It could have been me. People do get what is coming to them, and this man had been asking for it. It is a sad situation.

We are holding an election of sorts to choose our group leader this coming Tuesday.

Chuck, take care. God bless ya, and God love ya.

Dear Chuck,

I hope this letter finds you in good health and in good spirits. Thanks for the updated letter, my good friend and brother in Christ Jesus.

My life is on a very slow pace right now. I'm still looking for a job. Nobody wants to hire me because I just got out of prison, have no credit, and my age. This is not good. But, I still believe that God/ Jesus is in control and I just have to keep the faith. Amen.

I have to work because the Department of Corrections is making me take a Wednesday-night class for my crimes that cost me $50 every week, and twice a year, I have to take a lie-detector test for $250, which I also have to pay for. So keep me in your prayers, please.

I'm staying with my Kairos friends from way back to 1990. I cannot afford to go on my own yet. If they didn't come through like they did, I would have been in a halfway house in Richmond. But praise God for his continual mercy on me and my soul. Amen.

Maybe someday, Brother Chuck, you and I can come together for old times' sake and to show our friendship towards one another. If that sounds okay to you, my friend, please let me know. Amen.

Chuck—you did very well in the letter to the bishop. I hope and pray that he will answer it with great joy and support. When you see the brothers at church, tell them I said hello, and they are in my prayers. Always.

Until later, Chuck, take care, and I will always continue to pray for you and your family. Amen.

May God/Jesus continue to bless you now and always. Amen.

Dear Chuck,

This arctic weather really reminds me of my younger days living in Minnesota. It was a "dry cold." Jeez? When it gets into the teens, there is no water in any form other than solid. Great for skating though. Driving must be so much fun. St. Christopher must be working overtime.

Well, I haven't heard a peep from my biological mother since that first, and only, letter. I think she was overwhelmed by my first letter of response, coupled with the discovery of my current situation. The Lord will just need to continue to work in His mysterious ways on His schedule. Cool by me. All I have is her first name and an address in Michigan. It's probably a mailbox, i.e., P.O. Box . . . Yet another thing lost to me from this whole mess? Time will tell.

Your continued letters and updates are most welcome and highly appreciated. I'm kind of saddened that they're breaking up the core group back there. You're probably meeting all sorts of new members and spreading the love, as it were.

Well, for every tiny victory there's a setback around the bend at this place. I won back the ability to use a computer in order to complete my computer science correspondence courses, only to have my request for the subsequent lessons rejected. The lack of *true* commitment to education in here is disappointing. Actually, I think we've had a variation of this discussion before. The object goal seems to be to make sure educated inmates leave here less skilled and less able than when we arrived. Essentially, they are attempting to enforce a type of economic slavery upon us once our sentences are done. It's never going to be over, is it? *I'll* find a way to overcome it, but what about my brothers?

I guess that about does it for this installment. I'll try to write more often. You and your family will always be in my prayers. Say a few for me too. Heaven knows I need 'em. Take care, stay warm, and keep the faith.

Dear Chuck,

Thanks for your letter. I have had a wicked cold since last Wednesday and it is finally letting up, somewhat. I haven't been this sick in a long time. One good thing: I lost my ability to taste for the past three days, so the food in the mess hall just went down—*that* is a blessing from God!

I don't think the chaplain owns a TV—so it is possible that Father Rodus eluded him. I heard it on TV and on NPR, so I'm not sure how you can be *that* out of tune with the world. Our psychologist says he doesn't watch TV, listen to the radio, or read a newspaper. I don't get that, but hey, that is his choice.

CURE (Citizens United for Rehabilitation of Errants) is an excellent organization. I have been a member for three years now. Their newsletter is great, but it is sporadic in coming. I know they are short of volunteers and cash. National CURE is good and has a sex-offender subdivision, which I am trying to find out about. You will enjoy being a member of CURE.

You are correct about the current head of the parole board and her attitude toward prisoners. Your words are kinder than ours, she is an a—— to us. What gets me is that she is a crime victim. How can she be fair and impartial if she has been a victim? Where is the prisoner advocate on the board? I'm not eligible for parole, but this upsets me, and this woman needs to go. The time for "tough on crime" is gone—it *doesn't* work. Virginia needs to wake up. Most states have given up the 85 percent law as well, but it stays here, so Virginia can say it is "tough on crime."

Those eligible for parole should be given criteria to make it. Those of us under the 85 percent or "New Law" need to be given opportunities to earn extra good time based on behavior and participation in programs, school, etc. We'll see. Hope you can help concerning this.

Good that your letter will be published. I am going to write a response to it and have it ready to send in. I hope you can get more people to sign up for prison ministry. Many correction centers as well as local jails could use some help in gaining a Catholic presence. Good luck!

Okay, I'll close here, Chuck. God bless ya and God love ya! See you in March!

Dear Chuck,

Hey, big guy! Hope this letter finds you doing well. I can't believe how chilly the nights still are! It almost seems like fall is approaching. But I imagine I'd better enjoy it all because it probably won't be around for too much longer.

I spoke to my aunt today. She sounded good over the phone, even though she said she had a cold. She reaffirmed to me that it's okay to call her. She seemed very receptive to the idea, so feel free to do so, of course. I imagine my uncle and you may get along well in conversation.

Thanks a great deal about the movie contact. That shooting for me was very surreal, especially the scene at the roller rink in Virginia Beach. I gotta say, I wish I were around in my teens between the mid-1940s and '50s. Then again, there's the war. I'm not sure that I would have wanted any part of that! All three of those wars were terrible. Can you imagine being back in that time period and knowing what we know now?

Well, we're all ready for Good Friday. We have everything arranged, and it should be a moving experience. Next year—if this one goes well—we hope to invite new members and guests, as well as other inmates.

I really must apologize for my handwriting. I don't know what is wrong, but something is. I seem to have lost a bit of coordination in my right hand, and I don't know if it's a pinched nerve or something else that I don't even want to think about.

Anyway, a grasshopper walks into a bar and takes a seat. The bartender says, "Hey! We have a drink named after you!" and the grasshopper says, "What? That's the silliest thing I've ever heard of; who'd name a drink Larry!"

Your silly brother in Christ.

Hey Chuck,

Received your April 2 letter. Always good to hear from you. It doesn't take long for me to get rolling wherever I'm located with God in control. I am making the best of things. The food and the commissary aren't as good, but the showers are great, something that was a bit weird before. There are other positives and negatives, but I still lost more by the transfer than I gained.

At my previous residence, I had a Catholic roommate and a job teaching the academic side of the cooking school—talk about good food. What I lost was a close-knit Catholic community, weekly AA meetings with three great outside volunteers, and three other programs (Substance Abuse II, phase III, and phase IV). Over the years I have been a program junkie—taking all that was available. What I lost before that makes me want to remain here is the anxiety I felt for the five months while I was there. Clearly, my problem is the five and a half inches between my ears, the size of the group, and being outside the core members.

Monday was more of a business meeting rehearsal for our retired bishop's Good Friday visit. Yes, we are having a special service, and I have already cleared my absence with my new boss. I started my job five days early yesterday. Spiritually, I felt disappointed about Monday's service until they mentioned that they usually do the rosary on Mondays.

Tuesday, I felt better, but with the thought of losing our priest next month and the group's pessimism that a replacement will take six months or more, I wasn't looking at the positive. I met the two volunteers who visit twice a month. They seem like great guys. Evidently, one tried to get approval to visit weekly but was told not to push it. I was talking with them about other volunteers in the area in hopes of getting weekly visits like I saw at my previous facility. Considering there are sixty on our pass list with half as confirmed Catholics (the largest Catholic "prison" community that I have seen), I figure there should be more support. My enthusiasm to write letters was not well taken by some—especially the leader of the group. They have no 2007 missals, and what missals are available are in the hands of a few.

My roommate is seventy years old with over forty years in the ministry. He has only recently been incarcerated with a five-year sentence, arriving last August. He hasn't had the best of experiences so far. His first roommate assaulted him after several attempts to change rooms. That landed him in protective custody for a while—not a pleasant place to be.

Well, my friend, I must go.

Dear Mr. Brown,

Grace and peace. And thank you for the recent salvo fired into the conscience of the Church—I mean, of course, your fine column in the April 23rd edition of the *Catholic Virginian*. It is a great boost to my spirit to know that you have the courage to stand against the torrential tides of demagoguery presently being poured out upon the souls of sex offenders throughout this culture. That many within the Church walk arm in arm with blatant oppressors is a crime against the very heart of Jesus Christ and His embodiment of Divine Mercy. Public policy programs aimed at the virtual extirpation of sex offenders must be met with strong determination and moral indignation. I pray that you will continue to press the initiative against the pressure of Pharisaic politicians who so often prostitute their nominal associations with Christ's Church for the sake of power and ambition. Our Lord's words for such people are well known to those who love Him. Be strong and courageous! And do not be afraid. You have the Eternal and Almighty with you—and the prayers of all the truly faithful.

As a convicted "sex offender," I know well the pain and anguish of being marginalized as a leper. And, yet, I do not know it like most of my offending brothers. I am a new species of sex offender, convicted under a statue merely eight years old. I was sentenced to fifty years for my crime of Internet solicitation of an undercover cop. Demonstrating what I'm certain the judge considers mercy (how, I will never comprehend), forty-three years of my sentence for the "heinous" crime of illicit speech was suspended. I have a little more than twenty months remaining on my sentence.

I'm a recent convert to Catholicism, and am so very happy to have found my way to what I believe is the true Church of Jesus Christ on earth. Coming from a background as a Southern Baptist, I am still discovering many of the enriching aspects of the Church like a newborn babe. I praise God for prison, because I cannot think of another experience which may have produced such a dramatic self-evaluation and deepening of my love of Jesus Christ. In that process, I discovered the path to Rome. So God has shown me great favor and I am thankful to Him.

It is my prayer to be a vessel for God's redemptive and restorative power. I am particularly prayerful for the grace to work in the areas of justice reform and alternative punishment. And because I have been labeled a "violent sex offender"—and I think rather unjustly so—I am also feeling called to engage in the effort to defend what many regard as the defenseless. Sex offenders need an organization (or apostolate) strictly dedicated to defending their human dignity, their right to meaningful restoration, and to oppose the nefarious amount of invective thrown at them. Groups who are working so hard to pass tougher laws against sex offenders constantly make use of statistics that are inaccurate and also tend to lump all sex offenders into the same category. These things are unreasonable. Yet, little is being done to organize against the onslaught.

I am blessed in so many ways that I have an obligation to spend the rest of my natural life endeavoring to show the face and spirit of Christ to my brothers . . . those who have been orphaned from society itself: sex offenders. I know it will not be easy, and I know that I will be doggedly opposed and probably even threatened, but I also know that He who is within me is greater than he who is in the world!

Praise God for you, Mr. Brown. Thank you for the inspiration. Continue to champion the cause of God's mercy and true righteousness. Don't be afraid to kick the good of oppression and stir up the temple. Wake the Body of Christ from its material slumber. God bless you and keep you.

Dear Chuck,

Thank you for your last letter. Yes, I did read your article and the response. I already wrote a reply letter which grows longer every time I do a rewrite. They probably won't print it! I'm quite sure you'll have defenders from almost every prison in the system. Hopefully that provides you with comfort and encouragement.

Life here continues to offer the usual challenges. I'm still being blocked from taking my next semester's correspondence courses. This highlights my point (and yours) precisely! I'm paying for this, not "taxpayer dollars"! I just need these prison bureaucrats to get out of my way so that I can invest in my future. Do you wonder at my anger and frustration? At least I am blessed with a loving family who'll support me once I'm out if I'm not ready to do so at 100 percent. If that were not so, the temptation to seek retribution would be great, but for the fact I know that's what they want.

My folks just came for a visit last Saturday. They're getting way too white-haired for my tastes. What can you do? That, to me, represents the greatest punitive aspect of prison: lost time with loved ones. That's not enough for the get-tough-on-crime types, though, is it? All one can do is pray and stay in Christ Jesus as best one can. Anyway, despite getting older, they still have their health.

Hope your family is doing well. If ever anyone needs prayers of the faithful, do not hesitate to let me know. You've been busy this year, haven't you? Between writing, stained-glass window making, jumping out of perfectly good airplanes, and being a Eucharistic minister, you do pretty good. In all this, you must be spending quality time with loved ones. . . . I hope you're fitting everybody in. I, for one, am grateful for all your letters and good works. Thank you.

Well, Brother, I'll let you get back to your busy life. Say hi to everyone for me. I'll write again soon. May God bless and keep you and yours for all the days of your lives and beyond. Keep me in prayer.

Dear Chuck,

Hey buddy, it was great seeing you Tuesday. Too bad that things are so rushed when you come to see us, because it would be great to be able to just relax and hang out. Anyway, I think it's great that you were asked to join the Diocesan Prison Ministry Advisory Committee—good luck with that. I think we may see some real prison reform in the next couple of years. Many states around the country are looking to alternatives to warehousing inmates (i.e., giving out long sentences and little or no rehabilitation programs) because of the enormous cost involved. Hopefully Virginia will follow suit.

Also, as you've probably heard, former Virginia attorney general Mark Early has had a real change of heart. He used to be the stereotypical "tough on crime" and "law and order" politician, but now he is calling into question the practice of handing out long sentences with little emphasis on rehabilitation. That's awesome news because you would think he could be very influential toward the state legislature. We'll see.

P.S. Father told a joke Tuesday about an American and a Russian. It reminded me of one that they told us in marine boot camp: A marine and a Russian soldier, part of a "goodwill / get-to-know-each-other group," somehow became lost and isolated in the wilderness of Russia. Suddenly, a huge bear comes out of nowhere, running straight for them. The marine calmly reaches into his backpack and gets out a pair of sneakers and, taking off his boots, starts to lace them up. The Russian, panicking, says, "Comrade, what are you doing—you cannot outrun a bear!" The marine says, "I don't have to outrun the bear; I just have to outrun you!"

Dear Mr. Brown,

Thank you for your reply to my letter. As previously stated, my time in prison has been enlightening. The situation is also difficult. I have no family in Virginia. My father is in Maine and my mother, grandmothers, and sisters are in Florida. Since the distance is so great, I have seen my father one time and my mother three times during my two-and-a-half-year imprisonment. Prisons separate the inmate from their families and from the community, and this makes reintroduction harsh and a major factor in recidivism.

Prisons affect family members also, and not only by being separated from their loved ones. My mother has fought tirelessly to try to get justice. If someone is in politics or the justice system, she has written to them. This includes the President of the United States and the governor of Virginia. She feels that somehow this is her fault.

Our only hope now comes from a writ of habeas corpus. Things look good, but as you can imagine, I have little faith in our judicial system doing the right things. My only hope is God doing what he does best: bringing justice from injustice.

I would be glad to hear from you again. With regards to the documents sent, they are yours to keep. I have many copies. I appreciate your prayers in this matter.

God bless.

Dear Chuck,

I received your letter today. Thank you for your timely response. I did not realize you had never heard of *Prison Legal News*, which has been in circulation for about seventeen years now and was started in prison. Rather than just sending an address, I have decided to send one of my old copies so that you can see what it is about before trying to purchase it. I believe it will be of great assistance.

Yes, my mom really does love me, as do all my other family members. There is seldom a day that goes by that I don't get mail. I truly am blessed. It is unfortunate that I had to go through this in order to see how blessed I was and am.

I received a blessing today. One of my sentencing orders was incorrect, giving me an extra three months in prison. For two and a half years I have been fighting to get this changed. I first noticed this two weeks after my sentencing. I contacted my attorney about the matter. He told me the order was correct and that I was "just reading too much into it."

After that I ordered a copy of my transcript. In that transcript the judge states three times that my sentence is for twelve months. The Commonwealth Attorney questions the twelve-month sentence. The sentencing order said fifteen months.

Geared with this evidence, I wrote the court asking them to correct the error. Again I was told there was no error. If you read my enclosure with my first letter, you know the conflicts of interest and what I was up against with the court.

My mom then took up the fight by contacting DOC (Department of Corrections), the Supreme Court, and the attorney general's office. Neither of us had any legal knowledge, nor could we afford another attorney after being taken by the first one. DOC said they could not change my release date without an amended sentence order. The Supreme Court stated they could not do anything basically because it was presented in letter form rather than legal form. The attorney general's office just didn't answer.

Then I met another inmate who has become a good friend and he convinced me I had a decent chance at overturning my case through a habeas corpus. This became even more convincing when we found case law showing that I was really not guilty of the charges presented. He helped me with my habeas, and one of our grounds was my attorney's ineffective assistance in that he failed to recognize the error or fix the error once brought to his attention.

In the attorney general's response they concede that there is an error, that they will have it fixed, and then that ground will be moot.

A month later I get a letter from their office stating that his amended order per my habeas corpus is enclosed. Upon inspection of the document, I found it was exactly the same as the erroneous document. The only amendment was who had certified the document. I instantly filed a motion opposing the order. A week later I received a copy of a letter written to the Circuit Court asking them to verify that the amended order was indeed correct. One would think that if you concede that something has an error, and when the supposed corrected item arrives, it is exactly the same, then it is still erroneous. Instead, they asked if it was correct.

Today I received more paperwork from the attorney general's office. In it was a letter they wrote requesting the Supreme Court to enter the information in my case. The next thing was a letter from the Rockbridge clerk, stating that the amended order is indeed the correct one, and enclosed is a copy of the order and the arrest warrants where the sentence was written on the book.

Since I had seen the amended order already, I did not look at the attached order. Instead, I went to the documents that were sent as proof. These actually proved my case. Later, while going through the paperwork again, I read the sentencing order. It had been corrected. Why could they not simply say, "We found that the document was indeed in error. Please find a newly amended order which properly reflects the sentence." Instead, they try to slide it by that they did not make an error when first amending the order.

What I wonder is, did they purposely not make corrections to the document when doing the amendment in order to try to slide it by me? I mean, the last letter was clearly a save-your-butt move.

I tell you this as it is insightful of our "justice" system. You are right in that we need prison reform to be of a more reformative nature. I believe first we need reform in our justice system. Let's start with oversight committees that are approachable and focused on correcting injustices done by the courts. Let's face it: Judges have almost been lifted as high as God. Judges don't make mistakes. Sure, there is an appeal process, but only certain things meet the criteria. Even if they do most of the time, the appeal courts process the appeals so quickly that they totally miss the point of the argument. Second, they really don't want to overrule one of their judges. It is only the most obvious, grievous errors that get relief.

It is well known that the longer one is in prison, the harder it is to reenter society. We need nationalized sentencing standards to which judges must strictly adhere. We no longer live in a society where information is not easily shared. We are a nation of fifty states, not fifty different nations. My father's neighbor is an attorney in Maine. He did my dad a favor when I was trying for a pardon by reviewing my case. He found I was sentenced above the guidelines—this, even though I had never been in trouble previously. It is coupled with the evidence of the mildest form that may possibly fit under the statute.

Lastly, put the burden of funding for incarceration on the counties, not the state. That way, if a county wishes to take a tough-on-crime stance, or tougher on crime, they must pay for the extra time sentences.

It will be then that justice will actually be close to just. I hope all of this is understandable, and of course, I will pray for you.

God bless,

Your brother in Christ

Dear Chuck:

Howdy there. Got your letter. Good to hear from you. Hope this finds you doing well. All goes well enough here. With the 115-degree-plus heat index this past week, I had a busy work week (by our standards). Figures, after shooting off my big mouth about four-hour work weeks, I'm called to work all week in the blazing heat. No complaints, though; I enjoy my work, and I can handle the heat.

I agree with you: Our criminal justice system has evolved into a questionable system, or even an injustice system. And I agree that money plays a big part in that. Virginia has made an enterprise out of it. I think another big part is the political aspect of it. To be "soft on crime" is a taboo label and assured political suicide. Our legislators will sacrifice fairness, justice, constitutional rights, civil rights, whatever, so they can maintain a tough-on-crime persona.

In my case, the Commonwealth Attorney and judge were hard, but fair. I'm trying to get the court's ruling to be upheld, not overturned—a rather unique position for an inmate to be fighting for. But I, like you, hear many horror stories. Given my own experiences, I sometimes must question these stories, though. But I do know that injustices can and do occur. I think mostly they begin with the police, then no one further up the line (prosecutors, judges) wants to buck the system without the facts being overwhelmingly in the defendant's favor. If the wrongness, unfairness, and injustice don't scream and jump out to slap someone in the face, it's subject to be ignored. And let's face it: If someone is labeled by law enforcement as a criminal element, they'll use any means to get you on anything, because even if you didn't do it, you're guilty of something else.

Labels are a terrible thing, Chuck. And, if one is labeled as such, the police believe it is their job to get you off the streets by whatever means necessary, and the prosecutors believe it is their job to *keep* you off the streets by whatever means necessary. And, woe be unto you if the judge is swayed to their way of thinking.

That was one thing that helped me out so much: My parole officer and the prosecutor clearly saw that I had turned my life around and I was seen as an asset to the community. By that, and my voluntary admission, asking for help, and their investigation clearing me of any and all other allegations and concerns, I escaped being labeled as one they do not want in their community. I was fortunate and blessed that they were fair, even to the extent of investigating to find the truth. I had a top-notch attorney, and that was all I asked for—let the truth come out and make a fair decision based on that truth.

My attorney advised against such a course of action. He told me if they investigated and found the truth of all things, he couldn't object to anything once we get into court. You see, this attorney of twenty years' experience was accustomed to his clients *not* telling the whole truth. I asked him if all I was telling him was 100 percent truth, would I walk out of that courtroom a free man? He said yes, but… I interrupted. I told him, "There is no but; I've told you the truth, so prompt them to investigate." And Chuck, in court the prosecutor recommended I be released, and that's what the judge did.

The parole board, however, is not the least bit interested in such things. They have the documentation to prove it all, and they ignore it all. I am scheduled to go to the law library the 16th, 17th, and 20th. Thus far, the jailhouse lawyers haven't been of much help to me. I have found out there's a court-appointed attorney that comes here to assist inmates with their legal work, but he is limited in what he can do. I understand he can't even give advice. But I'm requesting to talk to him. Maybe he will sympathize with my plight and make a real effort to help me. Nothing ventured, nothing gained.

My dad has been sending me some pictures, as I lost my photo album when I got sent to prison. Here is one of my girlfriend and me, taken in 2003 in our den. Now you can put a face with the words, and thank you for returning it. It's my favorite picture of us. Well, my friend, that's about all the whatnots I know for now. Thank you for your letters; I always enjoy them, and they are always a boost to my disposition. God bless you.

Peace be with you.

Dear Chuck,

Hope this finds you doing well. All goes well enough here. From your letters it sounds like your plate is about overflowing. Didn't know retirement was so much work, did ya?

Oh yes, I'm a big-time dog lover. My girlfriend and I had a black Lab named Angel. When the parole board violated me, she went to a PETA shelter. It's now three years later and I still miss her terribly. My girlfriend and I stayed together until February 2006. We'd write, talk on the phone, and she'd come visit me at the correction center.

Yes, addiction is a terrible thing, and I can easily make a hundred valid excuses on her behalf. But I can't allow myself to do that. The danger of me falling into it myself is too great. I made a nonnegotiable boundary. I drew a line in the sand and said anyone who crosses this line with their drug usage cannot be in my life. I wish it could be different, but that's the way it has to be for my own well-being. My girlfriend understands that, and agreed that "I'm better off without her." I still pray every day that Jesus will bring His lost sheep back.

I'm on standby status with my legal pursuits right now. I need to see the institutional attorney. Here's what I found: At the end of the article that empowers and authorizes the parole board, it says, "The provisions of this article shall not apply to any sentence imposed or to any prisoner incarcerated upon a conviction for a felony offense committed on or after January 1, 1995." It appears to me I had a sentence imposed in 2005 on my technical violation, thus the provisions that empower the parole board to act upon that technical violation do not apply. But I want to talk to an attorney to make sure I am understanding this correctly. If I am, and this attorney tells me it appears that I'm illegally imprisoned, then it's a matter of them finding the right lawyer.

I have deducted that a law firm that does parole representations is not a good choice. They don't seem to be willing to risk getting on the wrong side of the parole board for the sake of one client. So anyway, this blind squirrel may have found the proverbial acorn. Looks that way to me, but I realize I'm not qualified to make that assessment. So I hope I'll get to talk to this ever-elusive institutional attorney soon.

Here are some more pictures, and thank you again for returning them. My house was in bad shape when I bought it, a real fixer-upper. After I finished renovating, it increased 55K in value in two years. It was in need of everything other than structural repair, and was just what I was looking for. It hadn't been painted in twenty years, all the exterior wood was rotten, and the inside looked like Custer's Last Stand took place in there. And, the good Lord willing, I look forward to being able to purchase another one in the not-too-distant future.

They don't have a dog program here, but they do have two "therapeutic dogs" they bring around, and they let us pet them.

Sounds like the format for your book is getting close to ready for print. I know you're excited. And I pray your book will bring about some positive change. I wish I had all the answers to the puzzle, but it is indeed a very complex problem. I think the root of the problem is that we, as a society, have removed God from our schools, homes, government, etc.; thus, logically, the answer would be to bring God back.

Well, that's about all I know for now. You and Lee are in my prayers always. God bless.

Dear Chuck:

My uncle got transferred here earlier this week. He is in a different building than I am, but we got to spend a couple hours together at the Thanksgiving Day worship program they put on here Wednesday night. It was truly wonderful to see him and spend some time with him again. What a blessing. We hope to eventually be able to get in the same dorm.

About lawyers: For many of them, practicing law has become a social/political relationship between themselves and the prosecutors and the judges. Usually the way it works is that the prosecutors will give them the little stuff, but they want the bigger stuff. Such is accomplished by a lack of assertive pursuit by one party or the other. If you'll allow them to do their thing, most of the time your attorney can tell you what the outcome of your day in court will be before you ever set foot into the courtroom. If you don't allow your attorney to do this, most of the time you're gonna get screwed. Your attorney's career is built upon their relationship with the prosecutor, and they're usually not gonna strain that for the sake of one client. Such is our legal system.

In my case, with what I'm trying to get done, I'd actually be going against the office of the attorney general. I'm not sure how that socially and politically plays out, but I'm sure it's not in my favor or done on a fair, level playing field. Such is my concern in hiring a lawyer. When I was in the receiving unit, I wrote a top-notch post-conviction attorney about filing a habeas corpus for me. He told me the court would view things in the narrowest possible terms, without even acknowledging the merits of my case. He said there had to be an outstanding and clear constitutional violation, and he did not see one in my case. But, that was his opinion, which has not deterred me.

I received a letter from a Virginia law group about whom I know nothing, really. They said they've never seen a violation quite like mine, though they've seen many; that it does not seem right or fair; and that they are going to have several attorneys that have experience with these types of cases review the information and get back to me. Mentioning payment did apparently make a difference. A couple other top-gun attorneys referred my letter to another attorney whom I have not heard back from as of yet. Also, I wrote to an attorney who practices federal law whom I haven't heard from either. But at least right now there are "several attorneys that have experience" looking for "a way to help." So right now I'm on standby.

Right now, to my novice mind, here's what I've learned: If a law would be detrimental to me, it means exactly what it says. If a law might be favorable for me, it doesn't mean exactly what it says. In plain English, the law says the parole board had no authority after the court imposed sentence on me. So, we'll see. I still believe there's got to be someone, somewhere who can bring some justice to my situation. How hard can it be to have a court's ruling upheld? I read an article in the Richmond paper where the House Appropriations Committee is recommending to lawmakers that something needs to be done about all the parole technical violators in prison. Nine hundred beds, they said. That just may be a voice that gets listened to. The budget is crunching in on them.

Of course, some delegate who didn't know the difference between parole and probation was saying we don't want to be soft on crime. He thinks a judge sentences parole, and he's in charge of some justice committee of some sort. Go figure! Maybe after his ignorant comments in the paper, someone will educate him. But who's gonna educate all the people who read that article and were misled by his statements?

Well, my friend, that's about all I know for now. Take care; you and yours are in my prayers always. God bless ya.

INMATE'S REQUEST FOR ASSISTANCE

Two letters follow—both address the same topic but from different perspectives. The first is the inmate's request for assistance that was mailed to a number of law firms and which pertains to the letter above addressed to Chuck. The second letter was written by the inmate's fiancé' at the time of the inmates incarceration.

I am seeking to hire someone who can help me in righting a wrong. In 2001 I was mandatorily released from prison and was on probation and parole. In three years I had bought a house, started a home improvement company, hired employees, and was engaged to be married. In 2004, I voluntarily admitted a substance abuse problem to my probation officer and asked for help getting into a substance abuse program. Instead, a dirty urine test got me put in jail for violating conditions #6 and #8 of my supervised release. The judge granted me a bond.

The probation violation guidelines developed by the Virginia Criminal Sentencing Commission, who is "an agency of the Supreme Court of Va. (17.1-800)," recommended 1–90 days' incarceration. At my original revocation hearing, my probation officer and the Commonwealth Attorney requested my release. The original sentencing court revoked my probation, then again suspended the time and placed me on probation again. I was sentenced and ordered to be released that day, attend outpatient treatment, attend AA, etc. . . .

Nine days after that, the parole board gave me a hearing on the exact same technical violation the judge had just sentenced me on, and twelve days after that revoked my parole for that violation and gave me seventeen and a half years in prison. My family and I feel that such a lengthy prison sentence is very excessive given my voluntary admission with request for a program, and the fact that two judges, my probation officer, and even the Commonwealth Attorney found no justification to impose a term of confinement. The parole board has conveyed to my family that they have no intention of changing their course of action with me. They even refuse to give me a hearing every six months, as their policy manual directs for technical violators.

What the parole board is doing with me just isn't right. Legal action is not an avenue I wanted to pursue, but it seems to be my only recourse. If it is the "duty of the Parole Board to release prisoners on parole when they have been found suitable for release (53.1)," I have a court ruling that determines I am suitable. People violated for new felony convictions have been paroled while I have not on a technical violation. Attached are some things I have come across in the law library which seem to have some merit. If not, hopefully you will know of something that would be effective. Two judges, the Commonwealth, and

an agency of the Supreme Court of Virginia have already tried to have me released. If you believe you can find a way to bring some fairness and justice to my situation, please do. My family and I are in dire need of your help. Please contact me concerning your fee requirements, or if you have any questions, you may contact me or my uncle at the following.

Thank you.

Letter from inmate's ex-fiancée:

I come to you on behalf of family and friends to ask for your help in righting a wrong. My fiance is currently a ward of the Virginia Department of Corrections. He was released from prison on mandatory release in 2001, and placed on supervision (probation and parole). He did the maximum amount of time the law would allow for the sentence he received. He paid his debt to society. He also became a very productive member of society, starting a home improvement company, hiring employees, buying a house, doing volunteer work through a local church, and completing all of his treatment requirements.

In 2004, he and I began using drugs, and he voluntarily turned himself in to his parole officer and asked for help with his substance abuse problem. Because drug use violated the rules of his supervised release, he was returned before the original sentencing court to be judged for violating these rules. The Probation Violation Guidelines, which are a risk assessment developed by the Virginia Criminal Sentencing Commission, assessed him to be no threat to public safety and recommended his release. The doctor, who had him in therapy for two years as a requirement of his parole, assessed him to be of no threat to public safety and suitable for life in society.

The Commonwealth Attorney at the time and his parole officer both requested he be reinstated to supervised release. The doctor and the parole officer were people chosen by the Department of Probation and Parole to deal with him on a personal level, to know the context of his character. And when the Commonwealth

Attorney didn't try to get someone any prison time, that speaks volumes in itself. Then, taking into account all factors involved, including his previous convictions and the circumstances thereof, as well as his violation of the rules of his supervised release and all circumstances involved, two circuit court judges ruled him as no potential threat to public safety, is suitable for release, and ordered him to be released with outpatient substance abuse counseling. The original sentencing court ruled that his original conviction, plus the technical violation, did not justify serving additional prison time. So how could he possibly be in prison?

After the conclusion of the above matters, the Virginia parole board interjected themselves, and in considering the exact same matters and issues, gave him seventeen and a half years in prison. This is in excess of 7,000 percent more time than what the courts and expert risk assessments deemed appropriate and just. In that the parole board is defined as quasi-judicial, we do not believe that any Virginia lawmaker ever intended that the letter or spirit of the law would empower the parole board to contradict, undermine, alter, or negate a court's ruling.

In the July 26, 2006, issue of the Richmond Times-Dispatch, Governor Kaine is quoted as saying, "I don't think politicians need to get in the way of a court proceeding. I don't think it's the role of a governor to kind of come in on top of a court proceeding." The governor is on public record making his position clear. Agree with it or not, a court ruling is a court ruling, and we tread upon dangerous ground when a politically appointed body can alter or negate a court ruling so they may further their own agenda. Even though the court is a separate (albeit higher) entity than the parole board, the actions of the parole board should never undermine or override a court's ruling. And now the parole board refuses to grant him parole, or even take him up for parole every six months, as their own policy manual establishes for technical violators.

Virginia state law as well as parole board policy states that it is the duty of the parole board to release people on parole when they are found suitable for release and such release is compatible with public safety and the mutual interests of society and the individual. Court rulings, as well as undisputed expert recommendations and clinical assessments, have concluded that he meets this criteria and should be released. In telephone conversations with the parole board, they can offer no logical rationale for their actions, but dispense rhetoric of the serious nature of his original offense (for which he is not incarcerated and has served his time and paid his debt to society), and his "failure" on community supervision, as if the courts and expert assessments knew nothing of these matters!

The parole board also arbitrarily asserts that the concurring sum conclusions of two judges, the Commonwealth Attorney, a doctor of psychology, a parole officer, and the Virginia Criminal Sentencing Commission are irrelevant, without merit, and somehow, beneath them. Who at the parole board is qualified to dispute the clinical assessment of the doctor, who had him in therapy for two years? The doctor was obviously chosen by the parole department for his expertise, experience ,and credentials, so why would the parole board dispute the very conclusion they paid him to render?

The risk assessment guidelines from the Virginia Criminal Sentencing Commission, which takes into account original convictions, were developed in 2004 for technical violators only. If these guidelines are good enough to give to every judge in the Commonwealth, aren't they good enough for the parole board also? And why wouldn't the parole board acknowledge the sanctity of a court ruling, or abide by the governor's publicly stated directive concerning matters of the courts? He has a court's ruling releasing him for exactly what he is incarcerated for, a technical violation. He is not a threat to society and is suitable for release; our courts have said so and that ruling has not been overturned or in any way invalidated. Is the Virginia parole board trying to imply that our courts are incompetent in their duties? He has now completed substance abuse treatment, which both judges ordered.

We strongly maintain that his continued incarceration is nothing short of a travesty of justice and misappropriation of taxpayer dollars. No one wants to release dangerous criminals onto our streets. By the same token, nor does anyone want to imprison those whom a court of law has ruled should not be imprisoned.

We, his family and friends, are simple, ordinary, taxpaying citizens of Virginia. We apparently do not have the stature or status to warrant the Virginia parole board listening to us or taking us seriously. They are calling wrong right, and basically asserting that they are beyond all reproach. We feel that we are being bullied and dismissed, and that there is nothing we can do about it. Thus, we appeal to you for your help in righting this wrong. We know it's wrong, if for no other reason than because the judge said so! Thank you for your time. Please feel free to contact me if you have any questions.

Dear Chuck:

Hello, my friend. Thank you for your letter, and the letter to all the brothers. It always makes my day to hear from you. I hope this finds you and Lee well.

I never take a flu shot either. My goal is to keep the flu virus out of my body, and the idea of injecting it into my body seems counterproductive to meeting my goal. I call that good ol', down-home, mountain logic, like my grandpa and grandma had.

Sounds like, between the driver's license and the volunteer policies, you're getting educated about the Virginia Department of Corrections. Ever seen the movie *Waterworld*? Well, I've dubbed this place *Backwardsworld*. No new policy or decision is ever going to lighten restrictions or make things better. It's not in the nature of the beast to do so. My philosophy is, Make the best of what you've got, step cautiously, and try not to draw any attention.

I've got a good one for ya. Two men from my dorm went home this week. One let me read his psychological report, dated this year, to be used to get disability checks. He's a paranoid schizophrenic, manic-depressive, hearing command voices in his mind, and diagnosed as having no regard for human life. They let him go—no hassles, and no questions. The other was evaluated for possible civil commitment because while he and his ex-wife were in a drunken physical altercation, he ripped her shirt off. Both are on supervised release. The former has the standard one page of restrictions; the latter has an additional four pages of special restrictions. I know which one I would not want living next door to me!

I never did hear from the attorney. Thank you for calling him, though. It doesn't sound like he's saying what I'm looking to hear. I've found in the law where the judge did impose sentence on me; where the parole board has no authority over sentences imposed after 1994; where after a court hears a matter, any further hearings on the same matter is barred; and where I should have been put into a treatment program. I now have a new sentence, and it is not into the custody of the Department of Corrections. How hard can it be to have a judge's sentencing order upheld and enforced? I'm thinking something simple ought to do it, like an injunction or something. So, I'll continue to look. I am rewriting my letter to the attorneys.

I think I've been misspelling some words here. I can't find the spell-check feature on this new Bic pen I bought. Don't ya just hate it when that happens?

My parole hearing date is scheduled for February. I was on the list for a January hearing. I've heard of another recent article in the Richmond paper about parole technical violators or dirty urines and the associated enormous costs. I am hoping something favorable will play out with regard to this by the time I have my parole hearing. Some states have made laws that prohibit technical violators from being sent to prison. I got seventeen and a half years for what in other states carries no time at all.

A friend of mine and I have been what I call "wrestling" for a couple of years now. She says I'm blaming the system for my current situation when it's my fault. I say I accept responsibility, but just because I relapsed and used drugs, that does not alleviate the parole board of their responsibility to fairness and justice. After I wrote her earlier this week, I realized that I need to forgive the parole board for the wrong they have done me. To that I said "What! Why don't you just ask me to sprout some angel wings and fly!" So, I've been asking God for his help because I'll never get that one on my own. This may take some time.

Well, another four-day weekend for the state employees. I don't consider this to be a good thing, but that's probably because I live in a dormitory of yelling and screaming adult adolescents. More *Backwardsworld* phenomena. It wears on my nerves and patience after a while. But, I'm not a *Backwardsworld* kinda fella!

Last night I got called out to work at 10:00 A.M. They paid me 45 cents for the hour. Two hundred feet away on the other side of this fence, I get $100 an hour for an emergency call-out. *Backwardsworld!*

I liked your message about Job. I've been working on trying to seek first the Kingdom of God and his righteousness, and letting him be concerned with the adding of all the other things. That was a revelation to my daily way of thinking.

Well, my friend, that's about all I know for now. Take care; you and yours are in my prayers always.

Three weeks after receiving this letter, I received the following from this inmate:

Oh yeah, the guy I told you about in my dorm who is manic depressive hears command voices, etc. . . . He's locked back up, in three weeks after getting out. Armed robbery, abduction, and several other charges. Sad, but expected.

Dear Chuck,

I hope you are well and blessed. I thank you for the two letters you have now sent me, and apologize for not writing back sooner.

I have been very preoccupied with working on my case. I have recently been blessed to have been visited by our mutual lawyer friend my mother has retained for me. Initially, he didn't think I had a good claim for ineffective assistance of counsel, but by the end of our visit, he was convinced that I do. I am honestly innocent of the two charges of attempted murder that I was charged, tried, found guilty of, and given eighteen years for. It all stemmed from an automobile accident on July 11, 2005. There were so many lies told before trial and at trial, and my lawyer just let it all happen. I have been struggling with drug and alcohol addiction for years. I didn't find out until 1998 that I have been self-medicating for a mental disorder (bipolar).

I was evaluated by a psychiatrist and team prior to trial. I was never made aware of any results, and it turns out the evaluators concluded that I was affected by bipolar disorder on the morning of the offense, but my attorney never said a word of this to me or the court. My attorney also neglected to call my only witness who was also a victim. She testified at my preliminary hearing and stated it was an accident, but for reasons I am unaware of, he refused to call on her against my pleading. I, on the other hand, am convinced that God has his hands on me, from the start of this whole ordeal, and still does. I have literally opened my eyes to the self-destructive path I was taking, not to mention I am more aware of my mental disorder and the importance of taking my meds.

I thank you again, and God bless both you and your wife.

Dear Chuck,

Hoooowdie, as Minnie Pearl used to say. Hope this finds you and Lee doing well. All goes well enough here, but I will say that the parole board courts seem rather reluctant to intervene in my case, and tend to view things in the narrowest terms possible. I'm still gonna try, though. I finally got to see the court-appointed lawyer that comes here. He told me I need to contact attorneys who specialize in probation and parole law. He also told me, as I had suspected, the letters I sent out would be ignored and thrown out because I neglected to mention payment of their fee. He said he gets letters from inmates all the time seeking free legal representation. Other than those two things, my situation was out of his area of practice and he was no help. So, it's through the process of going to the law library again to type up another letter and try again. My bad. I knew to mention payment; I just forgot.

The entire parole board needs to be replaced with folks who are doctors of sociology or criminology. Or even better, send inmates back to the sentencing court for early-release consideration. The parole board uses the ol' "severity of the crime" line to answer everything because within the establishment, it flies. Kinda like the military's top-secret line. It's the unquestionable answer that covers all. Throw that baby out there and no more questions have to be answered.

My dad and two uncles came to visit me last weekend. It was a very nice visit. My dad told me right now I should be living in Kings Grant (a very nice neighborhood), with a pool and boat in the backyard, a pool table in the game room, etc. . . . He knows firsthand how well I was doing out there, and is disappointed that I'm back in here. So I explained to him that I believe I did the right thing in trying to stand by my girlfriend. It just so happened that I ended up falling into the problem instead of helping her out of it. But that was certainly not the intent. We were to be married shortly, commitments were made, and to throw her out at the first rocking of the boat did not seem honorable or right to me. She hadn't tried to kill me, or harm me, or burn the house down. She just got high, for which she is tearfully remorseful.

Then six months later, when I came to acknowledge I had acquired the same problem, which by the way never left the confinement of my own house, I voluntarily admitted my substance abuse problem and asked for help getting into a structured substance abuse program. And after a rather thorough investigation into all matters of concern, even the Commonwealth Attorney asked for my release when there was twenty-five years hanging over my head, to do with at their discretion. Anyone who knows anything about the legal system knows that this alone is the tell-all for my situation. But on the other side of the coin, I knew that the parole board is a brood of vipers that will strike if given any opportunity, and I put myself before them and gave them the opportunity.

But that still doesn't make what they did right, and I'll never accept what they say and what they did. And if I'd been released when the judges said to release me (either time), I would not have lost my house, business, vans, tools, furniture, clothes, dog, etc. . . . But I told my dad, Don't blame me that the parole board can overrule a judge. I've never heard of that one either. And I reminded him that even after all that, last year I still had $6,000 to loan him so he wouldn't lose his house, which he now may not be able to repay. So I'm not the only one who does stuff and gets into situations. So, at that, all is well once again.

I saw on the news yesterday that the General Assembly exempted themselves from having to abide by the law of no smoking in state buildings. Our politicians would never manipulate the laws to advance their own personal agendas, though. Noooo, not them. Another brood of vipers, they are. I would bet they even promise not to raise taxes. The fox is definitely in charge of the henhouse here!

Well, my friend, that's about all the syllables I know for now. Take care; you and Lee are in my prayers always.

Dear Mr. Brown:

I received your letter today; thank you. I am so glad my son has had you to converse with. He thinks highly of you and perhaps one day you and he can meet.

I have visited him at the facility several times, and believe me, the prisons are nothing like what they show on TV. The media glamorizes it so much more than what it is. My son will have served three years in May, and to date has never had any kind of counseling. He was first offered programs while waiting to be sent to a prison but turned down once he had his placement. Every time he has inquired about something, the response is that he is on the list. The facility keeps inmates idle. What makes the judicial system feel that once released, the inmate will be a better person? From what I hear and see, it is no wonder they return back into the system, and perhaps that is really what it is all about—generating dollars for the facility.

I am so thankful that you are trying to open some people's eyes. I am afraid you are right: You will be greatly criticized for your work. I admire you for wanting to take on such a huge undertaking for the poor inmates that deserve a second chance. Not all inmates are worthless just because they made a huge mistake. Look at Johnny Cash; he was in and out of jail several times for misdemeanors, and he became a star. Today, unless you have money, you're labeled a nobody. I have wanted so badly to do something that might make a difference. I know I don't have what it takes to pursue such a task. Thank God for people like you.

Whatever you feel would be helpful in getting the message out to someone who might listen seems wonderful to me. I know I am not the only parent that wants to scream at our so-called judicial system. It stinks presently and really needs a going-over. Take, for instance, O.J. Simpson. Do you think if he had been an ordinary criminal he would have been allowed to leave jail and the state without paying bond? We both know the answer to that. We need standards for all, whether rich or poor.

One thing that upsets me the most is that everyone I contacted regarding my son's case told me whatever the judge did cannot be undone because he pleaded guilty. What was he supposed to do when the attorney hired to defend him told him that he had no choice but to plead guilty? And none of us knew any better, and that is why we hired him. We know now that we never should have, but that is water over the dam and cannot be undone.

The so-called lawyer cared so little about my son, his client, that he allowed him to go to prison under some unjust charges. I know because my husband and I saw with our own eyes 75 percent of the tape before the judge realized it. Even the President has to answer to someone, but all the Virginia officials contacted informed us differently. The Bar Association's letter in regards to my son's lawyer and legal misrepresentation was unfortunate. The lawyer was not that good. God will deal with all of them for the conspiracy that took place regarding my son's trial. I have learned a great deal and would never be taken again by a lawyer and his pretty words.

I am not saying—nor does my son feel—that he did not deserve a consequence for his actions, but his sentence was above and beyond his crime. The sad thing is that there are thousands of cases just like his, where there are decent human beings that just want to put the past behind them and move forward. The system offers them nothing but a bus ticket to who-knows-where.

Thank you again for being human and believing that not all criminals are worthless. May God be with you in your work.

PART III

FAITH

Dear Brothers,

Sometimes when we want our dreams to come to pass, we must convince ourselves to speak words of faith. Faith is the substance of things hoped for, the evidence of things not seen. Faith is an exercise of believing in something when you don't physically have it and you can't see it. Faith demands hope. Hope is the expectation and the anticipation of good things in our tomorrows. Faith is the substance that sustains us as we wait for those tomorrows.

Your words have enormous creative power whether you are saying positive words or negative. When you are downtrodden and speak negative words, you have just lost the battle and become your own worst enemy. We tend to blame everybody and everything else, and the truth is, we are influenced by what we say of ourselves.

Statements like, "I never do anything right," or "Why does everything bad happen to me?" will literally prevent you from moving ahead in a positive manner. That's why it is important to be careful of what you say and speak only faith-filled words, like—"I trust in God that something good is going to happen to me."

Sometimes, when problems occur, people will immediately think that God surely must be punishing them. They don't understand that God has a divine purpose for every challenge in life. His purpose is not to send problems to us, but sometimes He allows us to go through them.

Why does He allow this? It is because trials are intended to test our character, to test our faith. God often allows us to go through difficult situations in order to drag out those impurities in our character. I am convinced that God is more interested in changing *you* than He is in changing your circumstances. If we begin with faith and allow God to lead us, He will carry us through. It may mean making a change in your lifestyle—or your habits, your attitude, or your thinking—but God can make a way where there seems to be no way, when we put our faith in Him.

Although I am aging, I am still trying to learn. I have heard of two kinds of faith—a delivering faith and a sustaining faith. *Delivering faith* is when God instantly turns your situation around. This is grand when it happens. But *sustaining faith* is what gets you through those dark nights of the soul when you don't know where to go or what to do . . . but because of your faith in God, you manage. Faith in simple terms tells us that "the best is yet to come."

God love ya and bless ya,

Chuck

Dear Chuck,

Thanks so much for your many letters since Thanksgiving. I apologize for taking so long to reply. My affliction has slowed me down a great deal. At fifty-six, I would be hard-pressed to keep up with a man of seventy years.

Thank you for James's greeting. I send mine in return, with the hope that he is walking the straight path and immersing himself in catechesis and the prayers.

Since the escape at Dillwyn, ill winds have been blowing here. Our place is scheduled to go on a controlled movement scheme on Monday. It's too ambitious a plan for the physical plant here. The Department of Corrections boneheads refuse to think out a rational plan. Trial and error (and error and error) has worked for them for the last sixty years, and they're sticking to it.

Thanks for the update on the Second Chance Act. Please let us know if it passes. I don't remember the text of it, and I expect it has changed since it was first entertained in Congress. I hope it will give Virginia's aging prisoners relief.

You know, Chuck, when I came to prison, the state provided nearly everything: food, clothing, medical attention, writing materials, and one letter a week at state expense. Now they suck assets out of us with fees for everything, treating us in such a way that we must now pretty much pay our own way. It's costing me $11 plus change to call my wife once a week for twenty-five minutes. The phones are so poor we have to shout to be heard. I'm so weary of it all.

The bright spot in the darkness is the Presence of Christ in our midst. He shows himself in so many guises here. We are blessed to receive the sacrament here. I pray things will improve for the men at Greensville. It would be grand if even a deacon could be found to bring them Christ in the Eucharist.

Dear Chuck,

I know that I *very* much appreciate that you come here each month to share the Eucharist with us. I also feel that it's great that you want to correspond with us. It does feel good to know that others on the outside do care about us in here. Society may consider us the lowest of the low, but in the group, we support each other as best we can. We know we are no saints, but we are trying to change and want to do so within the Church and with its help. I would say that most of us recognize that the only way we can make it through this is with God's help, and that we need to turn it over to God and trust Him to do what is best for each of us.

Our Kairos prison ministry that we talk about has a great way to look at this. "The judge gave you a sentence; God is giving you an opportunity." The opportunity is to get to know Him better, and his son, and what Jesus can do for each of us if we invite Him in. I like this way of examining what has happened. I know that God has given me something I did not have as a free person—time to be with Him and to get to know Him.

You may also hear from time to time that prison is what *you* make of it. If you are miserable and blame everyone for your time but yourself, then most likely you will be miserable and angry at the world. And your time will probably be long. If you accept this and go with the flow and *try* not to let things bother you and keep busy, then the time can and will go easier. I pray to God for this peace and I try to live it. It is not easy, but I make small headway each day, and this is a miracle in itself.

Prison on a daily basis is like nothing anyone can imagine. You get a glimpse of it when you come in, more so than any other visitor because you come into the complex and see areas no other visitors see. Comparison is good, and we can ask for nothing more from you all. I appreciate you trying to understand what it is like. Just being open to us is good. There is no shortage of people like me who will tell you what we go through.

Your second paragraph in your letter "Dignity is Our Birthright" is so right on. Our problems are not very different from those on the outside. It is that I cannot physically participate in the goings-on. I am now divorced and my children hate me, but I could not explain it to them or have contact with them. I can assume my ex-wife now hates me as well. I am in control of NOTHING but how I react to and feel about what is going on in my life. God is in control. I lost

EVERYTHING. All I own now fits in my locker and footlocker in my cell. I do not even own my clothes.

One of my Kairos friends is a Catholic deacon and my spiritual advisor. He always says that the only difference between he and us is the geography. He likes to use "there but for the grace of God go I" because he realizes that in an instant, he could be right in here with us. Your observations are right on.

Thank you for you prayer. It is very moving and beautiful.

Thanks for the music comments. I am not a musician and never claimed to be so. My rhythm will always be off and I sound more like a wounded moose than anything else when I sing. That is my joyful noise to the Lord!

I have one of my colleagues who still writes me. She has some good analogies about what happens to some of us. We are kidnapped from our families by "the system" and not allowed to put our affairs in order. Also she likens living here to being in a monastery, and refers to this as a monastic life—not too far off. There are many similarities between prison and a cloistered life.

Well, Chuck, I will end here. Peace and love in Christ.

Dear Chuck,

Two of my Kairos friends wrote me recently that when they tell their friends they do prison ministry, they get all kinds of comments about them being crazy, but these men swear they love to come here, and they get more out of being with us than they do with their friends on the "street."

As for golf, it is not too bad. I played a *long* time ago—in high school and college. Not competitively, though. It can be fun and relaxing if you don't take it seriously and drink a few beers during the round. The scenery is good and you get plenty of sun. I would not consider you flaky, but a man who does what he wants and who doesn't care what others think. That's cool in my book!

Thank you for your prayer. It is very moving and I enjoyed it. If I may, I want to send it to some of my Kairos friends, with your permission.

I can't speak for the rest of the men, but I have no problem with receiving mail. Yes, I found out you *can* be busy in prison—amazing, huh? Beats sitting around all day and letting it all cave in on you.

I appreciate the compassion you show for us. I will always be branded by society as one of those "bad guys." New laws make sure I will never be able to forget my crime and that my name will be on some website for all to see. One of my friends who stuck with me during my ordeal was a physician where I worked. He is now dead, but he wrote me, "What happened is what you *did*; it is not who you *are*." I will never forget his words and what he did for me. He was a good man.

I now have God. I know that my now ex-wife and children . . . while I would like it if they would communicate with me, it's not necessary for me to find peace and happiness. I can get that through my relationship with God, and I have the men of the group to help me. My cellmate is a lifesaver to me at times. We jog together sometimes.

Some of us in the group live in the same pods. Other times, we eat together in the mess hall. We see each other in the recreation yards. We support each other as best we can.

I do always wonder, though, that those of you on the outside—and I mean *all* of you, not just *you* specifically—but all who show compassion to us in here, that when we get out, would you want one or more of us living in your neighborhood? This is a rhetorical question. I don't expect an answer, but some of us, me included, have done very heinous crimes. We are repentant and do not want to repeat our crimes. We have done that about-face and want to stay away from what got us here. I am making small lifestyle changes that I hope will carry me far into the future, if God lets me live that long.

God is directing my life now. I messed it up. I couldn't do it on my own. I realize that now. This was my wake-up call, and hence my opportunity.

Thanks for the words about my ex-wife and children. I am letting God take care of that. If He wants it to happen, He will find a way to make it happen. Another of my Kairos friends says it is love that heals, not time. If there is no capacity for love, healing cannot take place. I would add that the person wronged has to forgive, and the person who did the wrong has to be *truly* repentant; then, healing can happen.

My friend can't visit. She works every weekend, so that rules out any visits. She is busy during the week with her dissertation work. She writes when she has time and she can visit if she ever gets the time.

I still sound bad singing, but it is my joyful noise to the Lord!

Well, Chuck, thanks again for your letter. I appreciate you coming to visit us. I hope you try to visit on a Tuesday night sometime. The lay service we do is different from the Mass. I think you would enjoy it very much. I hope you can make it sometime.

Dear Bro. Chuck,

Thank you for your November letter. Sorry to not have gotten back to you sooner, but I finally moved into my single cell the day after I received your letter. This is a very good thing.

My single cell was a prayer answered by God. The Thursday and Friday before and the day of my move, I prayed to God that if He felt I had done enough Purgatory time on earth with my last two cell partners, to please get me out of the cell I was in and away from my psychotic cell partners. On that Friday, an hour after this prayer, the CO told me it was time to move. God is so good! He knew what I needed and he delivered me. Amen!

Chuck, you are in my daily prayers. I was sorry to read of your skin cancer and your other concerns. Another one of medicine's and God's mysteries. Why do some who spend most of their time in the sun develop skin cancer and others do not? I pray you will be okay and continue your visits to support us. May I assume you are going to a dermatologist at UVA? I liked your joke and the physician's reply—pretty quick of him!

("I suggested that the skin graft be taken from one of my feet and placed in my ear. He said, 'Why from the feet?' I replied, 'So that I could hear footsteps better.' He said, 'If

you had cancer on your mouth and I took a graft from your foot, you would be walking around with your foot in your mouth.")

You are so correct that concern brings fear and fear can paralyze. This is *very* difficult to break, since *we* want control, and we must realize that God is in control and we are powerless. It took me coming to prison to "get" that message. I fear much, and I am working on letting my fears go, allowing God to do His will for me.

I got some disturbing news from my parents regarding my son. When told I was never coming home, he said, "What difference does it make? All he did was yell and scream and make noise." Ouch. A heck of a legacy I left my daughter and son. They are sixteen and thirteen now. He was ten at the time of my arrest. So I have to go with the premise that I will never hear from my children again. I'm giving this to God. I can't do anything about it, and I have to trust that God will do what is best for all of us.

I loved the Alexander the Great horse story. This is so true! Only in God can we overcome our fears! I've lost it all, yet I am still here and I am living, thanks to the grace of God.

God bless ya, and God love ya, Chuck!

Dear Chuck,

Well, my good friend and brother, they finally sent me away. It had to happen sooner or later, what with my litigious ways. How's that for irony? I write you a letter encouraging you to maintain the fellowship, and now I won't even be there! In any event, do continue to visit with my brothers. They need your care and support.

How are you these days? I got your last letter, and you seem to be doing much better than you were. Life certainly throws us curves quite a bit, doesn't it? The trick is to just keep on swingin' away. That's often difficult when you feel like you're in a slump. Yet another reason why we pray . . .

At the moment, I'm far away from you. I'll probably be here at least a year, so I doubt I'll be seeing you anytime soon. Luckily, my parents will be dropping by on August 13. That will be a terrific ray of sunshine in an otherwise dismal place. As you might be aware, they execute people here. How'd you like to be at Golgotha? I couldn't bear to see Jesus suffer so. Even though the men they put to death are often "hardened criminals," two things give me pause: 1) These men are having the future opportunity to repent taken from them, and if they have already, why kill them; and 2) We are called upon to see Jesus in the least of these children; what we do to them, we do to Christ Jesus. Such are my heavier thoughts in my distress.

On a much lighter note, I'm all signed up to attend services here. There are supposed to be twenty-five or so guys! It should be a lively, vibrant, and hopefully devout group. I've gotta admit, I'm kind of excited to be meeting my newfound brothers in Christ. Just as in days of old, I bring glad tidings.... My faith has been so enriched by my time there; I know it will provide encouragement to those here, just to hear how my faith flourished even "under a bushel basket."

Please tell those I left behind to stay strong in their love for one another, and that I miss them. We are a family through Christ, no matter how diverse our backgrounds may be. Tell them to remember that, and all who have left them. I know I'll not soon forget any who sat among us, and that includes you. You brightened our celebration of the Mass with your enthusiasm and good humor. Thank you for that gift. To men in our position, such a simple thing becomes a treasure.

Well, this has gotten to be a rather long letter! Perhaps it's even a bit long-winded ☺. Allow me to close by saying how much I'll miss seeing you on our special Tuesday afternoons. Please take care of yourself and your wife. Remember me in prayer as I'll remember you.

Dear Chuck,

I got your last letter before our Tuesday service and couldn't help but feel shocked and deeply saddened by the revelations. Your letter has left us all with many unanswered questions and concern for you and your wife, which we all address in our prayers. Thus, I pray that this letter finds you in a better place in your life.

None of us want to pry into your personal affairs. However, we are desperate to understand what afflictions one of our brothers in Christ faces which can cause such separation. It's not contagious, is it? Actually, I can assure you it is, for the sad news you shared has moved us all. Whatever ill wind has blown through your life has cost us the fond fellowship of a kind man with a beautiful soul.

My life, too, has been filled with untold disappointments and frustrations. Even now I am faced with a maniacal administration whose hypocrisy is underscored by theft, corruption, and retribution. Moreover, no matter how boldly I may stand for justice or even compassion, I am thwarted by officials who know neither. I stand for the Lord, pick up my cross, and follow. In all, we draw only as much strength as we limit ourselves to accepting from a merciful God who understands the travails and tribulations of this world.

In all, when we come together in our little room to worship as part of the mystical body of Christ, it is *there* that we draw strength and encouragement. It isn't that the Holy Spirit is denied to us in any other aspects of our life. It is simply that Jesus wanted us to band together in the unity of our faith even as we receive Him in both species of the Eucharist. There's something to be said for belief in the "real presence." That's why we want *you* to be *present* at our next service!

Yes, I would still like to maintain correspondence (obviously). Your letters provide inspiration in a dark place—your intent, I presume. Keep them coming. For my part, I'll try to do better with the letters in the future. It isn't always easy without a word-processing program. Man, do I miss those. Nevertheless, I've enough pens and paper even though my schedule is so full.

Please continue to take care of yourself and your "trophy wife." You both will be remembered in prayer. Say a few for me too. I look forward to hearing from you again and hopefully to seeing you in June. May the Lord bless and keep you at least that long, and hopefully for years to come.

To Brother Chuck:

Happy Father's Day to you.

Last Friday I got a Father's Day card from one of my daughters.

It was a nice card and she signed it. It came with no return address (red flag). I tried calling home but no answer. So my heart is still troubled. What must I do for God to hear me? I pray with tears in my eyes, not for my sake, but for my wife and daughters. I take it that one of my daughters moved out, and I understand that both homes are up for sale. It is the breakup of my family. Sorry I'm telling you all of this; I just need a friend to write to.

I know you have your hands full. Sorry about your wife's condition. I write to you because you are about my age and won't answer my letter with quotations from the Bible. Just keep me in your prayers.

Dear Chuck,

Good to hear from you, and glad you have been able to return to us! I was called out for a dental appointment of all things. I put in for a mouth guard because I grind my teeth at night, and they had a spare moment and called me over. So no big deal. A heck of a time for it, though.

I had a visit this weekend from my dad and cousin. I had not seen my dad in three and a half years. We had a good visit. It was *very* difficult for him to be here, but we made it okay at the end.

I found out that my cousin has kept in touch with my ex and my children by phone and e-mail. At my mom's funeral he spoke with my kids. He said they are intelligent, fun, curious, well-behaved, well-spoken, and overall good kids. I got teary—I did something right in this world. Then, he just dropped the word that he had seen me and there was no shock or revulsion from them. He and my ex talked, and she told him that she fully expects that my kids will want to have a relationship with me in the future and that it will be good. So I have to be thankful to my ex for part of that. It made me feel better as well. It seems that they don't hate me after all. Time is what is needed, plus maturity.

The annulment rolls on. I was sent a letter by the Diocese that upset me. I felt I was not being heard or my requests addressed, so in return I got the questionnaire. Wow, it is involved! Fifteen pages, and I wrote twenty more pages in my personal history. It was good, and I am glad I did it. I realize I am still in love with my ex and would go back to her if she wanted me, but since she doesn't, it is time to move on. I have told my story and that is what I wanted to do. I feel good that she will get the annulment.

My cousin wants me to write a book about my case and experience. He feels it would help parents and teens understand the pitfalls of being online and how to avoid the sex talk. I am considering it.

Liberty University has some new distance-learning programs for college degrees and we can participate for free. I am thinking of an MBA, PhD, or EdD. I have some time to figure it out. I am not a fan of Jerry Falwell, but this is an opportunity and I need to consider it.

My dad's estate is figured out—at least that is what he told me. My brother and cousin are joint executors. There are grandkids involved as well, so it is not a fifty-fifty split. My dad said I will be taken care of; that is all that matters to me. My brother could sue. I don't think he'd do that, but one never knows. We have a heck of a family mess, Chuck.

I thank you for your letter and concern, Chuck. It means a lot to me to have someone care. I try not to let this place get to me, but it does at times. I have to remember that God is in control. I need to stop trying to control and let God do it. He will guide me to the right path.

Okay. God bless ya, Chuck, and God love ya! Take care and see you soon!

Chuck,

How've you been? I hope this letter finds you doing well.

I received your letter yesterday; it was good to hear from you once again. Thank you for understanding my reasons for not writing before. I do promise to keep writing even if it's only to say hi. I don't make promises I don't intend to keep as you will see in time.

I want you to know that I did have the prison chaplain add my name (again) to the list for our meetings. I will attend once again starting Tuesday. Maybe I will see you then, huh?

Your kind words were truly appreciated, Chuck, and so are those who care; it is a very sad world we live in these days, and we need all the friends we can find. I am only twenty-seven, Chuck, and I am very shocked at how things have changed since I was a small child growing up in Italy. Sometimes I wonder just how much worse things will get in this world before they get any better.

Please understand that I do not doubt the existence of God or our Savior, nor do I doubt God's willingness to forgive us our sins. I am the one who has been unable to forgive myself for my crime, sins, and failures, Chuck. I feel lost and confused a lot; I feel guilty, lonely, and basically unworthy.

I, with God's help, have made a lot of progress these last four years, but I have a long way to go yet. Today I can look myself in the mirror with just a little shame, yet still be present; I did many things and I don't understand why I made these mistakes. But one day, with God's help, I will learn the reasons why I did those things.

Once again, Chuck, thank you for writing; I will continue to keep in touch. Take good care of yourself and I will see you again soon.

Dear Chuck,

It is good to hear from you once again. Regarding the "Rule of Benedict," I am committing to leaving the past to the past and the future to the future—to live in the present and be thankful for all we have here and now. I think that evil is put to us at times to see how we react and to teach us a lesson. I've learned mine.

You are so correct about the love that animals have for us. My mom would echo your statement. I have often thought that I would get a couple of dogs instead of a woman when I get out—less hassle, and I would not have to worry about trust issues or returning here. They would be good hiking and camping companions.

My book is stuck for now. I'm still working it out in my head. As for the project, we are on hold until we get a new warden. Not a good time for new projects right now!

Yes, my friend, my friend from Kairos has a truly tragic family situation on his hands. I feel for you all who have these situations over what I consider trivial things. At least I know what caused my family to break up. I have to deal with being the cause of that. But these issues of strife in a family over non-criminal "stuff" is, to me, crazy. Something Dr. Phil says is a good thing I've learned: "Do you want to be right, or do you want to be happy?" If it is a trivial issue, don't always try to be right. Let your spouse go and just love him or her, flaws and all. Don't *always* try to be right. The principle sometimes is not *that* important.

You are also correct: I feel these things are for the best for all involved, and there is some reason for it, that as it goes on, we will see it and agree. God works for our best, always; I put my trust in that.

Dear Chuck,

More people should visit the incarcerated, the sick, and the elderly. You retain far more loving-kindness than the world may know.

Meanwhile, my transfer here has resulted in a great personal miracle. It's quite a story. You see, about a month ago, our local Catholic group watched a movie about the life of Saint Therese of Lisieux. We are fortunate enough here to be able to meet twice a week for worship such as this. Anyway, moved by her "Little Way," and feeling a bit blue about how things have been going here, I asked her to pray to the Lord to "change my heart." Saint Therese said in her writings that she would "spend her Heaven doing good for those on earth." She also said she would shower roses upon those for whom she prayed.

The very next day, I was called to speak with my counselor. She asked me if I had been adopted; I told her I had. It turns out that my biological mother, whom I could not find so many years ago (fourteen), no matter how hard I looked, had walked into the family court that executed my adoption, looking for me! She described it later as a "coming to Christ" moment in her life. Was this my miracle from St. Therese? When I got her letter (my mom's), I learned that her name is Rosemarie! Wow! That's quite a rose.

If that doesn't increase one's faith, both in Christ and the communion of saints, then nothing will. You must share this story as widely as possible. The world must know that we Christians *do* possess the keys to the kingdom. It also suggests to me that I *am* on the right path and God still loves me despite my sins—in short, all that I suspected already. Spread the word where ye may.

While you're at it, you might want to tell people to stay clear of this place. It is a dead zone. There's nothing positive going on here save for the Catholic group. They've even prevented me from continuing my correspondence course work "per institutional policy/procedure." So much for rehabilitation. I'm paying for the courses, and all I need is access to one of the fifty-odd computers they have in the classrooms here. They won't allow it. Every time I think that the battles are behind me . . .

Anyway, such is life. No rest for the weary. The wicked here seem to get plenty as they cause so many problems for those who try to serve the Lord. I imagine that's just as true outside of these walls and fences. Nevertheless, I'd still like to find out . . .

That's about it from me. I look forward to hearing from you again soon. I'll try to write again soon, myself. May God bless and keep you and your wife. Continue to keep his word and to share it. Keep me in prayer, too. You'll always be in mine.

Dear Chuck Brown,

I realize this letter is overdue, but I have many things to take care of and at the same time, get my head right. When I came here I was not in a very good mood. I hope you understand, my friend.

Now I'm writing to you to tell you some good news: I'm going to be released very soon. Like in a week or two. At least in the range thereof.

Please tell the guys at church the good news, and that I miss them all. I will be in touch with the brothers one way or another. Amen.

You are so right, Brother Chuck, I do give God all the glory, honor, and praise for what he has done for me, especially with what I'm going through. Amen.

Even though I lost my job because of my felony charge, I'm not mad. I will get another one by the grace of God. Amen.

God bless you for now, and always; good-bye and I'll see you soon. Amen.

Dear Chuck,

Thanks for your letter. Yes, my last letter I mailed out the morning of our monthly Mass!

I did want to comment on something we discussed at the Mass: the sex scandal and the embezzlement scandal. They are the "thorns" in the side of the church. But the church has had *many* thorns over the years, and yet it manages to always pull through. These will take a while to sort out, but in a hundred years, these will be a spot, like others, but the church will remain.

As a sex addict and sex offender, I see the problem from both sides. No one should be molested, but it happens. What are needed are programs to *stop* molestation or other sex offenses *before* they occur. When they do occur, help the victim, but also help the offender as well. It does *no* good to put the offender away and not treat him or her. I would like to see more restorative justice projects to heal both victim and offender, and to stop offenders from creating more victims.

The same for the embezzlers. They need help as well. It is a shame that these incidents happen.

We must remember that the Catholic Church is *not* the only church hit by such scandals. The media would have us believe this because the Catholic Church seems to be a target for the media. But I read in my Protestant Journal of Episcopalians, Baptists, Methodists, Calvinists, etc., all kinds of financial scandals and sexual scandals involving children and married men and women parishioners. All these stories are sad, but the mainstream media focuses on the Catholic Church's scandals. Media bias? Oh yes! Okay, enough of that, but food for thought.

Our mutual acquaintance, you know who, is an okay guy. He is very opinionated on issues, and he could use some polish on his people skills. He has not yet adjusted to how prison works and is resistant to people who try to control him or point out things he could/should do better in. I would pin him as having an issue with authority—*any* authority. If he has issues with his previous institution, *he* needs to write the bishop with his concerns/complaints.

A concern I have is for volunteers like yourself who can get caught up in inmate dramas. I have seen three volunteers basically banned forever from this place for not following rules or for getting involved in things that they should have left alone. It is really to protect you all. We will take advantage of people who show interest in us. There are master manipulators in here. I know you all want to help and that is *not* a bad thing. I just don't want to see anyone get involved in something that could lead to dismissal.

Great! About your article. I hope we will receive a copy! I'm sure it will be fine.

Okay, Chuck, I will close here. Take care and God bless you. You are in my prayers.

Dear Chuck,

Just to let you know, Chuck, that I did receive your last letter, and to tell you I'm a free man physically and spiritually. I have the Holy Trinity and I'm not in prison blues anymore. Amen.

Things are slow, but at this time I'm living with friends in Ashburn, Virginia, until I can get enough money to get my own apartment and a car.

I do believe I just have to be very patient and also believe in the Lord for his help. Amen.

I hope and pray that you are still going to the correctional center for church services. If you send me your phone number and what time would be good to give you a call, I will call if that's okay with you, Chuck.

Until more happens, my good friend, I bid you farewell until we meet again or hear from one another. God bless you now and always.

Remember, Chuck—God loves you, and so do I. Amen.

I do give God/Jesus/the Holy Spirit all the glory, honor, and praise every day for my life and my blessings.

Dear Chuck,

Thank you for your letter. You're rock solid in your love and commitment to your Christian brothers, and it's very much appreciated.

Father sent me a nice postcard and he encouraged me to continue to be a man of peace with God and my Holy Catholic faith. I appreciated his thoughtfulness.

Speaking of thoughtfulness, when I received your letter, Phil received his, and we shared your sentiments for us when we ran into each other in the chow hall. Phil works out on the yard crew, so it's quite easy to touch base with him when I need to.

When I arrived on Tuesday the 9th, I was surprised that evening when I was paged by the control booth that an escort awaited me outside to convey me to the Catholic group. I wasn't even unpacked yet, but the group here assured me, and were true to their word, that theft is not a problem in this dorm. So, off I went. Phil was waiting out front for me with a welcoming hug. I met the guys and our faithful volunteer, who comes twice a month. We have a priest coming on January 30, and apparently he's planning to come once a month. Since we have a longer program period, a lot can be done in our time together (6:00 P.M.–8:00 P.M.). We have a classical guitar available to us from Recreation, and one of our members plays and sings well, so he leads our songs. It's nice.

This place is something to get used to. After so many years in my sheltered life at my previous address, dormitory life is a complete 180-degree experience. Once I got used to the general flow, it became easier. I have referenced this experience as being like merging into traffic on Interstate 95 after driving on nice, easy country roads for twenty-four years. Once used to the flow and my niche in traffic, I can enjoy the scenery again.

It is sad to see so many men here who have wheelchairs, crutches, canes, and walkers. The dorm next door is the medical dorm, and they have men in there who are bedridden. The Protestant group has a choir that goes in there and sings to them once a week. And one of the psychologists, a really nice lady, has a dog named Suzy, and she brings her in to visit with the men. So we do at least have a dog here, and she loves to be petted. The men look into getting some dogs in here after all the moves have been completed.

Anyway, some of the men here are parole-eligible, such as myself, as well as most of the other men. Some are under the new law and some have life without parole. This is where they go when they get old. One guy here is parole-eligible and gets turned down every year. He gets around okay, but he's been down fifty-three years. There are also men here with visual impairments. So there's lots of need for prayers here.

I am convinced that God has me here because he wants me here. I will try to be an instrument of His wishes and just follow His lead. "Thy will be done."

There is such beauty in our surroundings. We have a small recreation yard behind each dorm which abuts the perimeter fence and road. Just on the other side of the road is a shoulder of grass and deep woods. The deer come out and graze by the road, and it is an awesome experience to watch them and be so near. They had a couple of youngsters in the group that were playing and chasing each other. There are also seagulls, geese, crow, turkey vultures, owls, eagles, blue heron, turkeys, and all sorts of other birds here. In the warmer months they say there are all sorts of other critters here. I look forward to meeting them.

For some reason, the sky is very active down here, and the sunsets have had some pretty spectacular displays. Even rainy days show various rain clouds, not just a drab gray sky. Spring should be something else!

I do like the aerobic equipment in the gym, and I have managed to get down there often. I'm a bit sore as I write this from my workouts. I have many friends here who I have known one time or another at my previous address. They have been very helpful in my adjustment.

Chuck, thanks for your love, my friend. Take care.

Hello, Chuck,

Hi! What's up? I hope you are well, and your family too. It's me again. I don't have any particular news, but I want you to know that I'm very pleased to hear from you and that my writing is good. To be honest, I didn't write everything by myself. I was helped by my friend in a couple of sentences.

I think the best way to learn is not to lose faith and to keep trying to reach what we want. But we must never forget to ask and give thanks to the Holy Son of God. Also, we have to keep practicing and take advantage of every opportunity to overcome difficulties.

I thank God for allowing you to come visit us in here and share His word with us. And I'm going to keep praying to God to keep you and your family in good health and fill your lives with happiness.

About our mutual friend, I haven't heard anything, but I think he is with his family, and wherever he is, I wish him all the very best. May God keep him in good health with his family.

About me, I'm okay. Trying to do my time the best way that I can. I hope to see you soon. God love you and bless your family, too.

Dear Chuck,

As usual, I apologize for taking so long to respond; last week my mother was supposed to have her second knee surgery but had to fly to Rhode Island on short notice because her boyfriend's mother died. I was worried enough about her surgery, but seeing that so many people are dropping dead left and right, I no longer know what to worry about anymore. I've always been a worrier, Chuck. I always worry about something, which takes my mind off of things I should be doing. My mother says I will end up worrying myself to an early grave, and she is probably right.

Anyway, I want to thank you for your last letter, the one where you told me how you and your wife met; I really appreciate your encouragement and words of hope. I want to believe that one day I will be as lucky as you were, but it is hard for me, Chuck, especially today when I can't even find a woman to write to as a friend. I trust that God has a plan and purpose for me. I am just not sure we see eye to eye on some things. What I want in my life and what God wants for me may not be the same things, and I worry about that too. I don't like to question God's ways, but I can honestly say I rarely ask God for anything, and never did—nothing more than some peace of mind, an end to my childhood struggles, and to be able to find a good woman who would be willing to raise a loving family and allow me to show I can be a decent man, husband, and father. I am thirty years old and none of the above has been granted as of today.

I am not pouting about it; I am not angry with God—or my father, for that matter. I am not complaining about the hand I was dealt in life. I may not like it, but I am not blind, and I can see others have even worse to deal with. Mostly I am baffled as to why I never get a single break. I have fought too many battles in my years, Chuck, and I am very tired in every sense of the word. I want a reprieve. I am aware of people who may call me burned-out or a quitter, but I honestly could not care less about people's views regarding my life; I am the one who went through it all, not them. I am the one who attempted suicide three times, twice before the age of fourteen. I am the one who's been beaten to a pulp countless times until I was fifteen. I was the ten-year-old boy who sat on a toilet while his dad was passed out drunk; I sat there with a gun contemplating whether I should shoot him or myself. I don't want to go on and on, but you get the point.

God knows I always did my best; I still am and always will. He knows that I made many mistakes. I made many wrong choices but I never meant to harm anyone. I don't know what else I could have done to prevent this whole mess, Chuck. I was never an angel, but I have done all I could do to be what people call a "productive citizen," but in the end, my best was not enough, and it was all for nothing.

Most people see me as a monster and a failure. They will judge me until death comes calling, and after that I will be judged yet again, and most likely I will roast for all eternity in hell. Once more, the future does not look too promising for me; judgment, loneliness, pain, and suffering. I see no end to it all. For me there is no reprieve, it seems . . . No rest for the wicked, huh? And people wonder why I am the way I am. No matter what I do, the end results are always the same: I screw up, it's my fault. I do good, someone else gets the credit. I can't win.

Aside from all that, I am doing pretty good, I guess. I am hanging on, once again doing my best, whatever that's worth.

Dear Chuck,

Thank you very much for your gracious words on the recommendation form. I appreciated that a bunch. I have no idea when Franciscan University will make a decision, since, because it is a "distance learning" program (i.e., through the mail), I'm not necessarily applying for any specific semester entry. Hey, what do I care? I've got plenty of time! Yes, a little prison humor there. We'll see—I'll keep you posted.

Another idea I've had for a while, and I think it's about time I go forward with it, is to make an aggressive push to invite a lot of the Hispanic inmates to join our group. To only have two guys from a large, growing group here just isn't acceptable—especially considering that almost all of them were probably baptized Catholic. I want to create some bilingual pamphlets to pass out to these men in our group, and have a bilingual service and a bilingual priest. If we get a few more Hispanic members, perhaps we'll put a greater emphasis on Spanish—have all our Scripture readings in both English and Spanish instead of one (or two). One Hispanic guy who came to one or two of our services told me that he didn't come back simply because his English isn't very good and, hence, he couldn't understand much of what went on. I sympathize with his frustration, so we'll get together and see what can be done.

Well, that's all I have for now, Chuck. Take good care, tell your wife I said hello, and we'll see you soon.

Dear Chuck,

Funny that you mention that our food sounds like stuff you ate in the service. My cousin, the retired Air Force general, said the same thing when I sent him the menu. I have heard stories of men in prison urinating into the food, putting ground glass into it to get back at someone, spitting in food, and other such things. Now we are served blind because of this. The servers can't see whom the food goes to.

Glad to hear your hip is better; also happy to hear that your doctor is in agreement with physical therapy as first treatment. I do know of the electrode—a TENS unit that stimulates the nerves and muscles and is a good way to loosen things up.

Citizens United for Rehabilitation of Errants (CURE) has trouble answering mail. I sent them my renewal dues and have heard nothing from them. I know they are short-staffed, but it has been a while since I got anything from them. Time for me to write to them. I thought the Quest Bookshop woman's name looked familiar. She is the one who sends us free books. Now I understand the connection! I am glad you are in contact with her.

I do hope the prison ministry takes off. I await my *Catholic Virginian* this week to see if you are published. After I finish this letter, I am sending one to the editor in response to your letter that you sent us. I am also writing the Diocese about the needs of prisoners who are Catholics.

Your letter to us all comes at a time when I have been reading about the worth of all of God's creatures, especially those who we find difficult. As one of my physician friends wrote me a while back—what happened is what you *did*, it is not who you *are*. Not letting the past determine our future is another way to look at that. Yet, as a sex offender, society will not let me put my past behind me. I am told where I can live/not live, who I can be around, where I can work/not work, etc. It is difficult to move forward when society wants to crush you, or doesn't want you at all. God really is all some of us have. I am learning to trust God and let the stuff I have no control over go. I kind of liken prison to purgatory on earth, and that if we are attentive to God and work on ourselves while we are in here, then, as you wrote, God will reward us.

I am enclosing a *USA Today* article from a couple of weeks ago on the Fr. Rodney Rodis case. It seems that this is more widespread than we thought, and it is *not* confined only to the Catholic Church. At least this is not generating the continuous daily press coverage that the sexual abuse scandal did.

Dear Chuck,

I saw your letter in the *Catholic Virginian*. You write well and have won many fans here at our correction center. I could become a chairman of your fan club. Of course we all agree with you. I also received your last letter and it encouraged me. Thank you!

How've ya been? You haven't been sharing as much personal info in your letters lately. I've been wondering about your stained-glass projects and your last skydiving adventure. Additionally, I'm always open to prayer requests. You simply need to tell me for what or whom to pray. C'mon! You've got your own personal monk who's already praying after your health and happiness. . . .

Some more wonderful news—my biological mother sent me a birthday card! It was my thirty-seventh birthday this past February 25. Her words touched me and greatly cheered my heart. As a matter of fact, the card arrived just after friends came to visit on the 26th, making that day perhaps the best day of my life since being incarcerated. God blessed me in many ways.

I've been able to continue my degree program on a computer they've provided me. So, I'm making personal progress and laying the foundation for others to be able to take independent courses too. The problem is that many of these guys can't pay tuition. Consequently, I'm trying to start a college grant program for inmates. I figure it'll require about 20K as a base investment. That way, the interest alone will pay for a decent grant per year = 1K @ 5% (greater if this were invested in say, a mutual fund, or other higher-yield account). I'm hoping for initial contributions from church members.

Keep in mind, I don't need this. My tuition's been paid. There should be hope for others in here who are worthy of a higher education but can't afford to pay. Since the DOC [Department of Corrections] has pretty much abdicated its role, perhaps our mother church can pick up the slack.

Well, my brother, I'll close for now. Don't be a stranger, and write back soon. Keep me in prayer. You and your family will ever be in mine. I'll be writing you again soon.

Dear Chuck,

It was good to see you yesterday! I'm glad we had time together. We are on lockdown as I write this—the usual—routine shakedowns to be done. We did not have a chance to do our P.M. service due to the lockdown. This one should be short, since they really only have three days to do it—Wednesday, Thursday, and Friday. They really do not want us on lock on a weekend. They have to give us three meals and that would cost more, so they like us to be off lock by Friday evening. We'll see.

Chuck, I am not surprised that only I wrote letters to the *Catholic Virginian*. As I look at the group and understand the personalities of each man and get more of their stories, it makes sense to me. Plus, some of the men are literate, but barely, or have learning disorders and find it difficult to write. I was surprised my letter was printed. I figured mine would be shelved. I am pleased it was not, and that the Holy Spirit moved a person in the Hampton Roads area to write that very nice card to me. God did that, not me.

As for actual bodies to come into the prisons and minister to us, Chuck, you have done an outstanding job of that. This is where the Kairos idea of planting seeds comes in. We have planted seeds. Some will take, some will be choked, some will grow fast and die, some will be eaten by the birds. We do what we can do.

One of the best stories is that of my spiritual advisor, a Catholic deacon in Fairfax who is now part of Kairos. His friend tried for six years to get him to come to Kairos, and he refused—he was fearful of the environment. Then, he reluctantly came to fill in for the music ministry—he plays guitar. That was all it took. He was hooked, and now this man loves to come here and minister to us.

People are scared to be here. God will call those He feels are worthy of prison ministry.

Don't be overly concerned with our membership. It will always be in flux and we are experiencing a blip toward the low end, but I feel it will come back up.

You asked about my friend. She has just completed her dissertation for her PhD. She sent me her intro—it looks very good, and I can't wait to read the rest. A lot of effort is in this work, and it is timely to health care in the death and dying area. I pray all is okay as her dissertation committee reads it. She is trying to work out a date with my cousin to visit me in May.

Thanks for doing that letter. We want it to get to as many people as possible. Thank you for doing your part.

Dear Chuck,

We are all Hokies in these tragic days. When I first saw the news, I actually started to well up. It has been too long since my college days and I'm sure I didn't know anyone, yet still I felt a profound sense of loss and sadness. I dated a girl who went there and I've been on that campus many times.

I understand why Cho lost it. After living in prison, isolated and at times reviled, I can relate to his terrible pain and sadness. The difference for me has always been my family and my faith, not to mention—in recent years—you. The little ways in which young people isolate their peers can be so cruel and vicious, and some poor souls store that for years. I've never allowed it to manifest itself beyond indignant anger. However, without a glance to Jesus's passion, one can imagine how one might be swept away into rage. If only Cho prayed . . .

I fully believe his imaginary girlfriend and his big-brother persona were demons. When you leave yourself open to such influences, they will come. He certainly needed psychiatric help, and a better, more-engaged support group. Thus, the need for more volunteers like you to let us know we're not alone in this world. Even if it simply amounts to you hearing our troubles and telling us you "get it"—how it hurts.

Validating someone's pain is the first step toward helping it to heal. Jesus knew this only too well. Sadly, we are often the cause of our own pain. Someone probably did reach out to Cho, but he didn't reach back. When we encounter such souls, we must pray for them.

My prayers go out there for all the victims and their families, but also for Cho and his. Perhaps Jesus, in His infinite mercy, can redeem even him. The thought of anyone suffering eternal damnation, even for such terrible evil as what Cho did, always filled me with pity and sadness. Even as a child, there was a *Tom and Jerry* cartoon where Tom is sent to hell. It always disturbed me, even while my friends would laugh.

We're on lockdown today. Apparently a sergeant in the next building couldn't resist insulting and harassing a fifty-plus-year-old inmate who has served eighteen years. He only had a couple to go. Not anymore. The sergeant was taken away in an ambulance. The inmate is facing twenty more years. All this could've been avoided with an ounce of common sense and compassion. Admittedly, the inmate could've just walked away. It's what I'd do. But, I do understand the frustration and anger. After years of it, there is always the temptation to lash out.

* * *

Please pray for us. We just got off our lockdown, but everyone is still frustrated. Kindness is such a rare thing in this place. I try to be a beacon of it by sharing food, keeping a smile on my face, and encouraging my fellow inmates to better things. Sometimes I fail myself—giving in to speaking harshly about our tormentors. So, pray for me too.

I'll close here. Please continue to take care of yourself and your lovely wife. Keep up the good works and the calls for prison ministry. God bless you and your family. May the best days of your past be the worst of your future.

Dear Chuck,

I've been trying to write you all day long, but was interrupted so many times. When I read what I had written, it didn't make any sense to me, so I figured it surely wouldn't make any sense to you.

Many men in here want to do things when they get out, such as get a tradesman license or a contractor's license and start their own business. I help any who comes to me, and today a future painting contractor and a future custom cabinetry shop owner had many questions. I always encourage them, let them know they can do it, and give them sound advice and accurate direction. Most have been given wrong information somewhere along the line, or are just clueless.

At my previous correction center, I often answered questions about tradesman licensing from the inmates and a wide array of home improvement questions from many staff members. Someone circulated my name amongst staff, but I'm always glad to help whomever I can. I agree that a book that would bring forth ideas, for change in our criminal justice system, is indeed a monumental undertaking. There is so much that is just outright wrong, or that could be done so much better. That would make for a lengthy, and, in part, unpopular list. And books could be written from just one item off such a list. It does seem that concepts such as *right* and *fair* have been sacrificed. I do believe that given your background, people will listen to what you have to say.

I usually begin larger endeavors with an outline, but the thought of an outline of what needs fixing in our criminal justice system is mind-boggling. I like CURE's slogan: Today's prisoners are tomorrow's neighbors. You know my philosophy: Follow your heart and your passion. I believe God put that passion in your heart. I used to do volunteer work and fix things for free for families that could not afford to hire a contractor. It was usually a single mom with kids. Between that and the work I did at the church, nothing brought me greater satisfaction. I believe we all have God-given talents and abilities, and when we use them in service to the Lord, God smiles. I must admit though, I did more than my fair share of fishing too. If I could find a job that paid me for fishing and playing with puppies, I would indeed be a workaholic!

Of course, the parole board maintains that I am this horrible, dangerous person. Ain't it strange that they are the only ones who seem to think this? I think it was one of the Roman Caesars that said "absolute power corrupts absolutely." Ironically, the state seal of Virginia says *Sic Semper Tyrannis*. Yet, they have created a fully functional, operating tyranny in the parole board. In a democracy in

America, a politically appointed body can't just nullify and ignore a court's ruling. Whoever heard of "You'll get your day in court, but it's not going to matter what the judge says"? Could that be done even in China or North Korea? I don't think so! And what's really alarming is that this doesn't seem to be alarming to anyone that this is being done here in Virginia! So here I sit, with a court ruling releasing me for exactly what the parole board afterward gave me eighteen years for.

Well, Chuck, its chowtime. Thank you for your letter and God bless.

Hello, Chuck,

I'm still working seven days a week. In October we are supposed to go on night shifts five days a week, plus the seven-day shifts again. These new prisons are keeping us busy, but at the same time they keep us from getting out. ☹

My mother and father are coming over this weekend (Sunday). I got an all-day special visit approved. I only see them four times a year. It will be good to see them. They've been there for me the last twenty-eight years, and I'm thankful to God in the blessings I have. Many families don't stick around that long after incarceration. I got locked up at sixteen, so I guess they still see me as their child, as I was when I came to prison.

Well, I know you have several letters to read, so I've bored you long enough. Take care and hope to see you soon.

Dear Chuck,

Greetings and salutations from my Corruptional Center. Got your letter; always a joy to hear from you. I am very sorry to hear that your wife has MS. I have a friend that has had MS for about twenty years or so. After much heartache and going against the grain of what I was being shown, I've come to realize and accept some of life's hard truths. I can lead a horse to water but I can't make 'em drink. And I can't change a heart. That's a job for Jesus, not me. Being on God's search and rescue team is not what I have been gifted to do. And though I live my life by the principle of love, that must be balanced by wisdom.

You see, Chuck, I did not have healthy boundaries. Someone would be harming me and I'd be hanging in there, trying to make it better, trying to fix it. But that was foolish of me. Now, if people are harmful to me, and I pleaded for some change but haven't gotten any, wisdom dictates distance from that person. I haven't talked to my mother since 2005, and my girlfriend since 2006. I love and forgive them both, but I cannot allow their negative impact in my life. I deserve better than that. My girlfriend and I were perfect for each other, like we were made by God for each other. It's easier for me to deal with the girlfriend situation, because her harming of me was not with the intent of harming me. She, like any other addict who is in the stranglehold of active usage, was just being selfish. Addiction really is, in many ways, insanity. But if getting and using drugs is priority one in any person's life, I can't have that person in my life. And I can't entertain "ifs" and "buts." That person is standing on the wrong side of my boundary, and that's that!

My attempts in the law library have proven what I originally suspected: I'm in way over my head. But I did get some encouraging news. My dad told me he may be able to replace some of the money I sent him. Maybe in a couple months, he said. That would mean I could hire a lawyer. Then my next dilemma would be how to find the right lawyer from in here. I fully, 100 percent believe, given everything in my favor, the right lawyer can get a judge to release me. Two judges already have; no reason to think a third wouldn't.

We do have air-conditioning in the dorms here, as more dorms in the state do, but the AC in the dorm I'm in has been down for over a week. They won't let me fix it because it is still under service warranty contract. I'm hoping the contractor will come fix it today. Not fair I keep everyone else's AC working, but don't have any AC myself. Something just don't seem right with that picture!

I have a request in to see the institutional attorney (I'm not giving up!). I want to know from where does a circuit court get its authority. It seems to me that the court's ruling on my technical violation disqualifies the parole board to be able to come afterward and do anything different than what the judge said. I'm told I'll find that in the Empowers Act from Congress, which the law library here doesn't have. I think the court's ruling is binding on the parole board, and everyone else too. I've just gotta find where it says so. I know what they've done isn't right. I just don't know how to fix it, anymore than the lawyer knows how to fix his heat pump when it's not right. I've done apprenticeships in carpentry, electrical, and heating, ventilation, and air-conditioning. Looks like I should have taken one in law also.

I've been recently pondering Jesus' statement: "Blessed are the poor in spirit . . ." *Poor in spirit*—what do you take that to mean? Theirs is the kingdom of heaven, so they're saved by belief in Him as their Savior. Yet, they're poor in spirit. What say ye?

Well, that's about all the stuff and whatnot I know for now. Thank you for your letters; they always brighten my day. You and yours are in my prayers always.

Dear Chuck,

Pax Domini sit semper vobiscum!

I have sixteen months left unless the good Lord lets me go first. My case is on appeal before the Virginia Supreme Court (has been there since May). I am praying for a miracle (which is what we call justice these days, sadly). I am keeping a special request for the intercession of the Georgia Martyrs (Pedro de Corpa and his companions Blas, Miguel, Antonio, and Francisco) who gave their lives in 1597 for the cause of Christ's Gospel and, in particular, the defense of Christian marriage. I also keep these hopes for God's favor before my special coterie of saints: Augustine (my patron), Thomas More, Jose Maria Escriva, Bellarmine, Philomena, and Anselm. It occurs to me that we sometimes neglect to seek the intercession of the apostles about whom Jesus said, "It is you who have stood by me in my trials . . ."

(Luke 22:28) and "... you have been with me from the beginning" (John 15:27). Surely their prayers are effectual if anyone's are? This aspect of my new faith is the most difficult for me to grasp at times. Help me to believe that the saints do hear me.

Please remember, of course, the sex offenders—especially those whose crimes are not quite so shocking as the public has been led to believe. The Diocese ought to be encouraged to speak out against the immoral "lumping together" of all sex offenders such that violent offenders are treated the same as those committed of porn possession, solicitation, or consensual sex with a minor. However reprehensible these things may appear, they are far from the sort of crime that involves the abduction, rape, and murder of an innocent child. It is an injustice to use labels which engender public fury against *all* sex offenders as if they've each committed a violent rape or dragged a child off the playground. And that is precisely what present policy does (not to mention those savage beasts at the newsrooms).

The church has an obligation to oppose blatant injustice—indeed, injustice in any form. It cannot shirk its moral duty merely because its own house has suffered from the detraction of sexual impropriety. Has it even occurred to anyone that it was God's will that the priestly scandal not only exposed the sins of Mother Church's holy spouses, but that it also made the church a registered sex offender? It is time the Church identified with the pains of the oppressed and stopped acting the hypocrite. It *is* possible to show compassion for victims without joining their crusades. It is possible to condemn sexual abuse without condemning sexual abusers. The Church has altogether forgotten the Master it serves on this front. Instead, I fear it serves Mammon—which I will call public opinion, in this instance. The church must do Christ's bidding, not the hordes and masses of men.

Please keep the Catholic community here in your prayers as we are struggling mightily against a number of adversaries. We have been meeting together on Monday and Tuesday nights in one of the three units (S-3). This has required those of us in the other two units (S-1 and S-2) to cross the center yard. Only the smaller faith groups are required to undergo this arrangement. The Protestants and Orthodox Muslims are able to meet together in the same units where they live.

Crossing the central yard has been more and more problematic as security measures have become tighter. We often wait for more than forty to forty-five minutes just to get a clearance. So, by the time we are all in one place, we may have twenty minutes of worship or fellowship time. Added to this is the fact that the Department of Corrections finally instituted the requirement in June that no programs may meet without a monitor (either approved volunteers of our own or someone assigned by the institution). The warden has recently informed the small religious groups that due to budget cuts, they can no longer afford to cover all the allocations of monitors. So, we are being asked to meet every other Monday, instead. We have volunteers from a local parish who come every Saturday. Nevertheless, the "outer unit movement" issue is the one we are having the most difficulty resolving. I have four grievances going on the issue. Two of them have been appealed to the deputy director in Richmond. One of them is at the "regular" grievance stage. And the last is at the "informal" grievance stage.

This past week I went to the law library and looked up the actual language of the Religious Land Use and Institutionalized Persons Act of 2000 (RLUIPA). It has some serious teeth in it. I would encourage you to familiarize yourself with this law in case inmates at other facilities begin to have the troubles we are experiencing. It would be wise for the Diocese to be familiar with it, as well (though I assume they already are).

Late last week, word came down through the S-1 chaplain that the warden believes the best thing to do is to split the Catholic group into three congregations—which is perfectly acceptable to those of us who have been required to wait the forty to forty-five minutes for permission to cross the yard. However, we do not presently have enough volunteers or monitors to cover all three units, so there is no guarantee that we will be able to meet in our individual units on a regular basis. No such concern is shared by our Protestant brothers, who have more than their fair share of outside volunteers. So the next thing I assume will develop is a disparity between the amount of time allocated for Protestant worship vis-à-vis all the other faith groups (excepting the Orthodox Muslims who, of course, nobody wants to upset in the least way). This situation will be a very blatant violation of the RLUIPA, which requires equity among *all* faith-based groups, regardless of their respective sizes.

On the positive side, splitting the group into three parts will help us to evangelize more effectively, since the whole "crossing the yard after waiting forty to forty-five minutes" has made each of us reticent to invite others to share in such a penitent rite of passage. Also beneficial will be the hopeful fact that our group is no longer used as a conduit for prison commerce. We have been besieged by people who sign up for Catholic services merely because they want to meet a buddy on the other side of the compound. This has caused no small amount of disturbances within our services. So, as I say, please keep these things in your prayer docket.

Thank you for your ministry to those of us who suffer the afflictions of our sins, rightly convicted or not. You are an inspiration to each of us, and we thank God for the gift. You are laying up great treasures in heaven where all of us will someday be rewarded with just recompense for our works giving evidence of salvation. Faith alone *may* be sufficient for a few—doubtful as that is—but, my goodness, who wants to be counted among the few who barely made it when it was possible to do so much more for Christ? The recent readings in Matthew seem to speak to this question (Matthew 25:14–30).

Dear Chuck:

Hello, my friend. All goes well enough here. My project for this week was to get some letters out to attorneys, which has been accomplished. I hope to get some responses in a couple of weeks. As I've said, I'm no lawyer, but I do believe I'm on to something. I'll find out here before too long now. Common sense says a parole board is not a higher authority than a circuit court judge, so they should have to abide by the judge's ruling just like everyone else. And overriding a judge is something I do not believe they have been empowered to do. So, we'll see.

I guess I'll go on record now as saying, given people's attitude toward convicts, and convicts' negativity and lack of understanding of society's interests, I do not believe letters from prisoners will bring about any positive ideas.

Asking for sympathy for a convict is akin to asking for sympathy for the devil. I believe the only way to approach the subject is to show lawmakers and society how they can benefit from making some changes. And there are numerous ways in which changes could benefit society. Society has multiple interests in the penal system, and all those areas could be improved upon greatly. I think I saw a promo for a show coming on in October on the Discovery Channel about how our prisons have failed. I'm not sure of the date or channel, but I'm scanning in October, looking for it. Prison can simultaneously serve the interests of punishment and treatment while being a contributor to, instead of a drain on, society.

As for injustices in the system, we must remember: it's prison. It's supposed to be punishment—a deterrent to committing a crime.

I believe the biggest injustice going on is old-law inmates who were sentenced when there was a swinging-door parole policy, but by the time they were parole-eligible, the policy had changed to a closed-door one. The judge believed that, contingent upon one's good behavior, one would make parole between the first and the third time up. Men are doing much more time than the judge ever intended. The judge is the one who has the responsibility to ensure that justice is served. Anything that enables the court's intentions to be altered in any way, lesser or greater, is in my opinion a miscarriage of justice. I think the abolishment of parole is a good thing. Let the court determine the length of the prison term. No politically appointed body has any business sticking their hands into the judicial sentencing process. That is not a matter for political appointees; they are not judicial. Some parole board members have had no more than a high school diploma.

As for incompetent acts and statements from prison staff,

incompetence is not unique to prisons. Possibly more predominant in prisons, but given the nature of the beast, such can reasonably be expected. Personally, I don't talk to them. What you say can and will be used against you, and it's too easy to put a negative spin on anything, if one is so inclined. There's a principle, Chuck, as old as man himself: Might makes right. Those who have the might get to say what's right. Virginia used to say slavery was right, and fought to the death for it. But when the Union armies usurped their might, all of a sudden, slavery was no longer right.

When we came to this country, it belonged to the American Indian. We killed him, and took his land and called it right. We had the might. And we must still call it right today because we haven't given him his land back yet. And look at the civil rights movement. States manipulated their laws of segregation, etc., so they still wouldn't have to treat a black man as the Constitution and Bill of Rights says a man is to be treated. Armed soldiers had to be present so six black students could walk through the doors of a college. Injustices, my friend? This country was built on them, and they're still widespread and thriving today. They're just hidden a little better in the complexity of our society's structure.

Pastor John Hagee once said that Jesus spent a quarter of his ministry casting out demons in a society ten times more moral than ours. He has also said that if God withdraws judgment on unrepentant America, He owes Sodom and Gomorrah an apology. Just some food for thought. And I am ashamed that I have been part of the problem. But I am repentant. And though that may not matter or be believable to man, one day there will be a righteous judgment, and it will matter then. So, until then, I'll love God and love my brothers, and do my best on the rest. Jesus told us in the world we will have troubles, and that offenses must come. But we have a better home waiting, my friend, and all of these troubles will be no more. So let us not take our eyes off the prize, and let us do our best to serve Jesus and be led by the Spirit this day. For we are not of this world, but we are in it. Chuck, may the grace and peace of God be upon you always.

P.S. I just want to add something regarding your book effort. There's a general bias toward a convicted felon, especially one who has not "paid his debt" to society yet, before the first page is read. Here's an example all parole-eligible inmates know. The parole board says, "Tell us of the circumstances of your crime." If I give just the pure facts, it's said I'm minimizing, rationalizing, justifying, and blaming others. If I say there are no circumstances that justify my behavior, that I was wrong and I take responsibility, it's said that I have no empathy for others and no insights into my past criminal behavior. It's a no-win situation. There is no good answer a convict can give, because they are predetermined to find the bad and see the worst. I do believe inmates should be heard, but not from their own voices. This belief comes from twenty years of experience on this side of the fence. But I respect you, and I trust you. If you think you can use my words in a way that would not bring a negative reaction, you have my blessing to do so. And I hope that you are right and I am wrong, my friend.

I would love to be wrong on this one. And you never can tell what God will reach out and bless. For with God, all things are possible. I have sent out letters to attorneys, but received no response yet. It occurred to me yesterday that I had neglected to address the matter of their fee in my letter (oops!), so they may assume I am soliciting for free legal representation. I have known many inmates to do this in the past. So it's back to the typewriter, which will take a few weeks to be scheduled for.

I am finally scheduled to see the court-appointed attorney tomorrow. Maybe he can tell me something that will be helpful. I hope so, in that he is an attorney and I am not. Did you see the special on the Discovery Channel about the California prison system? Very interesting. I saw a flyer for a new website: http://letoldlawgo.org. You might wanna check it out one day when you're retired and sittin' around doing nothing (ha).

Well, I'm gonna get my ducks in a row tonight for the attorney visit tomorrow. Take care, my friend. You and yours are in my prayers always.

Dear Chuck,

Thank you for chasing down the statement on prisons. It's good to finally have something I can show these guys. I will share it at the next meeting.

I asked that a copy of the bishop's letter be sent to you just so you would be aware of its tone and tempo. The letter went through several revisions and was the work of about five people. We even showed it to our volunteers who were quite supportive of its sentiments. The intent of the letter is primarily to motivate the Diocese to look more assiduously into the entire approach to its involvement at the prison level (throughout Virginia). Much of what we are facing here reflects a definite weakening of the Department of Corrections commitment to faith-based programs. This is more systemic than anything else. Our time has been cut and the schedule has become so sporadic that we don't know what we will be doing with our time from one week to the next. It is a death knell to our efforts at evangelizing for the faith, which is what vexes me most of all.

I know that the regular chaplaincy is concerned and has been fighting a holding pattern for several months, just trying to do all they can to prevent additional reductions of time and more regulations being added. It could not hurt for the Catholic Diocese to throw in its weight on the side of the chaplains for a greater frequency of religious services and an ease to the policies which appear to be aimed at frustrating the groups who are dogged in their determination to continue meeting as often as possible. We would ideally like to see the schedule revert to twice a week, every week, so that we have more time for Bible study, catechesis, and fellowship. I *know* that there are legislators who would be interested to learn that religious services are being treated as a privilege and not a right. I imagine both the governor and the attorney general would be interested in this as well. I frankly do not understand why we should not be allowed to meet *every* night for religious activities, since it would appear to me that this kind of preoccupation with faith could only serve to benefit the rehabilitative objectives of the department. They sure as hell aren't doing anything else to improve the lot of these men. The least they could do is get out of the way of those of us who are trying to help ourselves.

This compound has 3,000 "offenders." And yet, not one single pod is set aside for a faith-based initiative. That ought to be an embarrassment to the department. For a great many of these men, this place could serve as a monastic experience of spiritual enrichment and enlightenment. Instead, it's a freaking zoo.

Anyway, we are very appreciative and we thank you for the collateral blessings that come our way because of your service to God and us prisoners. Imagine what great and glorious things could be done if we had a hundred guys just like you spread throughout the Commonwealth. The Church would begin to grow inside these walls—in this crucible of penance, conversion, renewal, and reconciliation. People really have no idea of the intensity of one's spiritual journey within a prison. Sure, there are the fakers and the charlatan goats to contend with. But, I'm talking about the people who *really* turn to God at a time of abject personal pain and say to him, "Heal me" or "Restore me" or "Save me," or simply "Help me." Those guys really mean it. These are not convenient conversions! These are life-altering baptisms which cut deeply into the marrow of a person's psychological skeleton. If any of the guys who attend Catholic services has an ulterior motive for doing so, I cannot imagine what it might be. There are certainly no worldly blessings that come from it—as well there should *not* be.

Anyway, I am rambling away, as is my normal custom. God send us priests and deacons who will champion the cause of Christ's gospel with the passion and zeal of the Apostles! God give us priests who are not afraid to sound like Christ—or, at the very least, Ambrose, Bernard, John Vianney, Augustine, or any of a number of very fine preachers! Isn't it curious that so many Protestants believe that the next generation of church leaders will come from American prisons and that we hear nothing of the sort coming from the cavernous halls of so many Catholic churches starving for priests? Does the Catholic Church fail to see the same potential behind these walls? And, if so, ought it not be scolded? Especially when one considers that the Church of Jesus Christ was more or less a church *of prisoners* for the first 250 years of its existence? Which of St. Paul's letters wasn't written from a jail cell? I'd say it's time we rediscovered our roots. God will not give us priests if we are too proud to look for them in places where Christ makes his home. God will not be mocked by high-falutin' tartuffery all dolled up in the garb of saints who have forgotten the meaning of redemption, reconciliation, and restoration. We serve no God of prima donnas. We serve a God of mercy.

Well, Chuck, thanks again for getting that report on prisons to me. I hope that you will have had a fine Thanksgiving holiday by the time this letter finds you. May God bless you and keep you as we begin the season of expectation and light.

Dear Chuck,

Hello, my friend! Just a short note to let you know I am thinking of you, and to send you many blessings. As always, I hope and pray that you and the family are doing well, and that all else is just great!

Again, "I am truly sorry" for my past transgressions, and I pray that you will forgive me! I assure you that my past actions and conduct are not the true person I am! The demeanor I described was indeed an aberration of my natural self!

I have been wanting to send you the enclosed "Prisoner to Prisoner" daily devotional booklet (Kairos). I am not sure if you are familiar with it, but I wanted to be sure that you have a copy, as I find the writings from various prisoners very touching and enlightening. I am certain that you will agree, and find them very personal from within as they are reflections of feelings and experiences from different people and backgrounds, and various walks of life! I reflect on these writings—testimonies—quite often, and find them very helpful in dealing with my own personal grief and feelings of serious guilt and dismay.

I hope and pray that some of them will also touch you personally, as they define sincere inner feelings of others, and bring solace to many by staying close to God by trusting in HIS everlasting love and promises! True and sincere faith can and has changed many a good people in miraculous and most spiritual ways—personal will, desire, and love is all that is necessary to walk with God! God will right all wrongs, love all people, guide those who are astray, heal the sick, and bless the poor and lonely in heart! He is our strength, energy, light, and direction in life—through his love and grace we are drawn and shaped according to God's purpose, and do not walk alone, regardless of our sinful desires.

Being led by the Holy Spirit, I have experienced many changes within myself since my incarceration. Life has taken on a new and different meaning now—although, still physically the same, my inner being and spiritual self has taken on a new challenge. My ways of thinking and my natural sense have been transfigured and oriented away from the usual worldly aspirations and personal values of materialism, selfishness, greed, lust, and personification! Love itself has taken on a completely different meaning, as I have discovered new sensations of God's love and love for others. I have conquered and broken through the shell of deceptive and worldly love—it is more important to love God and others first, before one can find love, peace, contentment, and true righteousness within oneself!

Well, Chuck, my friend, I suppose I have surrendered enough of myself for now, so I guess I will stop rambling on, and get this into the mail. I am doing fine myself, and will enjoy the rest of this beautiful day!

Again, please forgive me and keep me in your prayers. So for now and always, take good care of yourselves, stay well, and be safe! May God's love, grace, peace, and many blessings otherwise, be yours this day and always.

Dear Chuck,

Thank you for the very fine Christmas card. Happy New Year to you and Ms. Lee. I pray that you are both well and prosperous throughout 2008. You may imagine that I am elated at the prospect of release in fourteen months. I am simply amazed at the passage of time. It seems of such recent memory that I was counting the years and calculating the months with a dread of unexplainable sorrow. I do not believe that I shall ever know again the depth to which the human spirit can plummet—the place where self becomes other, and even one's soul prefers to view its sheath of flesh from the angle of a hovering specter. When I think back on the worst moments I spent in jail, for instance, I am fascinated that I see myself in my mind's eye, as though I was a spectator to this scene. How is this? It is odd, I believe, to ponder one's self in this way. Perhaps it's what the ancients meant by being "beside himself"?

I am not so naive as to presume upon the future. There may yet await even greater trials than this. But I will have an advantage on them. I will already know the depths. And I will have confidence in my reserve of strength, the appreciation of preparation, and the calm reassurance which comes from knowing that darkness has not overcome it and that the gates of hell cannot prevail.

I want to bring you up-to-date on the status of things here. We have a new schedule for worship services. We Catholics will be meeting on Monday mornings from 8:00 A.M. to 9:30 A.M. We will meet again on Tuesdays between 1:30 P.M. and 3:00 P.M. This new schedule is right in the middle of the work week so that a few of our guys are worried that they may not get paid for leaving work. Others, like myself, feel as though it serves to chill evangelizing coworkers about the faith because nobody wants to be the cause of his friend's loss of employment.

The important thing to note is that this new schedule only applies to the small faith groups. Protestant worship services will continue to be held on Sundays (albeit moved to a daylight hour) and Thursday evenings. As a result, none of the Protestants have to deal with questions related to work. I believe this is, in both cause and effect, an unconstitutional policy that discriminates against the smaller faith groups and hinders them in their desire to grow. For the Catholic Christian, it's actually an impediment to his chief responsibility to Christ to go forth and make disciples of all peoples.

My employer is, thank the Lord, a committed Christian. However, she is unhappy that I will be missing work four hours a week, and that she is, according to rumor, required to pay me for the time that I am not there. She has said, in jest of course, that in the future she will hire only atheists. We say some of the most profound truths in jest, so it gives you a glimpse at the potential for inmates to be hired who are Protestant because they have no conflicts with the work schedule. Nobody needs to be a lawyer to realize that this new policy more or less promotes the Protestant faithful at the expense of everyone else. We are highly insulted over the situation and can't help but feel a certain persecution under the policy.

Like I stated earlier, I just wanted to give you a heads-up on this new schedule so you can make others aware.

Thank you for all that you do, and please keep us in your prayers as we do the same for you, pitiful as our prayers may be. In the meantime, I remain as ever in Christ and through him with the Father.

Dear Chuck,

I thank you again for remembering me. I hope your holidays were what you wanted them to be. I especially want to thank you for your story on Job. You see, I can relate to what Job went through. I too lost my business, house, family, and health (mental health).

I then subsequently lost my freedom. I was totally unaware of my mental illness and what it was doing to me and my loved ones. I look back now and see it, but couldn't at the time. Now that I have been medicated, I can rationally see it. I personally believe that God has put me in this situation to wake me up, so to speak. I believe God put me here to bring me closer to him, as I have.

I, being raised Catholic, never once said the Rosary. I now say the Rosary every day as of January 1, 2008, and I look forward to it. I still have my moments of weak faith, but as a whole it is stronger than ever and getting stronger. I had told you that my attorney was working on a habeas corpus petition. I have complete faith that we will prevail with it, not to say it will be easy. I expect a big fight from the Commonwealth Attorney the whole way, but in the end, I know God has the final say.

Dear Mr. Brown:

I am aware of your "many plights" in dealing with the Virginia Department of Corrections as a religious volunteer and as a Catholic. May I say that to deal with the Virginia Department of Corrections, it requires much patience (or becoming a patient!) and much prayer. As of this writing, I am in my thirty-third year of incarceration as a first offender (non-sexual), and sometime in March (unless they change the date again), I will be appearing before the Virginia parole board examiner to plead my case for the twentieth time. The nature of my case has not changed . . . only the political arena has gotten a little more outlandish.

Please do not despair. I remember many years ago while in the Virginia State Pen in Richmond, we had numerous volunteers coming in for a variety of services, and there was no difficulty and the program was flourishing . . . but over the years the system and the hearts of people have grown very hard and cold. People cared and wanted people to excel and make parole, but now it seems that it is controlled by "In God We Trust . . . and the Dollar TOO." I look at my situation as political and not because of my crime. I do not know where political correctness came into being, but it has had a terrible effect on people and their lives.

So you will know a little about me: I was incarcerated in 1976. I converted and was confirmed into the church in 1977 by Bishop J. J. Russell (retired). I have been incarcerated in six different Virginia prisons. I have crossed the state a few times and try not to get grounded in one place. I do not want to become comfortable and complacent in one place. At this point I am here, but here for a purpose, and when I think that I have fulfilled the purpose, I may be looking for another place to have a cell if the board does not release me.

I am presently enrolled in computer school and trying to learn all I can about the programs (Microsoft, etc.) as well as the hardware and attachments that can be used with them. I will turn fifty-four in February, and when the door does open, I have to make a decent living and survive as best I can. I do all the study and education that I can. I have already completed electrical school and custodial maintenance, so I have something to fall back on.

Please never give up, as that is what the system desires. I keep my faith close and do all I can to improve myself within my faith and my person as each new day comes by. I am not always successful, but it never gets to the point that I want to give up. I think that I watched too many episodes of *M*A*S*H* when it was on TV, because Hawkeye hated death, and I hate the system, and I will never let them win over my spirit.

I don't expect you to sit down and write a long letter to answer me; I just wanted you to know that there is someone who thoroughly understands what it is to be a person on the outside and to care about those on the inside; you even have difficulty with them, and you are paying their salary!

Please know that you are in my thoughts and prayers—that you will be given the strength to endure all that the Virginia Department of Corrections has for you, and that the holy presence of God will still enter those walls and fences that you encounter.

Dear Chuck,

It's Tuesday. I received a letter this morning and one this evening from you. Apparently, most of yesterday's mail found its way into a trash can and got fished out this morning. It is the talk of the town with many very angry campers. This isn't my first experience with questionable correctional officer behavior. At Sussex, I caught an officer stealing one of my magazines—he got three days off work in the end over that one.

As for your missing or unresponded-to letters, I have in the past seen the DOC [Department of Corrections] collect unauthorized letters and return them in bulk. Whatever the case, I now have you (personally) in my prayers. Yes, a slight change. Now I'm joking that I'm a saint-in-the-making. I figure I better step up to the plate. Time to run . . . Church night.

* * *

On November 8, church was canceled. No outside volunteers showed.

Wow, my week is getting pretty crazy. Sunday, I wasn't notified of a medical appointment (three weeks in the making to get my medication renewed). My lack of patience got me rescheduled for today, but no one told me. Divine intervention helped out and got me there. I was called to the mailroom to be informed that I had another $100 money order confiscated. While there, I ran into the nurse on her break, the one who got me to Medical. The price of incarceration keeps increasing for me. At least I should start receiving my over-the-counter meds again. Yes, my cup is usually half full rather than half empty, but my wallet has been taking a beating by a prison policy that has no penological purpose, since the criminal element can simply put any name or address on the money order to circumvent the policy (not to circumvent, but to comply). Life can be ridiculous, as you are well aware.

Upon my returning to my room for the day, my counselor returned the grievance I submitted concerning the first $100 confiscation. It was supposed to be forwarded to the grievance coordinator but got sent to my counselor. I have yet to get my grievance accepted for review at any level. So far, I'm getting the runaround. I need a grievance answered in order to notify the attorney general's office.

I hope you did something nice for the better half's birthday.

Pacemaker "L" is out of the infirmary and in the land of the living. One interesting note: "L" claims nine people died at the infirmary within his seven-week visit. I'll try to stay clear of that place. Unfortunately, "L" was moved to his original room. It will be interesting to see if I'll be able to spend Christmas with him. I had been hoping to spend some time with him before I'm transferred.

It does seem like I'll be transferred soon. The closer I get to Christmas, the more I think I'll be moved after the first of the year. I can only wonder.

My boss has plenty of personal problems. I think the prison

population gives him an outlet that he doesn't otherwise have. Plus, he's struggling with alcohol again more than he would like to. Trying to spar with me gives him an outlet, if he can push my buttons enough to get me to respond. At this point, I'm through with his antics.

Hey, I would have done the same thing as you did by enclosing a stamped envelope were I in your shoes. Unfortunately, I am well aware of most of the DOC's petty policies.

All your confusion about mail mirrors is what is happening with my money confiscation grievance. Sounds like we are a lot alike when it comes to grabbing the bull by the horns and riding it out—win or lose. That is how I feel about the money confiscation. I'm already looking ahead to district court. I already have one copy of a Warrant in Debt form. A few weeks ago, I spoke with an attorney to make sure I know my course of action.

Oh, the institutional attorney—I see I previously told you. One thing: the institutional attorney can advise me in my course of action but can't do anything on my behalf or for me otherwise. The notice to the attorney general filing suit and the serving of the summons are my responsibilities.

Second letter: I'm glad I'm not alone in letting my mind wander through all the possibilities.

Regarding X-raying: Each facility seems to have different concerns. They all have a portable X-ray machine similar to those used in airports. I heard Augusta started using an X-ray machine to X-ray TVs and boots, and Sussex regularly used it for TVs and boots. Here, I was surprised that they do pillows and mattresses. (They even X-rayed my head but couldn't find anything. Had they, they might have called it contraband.)

Well, my friend, I must wrap it up. As the temperatures have dropped below freezing and the heat has been turned on for most of this place, my building remains without heat as repairs to the system continue. With two outside (exterior) walls made of fine, cold, radiating concrete, the Lord is keeping my soul warm, but my toes need to get under the blanket and hide for the night.

Dear Chuck,

Got both of your letters last week: the one with the church address and the other one. Thanks for writing. No need to worry, we all got your church letter. As you said in your last letter, other prisons do not have these restrictions, or since it is on "the books" for all institutions, most choose not to enforce it. I suspect this is because there has been no incident between a volunteer and an inmate. Why this place is choosing to make an issue of this, none of us will really know. Again, I suspect there is more to the story than we are told.

I get the *Farmville Herald* local newspaper for the TV listings. They had an article on the twenty-fifth anniversary celebration of the opening of our Big House. What I read made me so mad. I cannot believe some of the things said. These people are delusional, and I have no doubt they believe every word they say. The lies and half-truths in this article are unbelievable. I fear for the souls of these people. I will see if I can find it and send it to you for you to read. They feel they are doing a wonderful job of protecting the people of the Commonwealth, and that they do good for the public and the inmates. It was all I could do not to vomit.

I wholeheartedly agree that once convicted, it is impossible to get an overturn. The stats say that 1 percent of all inmate lawsuits are actually heard in court. Bottom line, less than 1 percent of all inmate lawsuits are successful. One issue that bothers me is the innocent people who are exonerated of the crime by DNA or other evidence get released and have to fight to get money and have to petition the court to get their record cleared. This should be AUTOMATIC—no court should be involved except to sign the papers, and that should be Department of Corrections' job to do all of this, NOT the innocent ex-offender. The laws are favorable to the prosecution and the state. Virginia is a leader in unjust laws on evidence and post-conviction issues. I pray I can get out of this state when I finally get out.

Your writing on the book of Job was spot-on. No matter what happens to us, we are to bear it and trust in God. Unfortunately, our world is not just. The rule of St. Benedict also addresses this. We are to strive to be just. But there is no guarantee that the world will treat us justly—only God will do that, and it may take a while.

In my humble opinion, sustaining faith will become a delivering faith in God's own time. The Lord wants to know that we are ready to be delivered and continue with our faith. And the prize that we need to focus on, especially in here, is the next world. Yes, many of us will get out, but there will be challenges to that as well. We need to prepare for the future in the eternal world.

Dear Chuck,

You are so right: Even though we are in prison, we can experience God and get to know him. God is my comforter. He is my "Job." He is my hope. He is my life. He is my path to healing and feeling. He is my salvation. He forgives my sins. He forgives me and he loves me no matter what. So, Chuck, thank you for reminding me of my worthiness as a child of Christ. Even if society hates me, there are some willing to get to know me and love me as a brother in Christ.

Dear Chuck,

I am very sorry for not writing in such a long time. I don't have any excuse; I just got caught up in my own problems and neglected my friends. I am ashamed of my behavior, and all I can say is, I am sorry and ask for your forgiveness. I promise I will start writing as much as possible and I will not fall prey to my problems as before.

I am now doing well by taking care of myself and keeping out of trouble. You know, the usual things that we have to deal with. I admit I have backslid, Chuck. I have not prayed as much as I used to. I have not read God's word in some time, or participated in any fellowship with other Catholics. I intend to get back on track.

My family is doing pretty good. My mother is feeling somewhat better. You will be surprised, but she has begun going to church on Sundays with her boyfriend. My brother is still having some problems, but he does not seem to want to change his ways.

Do you remember why I am in prison, Chuck? Well, my mother was able to track down my sister. She lives in Massachusetts away from her adopted parents. She is expecting a baby within a month or so, and Mom is going up to visit her with her boyfriend and his family. She is twenty-one now, and doing pretty good from what I gathered. While she was with her adopted parents, she was physically abused by them. I was told it was a pretty bad situation. I wrote her a short letter last week; Mom said she was happy to hear from me. She said she will respond to my letter soon. I was also told that she does not hate me as I thought; in fact, it seems that she has forgiven me and wants me to keep in touch with her. She also said next year, if she can afford the finances, she will come visit me along with Mom and her baby.

I am so sorry, Chuck; I feel that now she has forgiven me, I can perhaps learn to forgive myself for what I've done. But now, maybe I can learn to do so and move on with my life. . . .

Not much else is going on. This place is pretty much as any other prison, but I am now doing pretty good. I do a lot of walking and reading, and I stay away from the majority of inmates (as always). I have approximately six years left to serve. I don't want to end up getting caught up in something stupid and end up getting more time. I've been in prison nearly eleven years now; I have had enough. Nothing is worth wasting away in a prison cell. I only wish this chapter in my life will be over so I can get out and lead as good a life as I can. Hopefully, I will find a good wife and raise some children of my own—if that is possible.

Well, my friend—and you are my friend, Chuck—that is all I have for now, but I will write again soon. Please continue to take good care of yourself, and may God bless you. Thank you, Chuck, for not giving up on me.

Dear Chuck,

You have been on my mind all day, so I'm writing to let you know that I'm praying for you and Lee, that all is going, and will go, well for you in whatever issues you may be facing. Trust in God's presence in your life and know that He is absolutely with you 100 percent of the way. Be strong and courageous and totally resigned to His will, for He is just in His judgment, and His love and mercy endures forever and ever.

It is such a thrill to see the Holy Father receive the kind of welcome he deserves as Peter's vicar and Christ's most visible spokesman to the city of God and man on earth. I am hopeful to hear some encouraging words. Do you sense, as I do, that many of the people protesting "pedophile priests" are actually more concerned about putting women in the clergy than they are with protecting children? I keep seeing signs, which say CELIBACY HAS FAILED and so forth. The priests who abused those poor children were certainly not celibate. My sign would read CELIBACY WORKS—JUST PRACTICE IT!

Let us both pray that the Holy Father will reflect on the circumstances faced by the 700,000 prisoners who are released back to society each year. In ten years' time, that's 7 million people. In twenty, 14 million. These idiot politicians are literally constructing a populist uprising that will inevitably reach such a critical mass that it will rise up and demand change in the way things are being handled. They have to be smart enough to see that. We felons are the next civil rights movement in America. Check that. All we have to do is sit back and wait for our numbers to reach the optimum point. The pressure will have to be released when there are so many ex-felons in the nation who live as second- or third-rate citizens.

I have roughly ten months left to serve. Don't know what I face. I'm stressed over how best to serve the Lord. I am frank about my talents. There is no doubt that God has blessed me with the gifts of writing, speaking, teaching, and administrating—I have always excelled whenever I have been required to meet these tasks. All I've done is work to improve areas where I've received particular graces. And, of course, I pray for additional grace all the while.

It is only natural for me to gravitate toward greater involvement in the life of the Church. I am obliged to spend my talents in the furtherance of God's Kingdom, and it's an obligation I take very seriously.

Five years ago—working on six—I did not have the focus I have now. I had all the same talents, but I was sure my "calling" in life was to public service. Everything I did was calculated toward that end. Sooner or later, I was going to be elected to something in order to serve a cause larger than myself. At the time my affections were in solidarity with the Christian/Conservative brand of political ideology for which I was well indoctrinated. I can now see more than a few flaws in that perspective—but, I also see a litany of flaws in the whole dualistic structure of American politics. I don't see a comfortable home with bloviating Republicans anymore. But, I simply can't make a home with extreme relativism, either—and that's more or less how I view the Democratic Party.

Now, you're probably thinking that this whole consideration is an academic exercise. What does it matter? I can't even vote (though, in reality, as a first-time felon, I can vote back in my home state of North Carolina). Virginia's the state with its head in the sand on this issue. I'm simply saying that all the passion I once had for politics, and the talents which redound to it, has been redesigned and refocused toward the building up of God's Kingdom on earth, the Church. In fact, I'm fairly certain that God's calling me toward some form of dedicated commitment in this area, though I haven't yet discerned His precise will.

Unfortunately, as I have shared with you before, and as I hope you will share with other Catholics in particular, the "blowback" against the priestly scandal is so severe that I dare not suggest what I'm strangely convicted is God's desire for my life: a special relationship to His Church. Institutionally, the Church is responding to the scandal by battening down the hatches and vetting everyone who lives and breathes. This is not an unexpected reaction. The only problem is that it lacks objectivity. People are being consigned to status based upon criteria that makes their present standing the captive of prior sins, or, in some cases, sins assigned to them which they may not actually "own." I wonder if the Church ever even considers, for example, that when background checks are done, they may recover records that are not completely reliable, or else reflect the outcome of cases, which, by the Church's own canonical standards, were secured in circumstances that fell short of a fair and juridical process. This may not occur to Church authorities who, like most Americans, simply assume that anyone who is convicted in the United States got a fair shake. We ought to know better by now!

I believe Catholics such as me ought to be provided with a canonical process to clear our names as it relates to, and affects, a relationship with the Church. It is wholly inapposite to the message and purpose of the Gospel to render a child of God to second-class status in the Church based purely on the fact that some state or jurisdiction in the United States managed to win a criminal conviction against him. Where in Church law is there a presumption that secular law is superior in assigning guilt? Is it not the Church's duty to deal in matters of truth rather than appearance? How can the Church be honest with itself if it sets purely objective standards in determining who is "fit" to be called by God to Holy Orders or religious life? Can the same Church that claims sinners like Mary Magdalene, Saul of Tarsus, Dismas of the Cross, and the woman caught in sin turn a blind and judging eye to convicted felons—or even "sex" offenders—without inviting the wrath of God?

My talents and gifts are to be used in the service of God. No doubt, there are a multitude of ways to do that without becoming a deacon or priest. But, if the only reason I fail to serve God in these ways results from an unforgiving and dismissive policy of the Church, doesn't that make the Church an impediment to God's will? I realize that the Church may bind and loose as she is so inclined, but her chief charge is to make disciples, baptize, and teach (and it would appear, at least, that she needs all the help she can get).

I actually wonder at times if I hadn't ought to pursue a stricter service to God in another "ecclesial community" (Lutheran, Anglican, or Episcopal—or maybe even Eastern Orthodox) simply as a means to an end. I would remain Catholic (in secret, I suppose), but serve at schismatic altars (maybe I could convert them by stealth?). Do you see how vexing this is? I've spent serious time contemplating how I can respond to God's call to serve, at the very least, as a teacher and evangelist, by imagining scenarios that will allow me to remain Catholic while serving at the altars of my separated brothers. Why? Because my separated brothers will accept me, will give me a second chance, will even trust me to minister in "mixed" company, while my Catholic brothers are unable to be so forgiving because of all the bureaucratic mumbo jumbo connected to the priestly scandal. In some respects, this comes down to a difference between a community of believers who act and sound like Christ, and a Church that sounds surprisingly similar to the Pharisees.

Perhaps I'm being harsh. Please forgive me. I love my Church, Christ's Church, and I can't deny her. But, I want her to love me *despite* my flaws, my old sins, my criminal record. And right now, she isn't acting as if she really gives a damn about my special circumstances. Am I being unreasonable? Self-absorbed? Too concerned about my own feelings and not concerned enough about the Church's immediate crisis? Just tell me what you're led to say.

Well, brother, I appreciate the opportunity to vent. I trust you will pass along my frustrations and remind those in authority that "All members of the Church, including her ministers, must acknowledge that they are sinners." Ministers are sent by Christ, not screened, vetted, and selected through a process of socially acceptable norms. There are easier ways to ensure against priestly abuse than barring anyone who's ever been convicted of a sexual crime, wrongly or rightly, from taking Holy Orders. It will suffice merely to enact the following canon: "No priest or deacon shall ever be alone in the presence of an underage child." This would be a simple, prudent rule which would serve to protect *all* priests from false accusations and to prevent scurrilous ones from taking advantage of close quarters. More important, it would make possible for an individual who has a record such as mine to respond to God's initiative in sending out laborers for the harvest.

May God bless you and keep you in all that you do.

Dear Chuck,

How are you doing my friend?

During the week of Father's Day I was beginning to get nervous as to whether I would receive a Father's Day card. I haven't heard from or seen my youngest in over three years. I wrote them and sent them a book of stamps and had a necklace made for each of them. I received no response from them and I can't call them because they only have cell phones and the connection is bad.

So all of this is eating at my nerves and I asked myself, if I am spending enough time with God. That's one of the reasons I am in prison because I didn't. I ask myself, do I have to let go of my loved ones? Is what God wants? Even my ex-wife has remarried. I wonder how much do I have to endure to stay on God's good side.

Well Sunday morning came and the C.O. came to my cell and told me I had visitors. Yes, I had a lovely visit with both my daughters. And with the high cost of gas they made the three hour drive to see me.

When I saw them together, my eyes swelled up with tears. I was so very happy to see them both. We had a visit together and when they left, I went back to my cell and I thanked God from the bottom of my heart for the wonderful blessing He gave me.

God is very kind to me. he has given me many blessings each day. I hope you are doing well my friend and God bless you.

Dear Dad (Chuck),

It's good to be the King. I know how you feel. I received your letter this evening. Even though my grey matter doesn't seem to be happy with me, I'm forcing the stuff into labor. In short, I thought I would begin a response in hopes that my brain cooperates. It hasn't so far. This is my 3rd attempt to get started. Words have never been my strong suit. What God gave me was plenty of love to share. Please give mine to Lee. I can feel hers all the way from your home..

You know the saying, "waste not; want not." Wasting time is a crime of the procrastinator, so without any further a do....

Today, in church, I gave a special prayer for Lee and you during the Eucharist service. There were six of us in attendance, and I have good news. Starting next month, my Tuesday church gathering will move back to the evenings (1830-2000), which will make things easier for all those guys who aren't able to get away from their jobs during the day. Plus, one of our volunteers, says it should make it easier to recruit more volunteers. She also said, the priest we have been hoping for and expecting will begin the process for approval to visit us on July 7th.

Yes, of course, I knew you would receive my Father's Day card on time. Why did I ask? You see, this is a prime example of the grey matter problem I have. An 8-cylinder brain running on 4. It must be the fuel I am feeding it. Speaking of feeding, prison food is like Chinese dog food—it will kill ya! Plus, they taste about the same.

Did I ever tell you that I am one of eight guys who attend the therapy support group? True rehabilitation is difficult to come by in Virginia. At my previous correctional center, I was one of ten. Less then one half get any type of cognitive therapy that will stick with them. I've been lucky that I have been able to get into these special groups, courses, classes and plenty of one –on –one from the very beginning of my tour with the Department of Corrections. (The early bird got the worm and I have been pushing for more everywhere I go. What can I say? I want my money's worth out of this one time tour.)

I think (a grey matter problem), I told you about Virginia Beach suing the DOC. There are currently 1800 or so, state prisoners in local jails waiting to be moved to a state facility. About two months ago, Virginia DOC took in 296 Wyoming prisoners for $130 per day/ per prisoner while paying local facilities $14 per day for state prisoners. The local facilities claim it costs them $60 per day. In my eyes, this practice burdens the local communities. Anyway, last week the DOC announced that they would bring in 700 more out-of-state prisoners. That didn't fly to well with the Sheriff's Association, who spoke up, forcing the Governor to fix the problem at the states own expense.

Just five years ago, there were over 3,000 state prisoners in local facilities waiting to be moved while the DOC was leasing 3300 beds to other states averaging $65 per inmate. By late 2004, Virginia got rid of all out–of-state prisoners and emptied the jails. It now looks like those jails are filling up with a backlog of men waiting to be moved to state facilities—now at 1800. (This sums up the latest article I read this week). Therefore, there are no more out-of-state prisoners at the expense of our local communities.

Dysfunctionality (Yes, I made that word up. It's good to be the King). It has such far reaching impact on families. In my last letter to my niece, I teased that I was the last to know of her engagement. In response, she wrote, "*You are not the last to know. Grandma and the rest of the family have not yet been informed. I guess it is just odd calling them out of the blue and saying I'm engaged. It's not like any of them have kept the lines of communication open with me. I always send Christmas cards and I sent a change of address card to all of them, but no response. Grandma feels satisfied and connected if she sees me at Christmas and my birthday, but hey, it's worth 200 bucks a year.... Who says you can't buy love!* ☺. *Maybe I'll send out an engagement announcement.*" It is a shame the impact my alcoholic grandmother had on my mother. And, I thought it was my fault for my mother not loving me. I didn't know it was only her inability to show love. What a simple concept that can free a lifetime of torment. Fortunately, I can change my world by changing the way I look at things. It's unfortunate that many are stuck in dysfunctional patterns. We can try to bring them enlightenment, but they must be willing to change. In the end, we must accept them for who they are and at what point they are in their personal growth. Acceptance has made me love my mother even more. And to think, she only made baby steps in opening communication 9 months ago. I didn't even get a Christmas card.

Monday, I wrote my biological mother. There is progress there. In her letter, she mentioned for me to acknowledge if I received her letter to my letter. A nice turn of events from, "Don't give any indication I'm writing you," she wrote last year.

Well, I better wrap up while it's "Good to be the king."

P.S. Sorry I didn't call for Father's Day, but I didn't have the number. Yeah, I can get away with that one.

PART IV

ADVERSITY

Dear Brothers,

I can imagine that trying to live your best life right now is categorically challenging. Let's face it—it's a grueling, testing, demanding, and strenuous state of affairs. It is a fact of life that many people give up far too easily when things don't go their way or they face some kind of adversity.

Pain has always been a part of life. A mother carries a baby in her womb and with difficulty a child is born . . . but that knowledge of pain has not resulted in fewer babies born on earth. The first experiences of life consist of pain—the first slap on the behind; growing your first teeth; learning how to walk—and all of these are part of life's experience. And as we grow up we discover emotional pain as our tender emotions of childhood are turned upside down as we grow to our teen years.

None of us really enjoy adversity, but we need to recognize that some of the greatest decisions in life have come as a result of adversity. The early church responded to adversity by spreading the Gospel of Jesus Christ further than it had gone before! It is often in adversity that we pray more, believe God for greater miracles, and yes, we often submit ourselves to Him in repentance and a greater commitment to obedience when we face those difficult times. God does use the adverse circumstances of our life to bring about His perfect plan!

Times of adversity are often used by God to help us see the deep places in our hearts—the places where we are tormented and driven. It is out of this poisoned well that we frequently hurt others, say things which damage relationships, and we wish we could change. We are caught in the habit of kicking against the sharp sticks of life . . . we damage ourselves and others . . . and Jesus is waiting to get our attention to change us!

So when we face adversity, we need to find strength through it. Perhaps it's there as a reminder to help you find the plan God has for your life. We need to take on a victor's attitude and mentality and say, "God, I may not understand this, but I know that you are still in control. And, you said all things would work together for my good. And, you said you would take this evil and turn it around and use it to my advantage. So Father, I thank you that you are going to bring me through this."

So brothers, no matter what you may have faced or are facing in life, let God make your hard times into harvest times!

God love ya and bless ya,

Chuck

Dear Chuck and Lee:

Hope this letter finds you well.

I have enclosed an article that my son wrote for *Paddler*—thought you would be interested in it. I think it is pretty good. He told me that it is nothing and I only feel that way because I am his mother.

Chuck, as a mother, I am so frightened as to what will happen to him once released. I have been on the computer and the information I have found really frightens me. It appears he will have to pay for supervision and it ranges from $40 to $103 a month. How on earth does an inmate make it back out in society? He gets absolutely no breaks at all. He will have back child support from his daughter in Maine and will have to begin child support for his daughter, which was set at $383 a month, and now an additional amount, as well as 500 hours of community service. What he did was wrong, but, my gosh, he will be treated worse than a murderer. My husband and I aren't made of money and can't support him forever. I have tried to find out how difficult it would be for him to come to Florida and then be transferred to South Carolina, and Florida seems to imply it would be very involved. It appears that he has no place to go and may have to stay in prison longer in order to stay in Virginia, so that when we *do* move, he can be transferred directly to South Carolina without a hassle.

The prison asked him the other day what his job plans were going to be. How on earth can he have job plans when he has been in prison for three and a half years? He won't be able to support himself in Virginia with all the other stuff too. Wouldn't you think that the DOC would want him to be anywhere his parents are? I pray every day that our home sells before his release, but things don't look very good. If our home sells, it would eliminate all this hassle.

I am sorry to unload on you. I felt you would know where I am coming from better than anyone because you most likely have heard it from other inmates.

Dear Chuck,

Hey! I guess timing is everything. I was waiting until I received my "official" answer from the parole board before I wrote again, but then also, I just read the letter you submitted to the *Catholic Virginian*. So this letter will be at least twofold in purpose.

Well, let's get the bad news out first. As I expected, I received my second turn-down just yesterday. Coupled with it was a three-year deferral. That is to say, I won't go up for parole again for three years. This was also a second three-year deferral.

So, six years! It's as if I didn't go up for parole at all. Funny thing, though—when I was being sentenced, everyone was discussing the fact that I'd be eligible for parole in twelve and a half years. Also, the judge suggested I'd probably be out at fifteen to sixteen years. So I find it interesting now how everyone disowns that same ideology. They say, "Well, you do have a life sentence!" or "You know, they don't have to let you out at all!"

I was hoping at least for a one-year deferral, but this three-year situation very well may be fatal in a number of different ways. I myself am confident that I'm not in the best of health. Both of my uncles (at least) have had heart problems around my age; and because admittedly I haven't had the mental strength to continue to take care of myself, I could also be a prime candidate for a stroke, part of which has already come true (silent strokes). Then, there's the issue of the effect on my aunt and uncle, and my son. Personally, and with the same aforementioned confidence, I fear my aunt and uncle won't make it through these next three years.

My attorney has put a great deal of time and effort into trying to assist me with representation, and it seems, in one respect, all for nothing. We're not going to win the hearts and minds of the parole board. No matter what I do, I can't change the past. There are people in here who have done things much more terrible than myself—maybe in some cases not as frightening—but many of these people received sentences far below what I received. And these people haven't done a thing to help themselves change for the better. It's all sad, really.

I am a firm believer in karma. The laws of nature and the universe are intertwined with the will of God. The arrogance of the parole board, and those who fabricated the evidence in my pre-sentence report, will not escape God's eyes and judgment. I take solace in that! I've accepted all of this and will continue to try and gather strength to carry on. But each year, it gets harder and harder.

Now, with regard to the article you wrote in the *Catholic Virginian*. I guess the most appropriate thing to say would be "Thank you!" Embarrassingly, I must say that when I got to the fifth paragraph, that damn tear welled up in my eye again. Please forgive me, but when I finished reading, I said to myself in a self-hatred, unworthy kinda way, "How dare he be so kind in saying such compassionate things about us in here? How dare he be one of only a few who do actually care about us?" It all seems so unfair that God has chosen so few to do this work! That makes you one of the chosen few—carrying out one of Christ's direct requests, to visit those in prison.

I could never express well enough how honored I am to know you, Chuck. Many in your former profession and background—after retirement—would simply go to their dinner parties, drink their evening martinis, vegetate, and complain about how the world is so screwed up by the poor people. You have chosen to do amazing Christ-like things with your life! You are truly a disciple of Christ!

Anyway, I really look forward to seeing you again. Just to see you sitting in the room at service is so good!

"Far better it is to dare mighty things, to win glorious triumphs, even though checked with failure, than to rank with those poor spirits who neither enjoy much, nor suffer much, because they live in the gray twilight that knows neither victory or defeat." —Theodore Roosevelt

Dear Brother Chuck,

Hello, my friend—how are you? I hope and pray that you and family are well, and that everyone is filled with ardent spirit!

It was great seeing you and the other wonderful volunteers for this month's Mass, as per usual, on the second Tuesday of the month. You people are just extraordinary and super! It always brings our group great joy to have you fine folks care so much about us inmates. Your sincerity, love, and compassion are indeed noteworthy and deserving of utmost praise. Many of us see all of you as members of a true "Family in Christ" and feel greatly *blessed* to have you all on board in our continued journey in faith. God bless you all!

As you know, I am very glad to hear that you have decided to pursue your book venture, and pray that it will be a most exciting challenge, and a rewarding experience and success. I have great hopes that your book will provide undeniable and unconcealed truths and insight, regarding a life in prison from a prisoner's perspective, and the pressing need for rehabilitation and restoration of true purpose and worthiness of people behind bars. Yes, prisons are needed in any society; however, it should never be for a purpose to vindicate warehousing of people for unrealistic, unreasonable, and greatly disproportionate periods of incarceration, nor for reasons of exaggerated public safety concerns. Although it is necessary to confine certain criminals to lengthy prison terms, as based on seriousness of crimes, it is not always justified to totally condemn someone to a "living death sentence" for a crime alone. All human life is sacred and worthy of God's love, mercy, and compassion, and always deserves a sense of dignity and respect for life, regardless of a person's failures, disabilities, sins, or social shortcomings, for we are all "children of God."

I have now been incarcerated for five years, a time lost to confusion, shame, and loneliness. It has been a most trying and difficult period, as I had never been incarcerated, or in any serious trouble of such nature, before. I have discovered that FREEDOM is the essence of life, joy, and wholeness; without it, a person is deprived of social worthiness, esteem, and ineffable personal development, affecting both physical and emotional soundness.

To me, being in prison is an absolutely disheartening and dismal experience. One must humble themselves to harsh and greatly humiliating extremes, in order to maintain a sense of humanity and personal dignity. The environment offers scarce and minimal opportunities for self-reliance, self-determination, and self-improvement, which of course contributes to a negative attitude and despondency. Such an environment exposes one to existing criminal behavior and activities rampant within, and as such poses inherent risk to security and personal safety. Virginia's prisons are not run in ways conducive to, or that foster, objective and purposeful means of rehabilitation, nor reasonable and productive means or purpose for restoration of errants. It is my sincere opinion, and experience, that misconduct and subversive activities are in most cases tolerated. Such, of course, does not support any great hopes for rehabilitative initiatives or incentives.

Although various programs are available and offered to inmates in support of viable rehabilitation efforts, they *do not*, in most cases, afford core essential development needs beneficial to improving individual character and behavior attributes. The focus appears to be mainly in support of common expected standards of personal aptitudes. I have not personally experienced any great practices which have had a direct bearing upon a person's development needs essential to basic human and social values, i.e., discipline, respect, integrity, faith, and responsibility, etc.

I find that most prisoners come from wretched and dysfunctional backgrounds and social environments, which indeed influence individual behavior, and thus, in many cases, contribute directly to an individual's criminal mind and character, social conflicts, and, unfortunately, lengthy periods of incarceration. However, such people should not be construed as total failures, or unworthy of another chance in life and good social standing if a willing, honest, and sincere attitude is evident. As such, rehabilitation of prisoners warrants a social expectation and civic duty to promulgate worthwhile programs and initiatives, which augment already-established objectives and incentives for restoration of inmates.

Such programs and initiatives should focus on psychological and sociological barriers and social expectations, in order to reshape and nurture individual needs, as well as social attributes, meeting standards of social responsibilities and expectations of a proper and well-functioning society. Rehabilitation of errants is indeed a public and social responsibility, which can no longer be ignored, or disguised within the fibers of our society, as it greatly impedes and infringes upon the essence of human values, morals, and individual liberties.

Social neglect and warehousing citizens in prisons is neither a viable nor financially sound solution to our current overpopulation in prisons, due to a harsh stance on crime punishment versus rehabilitation. More prisons and their high operating costs are a public taxpayer nightmare, when millions of dollars are expended yearly for unprofitable, unproductive, and otherwise questionable *material* reasons. The real values and public concerns should be for humanism, dignity, liberty, wholesomeness, and worthiness—as *all people*, regardless of background, need to be rightfully nurtured and valued, as contributors and purposeful elements of society. Even though not every inmate can be rehabilitated, *everyone* should, as a minimum, be afforded a *second chance*, or at least, an opportunity for reform and restoration. As a caring and responsible society, all citizens have a duty to invest in and promulgate a respect for human worthiness and values. "A defective system in need of desperate repair"—now!

The following is a synopsis of personal background and criminal case summary.

Personal Affirmation:

It is with profound shame, extreme remorse, and deep sadness that I make known some facts regarding the crimes I committed, and circumstances thereto involving my ex-spouse in a domestic dispute. I understand and confirm that my criminal actions and behavior were unwarranted, and indeed an aberration of my normal character and true persona. As such, and for reasons thereof, I am to blame for my present condition, due to gross errors in judgment and lack of anger control on my behalf, resulting in my criminal status, and the extreme pain and suffering caused to my loved ones and family members. I hereby assume full responsibility for my actions!

In my present life in prison, I continue to pray to my GOD daily for forgiveness and redemption, and for hope that my wrongs can be corrected and absolved, as I truly desire to seek a new beginning and closure to a most terrible experience. I continue to pray to stay strong in my faith and to seek my needed daily strength and energy from Our Lord, in order to maintain hope, vigor, and a positive outlook on life. Loss of freedom and lengthy incarceration can destroy the soul!

Personal Profile:

- **Born and reared in (West) Germany**
- **Attended German school up to grade seven**
- **Immigrated to the United States of America at the age of thirteen**
- **College graduate, plus many various military and civilian specialty skills training; other social and academic curriculums**
- **Area of expertise: Communications and Electronics/Telecommunications**
- **Vietnam War era veteran and Retired U.S. Army Officer (1988)**
- **Previous Virginia State Employee (State Police); thirteen-plus years (up to September 2002)**
- **No previous criminal record; first-time offender**
- **Exceptional work experience**
- **Social Security–eligible (if released from incarceration); VA State Pension eligible**
- **Devout Christian and upstanding citizen (was active in church and community); previous member of Knights of Columbus (third degree)**

- **Two previous marriages with children (first marriage lasted twenty years, with two adult sons, ages thirty-four and thirty-seven; second marriage lasted twelve years, with two minor daughters, ages nine and twelve)**
- **gentle, kind, compassionate, and sincere (I am not a career criminal, or rogue or reprobate-type person); righteous and trustworthy nature**

Brief Case History:

Preamble:

Prior to my state of aberration and commission of my criminal acts and unfortunate behavior, I was under medical care (for approximately two years) for severe depression, stress management issues, and alcoholism. Problems within the workplace and home environment were evident, and contributed immensely to disruption of work and family responsibilities. As problems escalated, I attempted to soothe and cover up my troubles by drinking excessively, which in turn greatly aggravated my already-serious conditions within the home environment.

In September of 2002, my then wife decided to pursue legal action by obtaining a court-ordered "Protective Order" with the most restrictive conditions. As such, I was required to remove myself from my home, and was not allowed any contact with my spouse. The order permitted me to have two hours of supervised visits on Saturdays, 10:00 A.M. to 12:00 P.M. only, in my mother's presence. This tragic and devastating situation added to already-existing problems and dismay, and caused me to rebel and act out against my wife, as I could not cope with my emotions and state of anger. As I dearly loved my wife and daughters, my passion for them was uncontrollable, and forced me to violate the "Protective Order," as I desperately needed to converse with my wife about our present situation and the well-being of our children. I was extremely intoxicated that night when I entered my house, in order to converse with my wife. She notified the police upon my entry.

(Note: There was no history of any previous domestic abuse in any incidents. I have never physically hurt or abused my wives.)

Upon the arrival of the police, I willfully surrendered without any resistance or altercation. I was charged with "Breaking and entering, with intent to murder"; "Abduction" (asked wife to come with me from bedroom down the hall to the living room); "Malicious wounding" (I was in the possession of a knife upon entering the house proper—my wife attempted to get hold of the knife, grabbed the knife by its blade, and cut her hand as I pulled it from her hand); "Property damage" (damaged vehicles parked in the driveway).

I was tried and sentenced in circuit court during April/May of 2003. I had entered an "Alford Plea" (without jury) at the recommendation of my counsel (retained).

In accordance with established Virginia Criminal Sentencing Guidelines, my sentencing range called for 5 years, 8 months (low side) to 10 years, 1 month (high side), and with a mid-range of 6 years, 11 months. As per Virginia law, guidelines are "discretionary." Since I had a bench trial, the judge had the option of sentencing me under the sentencing guidelines, or applicable (still-valid) statutory sentencing laws, as applicable to my felony charges.

For whatever and unknown reasons and purpose, the judge chose to ignore the sentencing guidelines and sentenced me under the statutory laws. He gave me the maximum permissible sentences for all four charges. In reality and finality, he imposed a total sentence of "life, plus 35 years." With all suspended time, I ended up with 60 years to serve, without possibility for parole. This is under the "New Law"—Sentencing after 1995. Anyone sentenced prior to 1995 is under the "Old Law," and parole-eligible. Under the "New Law," one has to serve 85 percent of non-suspended time (in my case, 60 years). My current release year is 2055!

In my case, a definite "cruel and unusual" punishment! It greatly surpasses "reasonableness," "fairness," or "judicious" applications if law. My punishment is "greatly disproportionate" when compared to the sentencing range of applicable guidelines. Roughly six times the amount of the high side of guidelines. Other things to consider, or things that should have been considered, are my age (I am sixty years old now); running my sentences concurrently instead of consecutively; way more suspended time, or lower-range sentences. I am a victim of extreme and gross injustice! A most atrocious example of the Virginia Criminal Justice System! Who can HELP ME?

(Note: I have been pursuing habeas corpus relief through state and federal courts for over two years now, and so far without much success. My attorney is filing a petition for review at the U.S. Supreme Court this month. It is my final and last option for possible relief.)

Dear Chuck,

I pray your health and spirits remain good and that His graces continue to be upon you. Seeing you come to celebrate Mass with us is certainly a blessing for all of us. The more the merrier aptly fits the occasion. Hopefully, one day I'll be able to come celebrate in your church. When I am free, four and a half years hence, I shall certainly make it a point to pay you a special visit!

As to your appreciation of the challenges we as prisoners face, it's not quite what you think. Unless you pay close attention to the Discovery Channel when they do shows about current facilities, you might be tempted to think we still call guards "screws" or face violence here. That isn't the case here, but for the occasional fistfight. Even *that* is pretty rare. The main challenge for me comes from fighting abuses by the administration. You'd be surprised by the ridiculousness of what they do, to say nothing of the "obligatory" graft and corruption. Suffice it to say: Your tax dollars are *not* at all hard at work here.

The real outrage, however, is the utter lack of a true commitment to rehabilitative programs, regardless of what you might be told. Case in point: The Department of Correctional Education. They won't hire me to teach despite my having a bachelor's in economics and lots of teaching experience. The failure rate for the GED (high school equivalency diploma) approaches the abysmal! In plain fact, these folks prefer that inmates leave prison just as ignorant as they came in. The strongest crime-prevention technique *is* education, and it's given the lowest priority!

I don't want this letter to be filled with complaints and negativity. There are, as you've seen yourself, moments of extreme grace. After all, I *can* sleep in every day if I so choose. However, I tend to keep busy in a positive way. I'm taking a correspondence course in computers; I do plenty of craft projects for friends and family to let them know I care; I'm *very* well-read; and I even make time to write letters—a lost art these days. While this certainly isn't a life anyone would choose, one certainly has a choice of what to do with it. I choose to maintain a positive attitude and to continue to be constructive in whatever ways I can.

In a way, that's what we all must do, free or not. Truthfully, one is never truly free of responsibilities, expectations, obligations, or restrictions. It's all just a matter of degree. Regardless of condition, we are ever called upon to acquit ourselves in the way our Catholic faith instructs us. It's not important *where* we are, but rather, what we do while we're there.

With that bit of wisdom shared, I will close here. You shall ever be remembered in my prayers. Please do the same for me as for us all. I'll write again soon. Take care of yourself, and by all means, keep coming to see us. I'll always be present to greet you.

Dear Chuck,

I hope that this letter finds you doing well regardless of whichever circumstances you may be experiencing.

In my life, I've always had trust issues. Practically everything I've ever been involved in and people I've grown to love and trust seem to never be around very long, or—through human nature—I find myself somewhat betrayed. I've come to learn to trust; it's not about the other person, it's about your ability to handle the situation should the other person break that trust. Trust, like respect, is earned. I believe you already know this, of course, but it never hurts to reiterate the fact. To trust in others is the ability to trust in yourself.

In closing, I wanted you to be aware that although I don't know you well on a personal level, what I do know of you I admire very much! I'm proud to be associated with you for a number of reasons, and I don't want our contact to end. When you write to me, it's not necessary to try and expend great effort in telling me about Christ's work in my life—I'm aware of his love for me. I desire instead to know how you're doing and that you are okay! You are a brother in Christ, and I want to be there for you also.

Dear Chuck,

Thank you for your letter and your encouragement on the book. You are correct: Kids today are *very* Internet-savvy. However, they are also life-savvy and curious and wind up in situations that they are not ready for. I'm still in the idea phase right now, but I hope to have something in outline form in a few weeks.

I received a letter from my advocate in the divorce about my annulment. It seems that they will use my testimony and *only* my testimony as the grounds for the annulment. It appears that my inability to see marriage as a sacrament was an issue for the Tribunal to seek grounds. Therefore, whatever my ex-wife wrote will not ever be considered. Good news, right? Not really.

The judge in the case wants to shield the testimony from me. My advocate can summarize it for me, but even then, the judge will censor parts he feels that I do not need to know. I am *very* upset at this. I do have a right to review the testimony per "the rules," but "the rules" also say that the judge can close parts or all of the file if he feels that it will or may cause harm to either party.

I have had it with people trying to "protect" me. I don't need to be protected. I need some truth in my life to help me with my therapy. I want to read what she wrote and I think it will give me some closure to our marriage and help me. I wrote my advocate to explain this to him and asked him to advocate for me. I'm willing to go far with this. I do not understand the secrecy over this.

Finally, I feel validated in my decision to participate in the annulment. My wife could have avoided all the pain she wrote me about by answering the questionnaire. If she had let me read this, she would have not even had to participate at all in the process and gotten what she wanted without the pain. She chose to ignore me on this and the consequence was the pain. I'm sad for her on that, but I'm not really sorry. It was her decision to do as she did. Unnecessary angst.

My spirits go up and down. This annulment issue is not helping, nor is the weather. I will continue to pray for us both, Chuck. We've had a lot and have a lot going on in our lives that cause pain. I know someday God will reward us both for our suffering. In the meantime, we must keep trucking along and trust in Him to do what is best. Thanks for your support, Chuck. God bless you, and I hope to see you soon.

Peace and love in Christ.

P.S. Go ahead and write our mutual friend. He has asked about you in a couple of letters. He won't care that I shared with you. What happened was, he was minding his own business in a halfway house, and a local TV station decided to do an exposé on sex offenders in his halfway house. They put his name, address, etc., on TV, along with his crimes, and he was fired from his job at McDonald's. He was up for a manager's position. He was upset. I got another letter; he is working with his uncle laying carpet, but go ahead and write him. He could use some encouragement.

Dear Brother Chuck,

It is always good to hear from you, my friend.

Brother Chuck, what I'm going to tell you is a very touchy subject, but I do believe you will understand and will not turn your back on me. I was charged twenty-two years ago with a sex crime, and certain people are trying to keep me in past my max date, which is July 21. Please keep me in your prayers because I do need them. As I know more I will tell you.

Now, how are you doing, my friend? I hope your health and marriage are doing just fine.

I realize that I'm never alone and Jesus has my back, front, and sides of me all the time. I just wish people in general would be more understanding and forgiving. There is enough hate in this world. Must we turn on each other here in the United States of America? God help us all!

I have been punished dearly for my wrongdoing, and now they want to keep on punishing me for the rest of my life in prison. I'm not a threat to society, but if you don't give me a chance to prove it, how can you judge me on what I might do or not do again? There is something very wrong with this picture, and they don't care about me or others in prison.

I don't like it here. I went from a very good pod with single cells to a dorm of sixty-five people. Not nice at all. I am not happy at all at this time, or will I be until I get out—hopefully.

I wish you well, my friend; take good care of yourself, and may God be with you always.

Miss you, my brother in Christ Jesus.

Love always, brother.

P.S. I hope you can read this. I'm writing this letter on my knees at my bunk.

Dear Chuck,

Thank you for your letter.

I am sort of depressed, this being my son's fourteenth birthday and me not being able to be there, while the man my ex is going to marry most likely *is* there. That sucks. I can't do anything about that fact. I wrote him a letter, which I will keep with the rest of them until he wants to read them or asks for them. It is all I can do; that, and pray, which I do a lot of.

I understand about MS (multiple sclerosis). One of my lawyers has it. He uses a walker to get around. Rich was really good. I wish I had him for my other two court cases. I may have fared better.

Well, I am TV-less and radio/cd-player-less. No electronics for me. My TV went supernova on Memorial Day—I gave it a fitting service. My CD-radio unit, I'm trying to get a better one, so I sent it back to GPX with a letter of complaint about the radio and an "intermittent" problem, and $25. So I'll see what comes back. Others have done this and gotten better units. I pray that happens to me.

My dad is sending me the cash to buy a new TV: a seven-inch color LCD. He felt it was not worth $65 to fix my other one, which failed now for the third time in nineteen months. They sell us junk off our commissary. We pay inflated prices and no one does anything because no one cares how we are ripped off in here. One of my friends bought the black-and-white TV. Warranty: 90 days. Broke down: 96 days. He has no money. Tries to get it fixed in here by another inmate—that man is shaken down, TV confiscated, and he gets a charge. Stupid. The system is stupid.

Now I have to wait until June 16 to order the TV and another two to three weeks for the order to be filled. What a mess. At least this is allowing me to catch up on reading, writing, and allowing me more "God" time and prayer.

Then I find out that my brother *really* wants nothing to do with me *ever* again. This from my father—and we know that my brother holds grudges for a long time. For some reason, he sees what I did as an affront to *him*. What twisted thinking that is. So this changes how my father's estate will be settled and what will happen to my "share" and who will control it. A trust now will be set up with my cousin in control. More mess.

Oh well, enough of that. God will see me through. God bless you, Chuck, and God love ya! Take care. Hope to see you in person sometime soon. Hang in there; God will guide us to the eternal reward!

Dear Brother Chuck,

I hope you are doing well these days. I wish I could say the same. I have a troubled heart.

I love my family on the street very much. My wife and I have been soul mates for nineteen years while serving time. I pray to God to watch over them always. Being separated pains me so much, and I know I'm not the only guy in here who has been hurt or abandoned. I don't share my problems with anyone in here. I thought I had a handful of problems when I came here. Not one person in here had the same lifestyle that I had when I was on the street. I had so-called friends who liked to talk about you behind your back. Again, I pray to God, but it seems like he doesn't hear my prayers. I don't pray for myself, only for my family.

I know God has his plans for me and my family, but it hurts to see them suffer. To me their lives and welfare are more important than my own. I have some kind of depression because it hurts me so when my wife suffers. I feel her pain as well. There is no one inside I can talk to privately about my family. All I can do is pray, but that doesn't seem to work right now.

This place is tearing my family apart. I need time by myself to try to hear what God is telling me.

To Chuck,

I was glad to get your letter today. Sorry it sounded like I was venting. It is good to know that I have a friend I can communicate with, and I would not ask you to do anything that you're not supposed to do.

I'm sure others have asked or tried. First of all, I did something stupid to get myself in here. I am guilty and I know I have to do my time. I had it made on the streets outside, a good home, family, and job. I moved down from Maine to Virginia and got a job in northern Virginia, and shortly after met the lady of my dreams. We bought a home in Fairfax City. It was a house in bad shape. I fixed it up. It took me five years. I know I had the best BBQ grill in Fairfax. I spent $6,000 just on materials. The house looked good and the value went up. Shortly after I got arrested, my wife had to get a small deli to get a better income. It just made enough to pay the bills.

An opportunity came up for her to get another house next door to her godmother's place. She thought she needed a change. She put the house up for sale and made a contract for the other. She was very happy with the new home, but the other one did not sell. So she has been struggling on running two homes for seven months, and still it did not sell yet. So anyway, she is about to lose both homes.

I talked with my daughter who sent me the Father's Day card. She told me she forgot to put the return address on it. She told me that she was going to move out on her own on July 1. This hurt me. She is going to school at George Mason University and working, so it is harder on her. My oldest, she is twenty-two, so there's a lot on her shoulders. I have another daughter who is twenty and does not have a clue about the real world. My wife has too much to worry about now. I pray for them every day.

They say when you are in prison, you should only worry about yourself and don't worry about your family. So far I have eighteen more years. So my wife said she'll have to live for herself. Maybe relocate and even go through the process of remarrying. She said if I love her, I should let her go. I know deep down she doesn't want to.

Well, it's getting late. Thank you for being a friend and having an open ear.

Dear Chuck,

I am sorry for not responding to your recent letters, I know there is no excuse. I really wanted to write before, but I did not know what to say. I am no good when it comes down to meeting new people, and have never been what you would call a social animal. By nature and circumstance I have always been kind of a loner. I don't feel comfortable in crowds or groups, so I missed many services with our Catholic group. In fact, the last time I saw you was the first meeting I went to in a month, and consequently I am no longer on the list.

Because of my past, I carry around a lot of guilt, and my faith is not as strong as it should be. I have never been a religious man. I try my best to stay on the path, but I stray a lot. Due to my past and also my intellectual nature, I don't believe in all I should.

I deal with many personal problems and I have yet to find it in me to forgive myself for my sins. I carry a lot of weight around and tend to do so without requesting help from anyone. I am not a bad person; my heart is in the right place, and I did my best to be a good man. Life threw me some good curveballs.

My point, I guess, is that I do appreciate your volunteering your time for us. Too many have simply given up on us, and it is good to see that some still care.

I will say that I will make more of an effort to respond to your letters and come to the meetings. Once again, I thank you for your patience and kindness.

Dear Chuck,

Your assumption of me being in low spirits is correct. I will not deny it, and I don't mind sharing my feelings or talking about them. I carry around a lot of guilt and let many people down, myself included. What I am about to tell you is not to alleviate that guilt, and is not an attempt to make excuses or receive any pity—please know that, Chuck. I am only giving you a way to perhaps understand why I feel and think the way I do today.

I was raised in Italy from when I was six months old until the age of fifteen. My father was, for lack of a better word, disturbed. No religion was taught in my family. My father provided for us, I will not deny that. He worked his butt off to feed and clothe us all. I have two brothers and one sister, all younger than I am. My dad was very abusive to us all, both physically and mentally, and my mother was too scared to leave. I was the oldest, and I grew up assuming the role of protector. I felt it was my duty to protect my mother and siblings; therefore, when Dad beat my mother or the kids, I would anger him so he would stop beating them and take it out on me. In that I did a good job; by beatings, I mean, with whatever was within reach: chairs, broomsticks, etc. He tried to throw me off a bridge, pointed a gun at my head, tried to strangle me, and on and on.

I will show you my scars if necessary; I have no reason to lie. I tried to kill myself when I was eight or nine by jumping in front of a car. I was too overwhelmed. Too many times I held my mother in my arms as her blood leaked to the floor, and today she still credits me with saving her life more than a few times, as well as did the kids. Personally, I take no credit for that. In fact, I believe there was more that I should have done. Looking back, I did not do enough in my mind.

I never experienced childhood. I was always too concerned with more important issues than to be involved in games. Reality was all I knew. I learned and understood too much too soon. No love from anyone other than my mother; very few good memories, no friends, no hope, and only one dream to hang on to, which is now impossible to achieve. All I learned I did so on my own. I survived; I always have been stronger both mentally and physically than my mom or siblings. With all I have been through, it is a miracle I am alive, even more so because I am still sane. I took on more than them and I am ashamed to say that I failed.

My life has been nothing but a continuing battle. Today at the age of twenty-eight, I feel fifty-six. I am very tired, my friend, too tired. Sometimes I wonder how many more of these battles I can fight before I am laid out for good. How much more can I withstand? When will I be able to rest a while and be happy for once? At peace.

All my life I wanted to one day marry a good woman and raise a family of my own—be the kind of father my dad never was, and be a good husband. Have a healthy family life, that has always been my dream—the only dream I ever had. That was all I ever wanted. Today that dream is dead, and I have nothing else. I will be out at the age of thirty-six, but with my crime, no woman will ever give me a chance again—no need to even hope.

I met a twenty-nine-year-old woman from Waynesboro, Virginia, a month ago through pen-pal writing. All seemed well; we had a lot in common and we got along. She asked for my picture, I sent her one. And now three weeks later I've yet to hear from her. Now I am close to giving up on finding a female friend in my age range too. What's the point anyway? I will die alone and cold. I know that, and the scary part is, I am about ready to accept that reality, and I am no longer scared or bothered by that.

There is more to tell; however, I don't want to make you depressed, so I will close for now. I want to thank you again for writing and listening, Chuck. Take care of yourself, and may God continue to bless you.

Dear Chuck,

Thanks for your letter. Yes, it was not good that they chose to lock down on our services week, but they must remind us who is in charge from time to time, so it happened. Plus they needed to do it before Thanksgiving.

No word on the bells you purchased for our church service. It might be a surprise for our next service.

The sex offender group is a separate group that meets once a week. I am not at liberty to disclose who is in that group, but there are a few men who are in our Christian group who are in it. Most of us have some church or spiritual background. You are correct, there are many sex offenders in our group. This correction center has approximately 50 to 65 percent of men who have committed a sexual crime. Unfortunately, there is only one treatment group because it is voluntary. The DOC cannot force anyone to be in group therapy while in prison, but *can* upon release. How crazy is that? But a reason I have heard is that some inmates truly are innocent and refused to be forced to take treatment when they say they did not commit the crime, so they sued DOC and won. Hence, only one phase of treatment is mandatory, and any actual therapy is only voluntary. Weird, I know, but that is how it is.

I had a visit that Saturday after Thanksgiving from my cousin and a friend I used to work with. It went well. I got to eat well and had good company. I was denied an extended-time special visit, but we had four hours together, so God was definitely with us to give us time to talk. I won't get another visit until April.

In that visit, I found out my ex-wife has already remarried. I am okay with this. It supports my theory on why she sought the annulment in the first place. But hey, that's on her. I told this to the priest who visits us and he was upset that she had married before the annulment was decided. According to him, she had no business seeking it unless she was going to abide by the rules and stipulations of the process, which clearly state no remarriage until the annulment is actually decided. He was disappointed that she would do this. Well, I can't speak for her, and that has to be on her conscience, not mine. I have my own issues to deal with. I just hope she is happy, and that my children are taken care of.

Dear Chuck,

Regarding the criminal justice/prison system, I understand your concerns. There is a percentage of us that are *truly* innocent. A look at the recent DNA analysis and overturned convictions attests to that. You are correct: The judicial system looks bad when these things happen. Our system is not fair, and its adversarial nature enhances that. The truth is not what anyone is after. Convictions for reelection is what a Commonwealth Attorney wants—usually with a look toward a judge's position or political aspirations. Defense attorneys want acquittals so their reputation is established and business comes in. All a trial is about is different theories of what happened in the absence of DNA or other damning evidence.

I pleaded guilty, I *was* guilty, and thought that would help me. It actually hindered me to tell the truth. I would have been better off pleading "not guilty" and forced things. I doubt I would have gotten the time I did if I'd played it that way, but my conscience got the best of me and I wanted to play it straight and tell the truth, and I paid a heavy price for that. But I think I did the right thing and I stand by what I did in telling the truth and confessing.

In the movie *The Shawshank Redemption*, there is a line where Morgan Freeman tells Tim Robbins that, "In prison, everyone is innocent." Not owning up to your actions and taking responsibility for yourself is why men keep coming back here. One of our Christian group members who has been transferred was like that. I was his cell partner for almost a year, and everything that went wrong was always someone else's fault, when it was him who created his own problems. When that man is released from here, he will have a difficult life unless he owns up and takes responsibility.

Yes, the prisoners won the case against forced treatment, but at what cost? Their cases could not be reopened. Once you are convicted and sentenced, it is *very* difficult to get a case back to court unless it is a DNA case. The system "worked" according to the powers that be. Less than 1 percent of prisoner legal cases make it to court. Unfair? Yes. Wrong? Yes. But try to get a politician to change it—oh, no, that would be political suicide. So it is tolerated as "it is the best we can do."

My eyes have been opened. I have *no* respect for our criminal justice system nor those who work in it. Prison is just warehousing humans and modern-day slavery. And we sex offenders, forget it. With all these crazy restrictions I will be hard-pressed to find a job and a place to live when I get out. Phil is lucky. Time will tell if he can make it. We are praying. We did hear from him, and so far, so good.

We just got a huge dose of bad news last Wednesday. We are going to get, to start, ninety-plus new inmates as an expansion to increase our inmate population. To do this, we will be losing our single cells. The only single cells will be in the honor pod. So I will have to live with someone again, and I am none too happy about that. None of us are. They took away the *one* incentive we have to behave ourselves. So now we will join the overcrowded ranks. The supposed goal is to increase our population by 136 to 150 inmates.

This will overwhelm us. Chow hall, laundry school, property, vocational classes, library, barbershop, jobs, etc. The COs don't like it, we don't like it, but it is what it is. We can't change it, so I'm looking for a cell partner that I am compatible with. That is all I can do.

Dear Chuck,

I received your monthly letter as well as the copy of the letter you sent my mother. I appreciate your kind words and the fact you understand my core problem. I spoke to my mother on the phone and she also thanks you; she will respond, she said, but she wanted to make sure you were who you said you were with me first.

I am doing okay, but I have been bored out of my mind lately. I've also been more depressed than is usual, so I am sleeping too much. I can't pinpoint the cause, but I pray for an answer anyway. I also am still attempting to find a woman around my age to write to, but no one seems interested. I read and write still and study the word of God; however, lately it all seems too monotonous. I continue to stay active but I seem to be losing another battle, honestly, I don't know what else to do.

Dear Chuck,

I received your letter Thursday. Thanks; it's always good hearing from you! Let me fill you in on what's happened. Yes, the guys voted me as new leader of our church group and I humbly accepted. So far it has worked out very nicely, especially our service on January 30. Last month I had asked Father if he could give us confession on that night, since it had been well over six months since we last held penance.

I figured that instead of holding our usual service that night, that maybe we'd be better served doing something else, something more tailored to confession. Our service consisted of a couple of songs from a CD—a combination of classical music and Gregorian chant, followed by one of the men reading the missal readings for the day. During the serene music, we contemplated our sins, the Lord's forgiveness, etc., until time for the next reading. All the while, as one man came back from confession with Father, the next man would go out. I loved it! I thought it was perhaps the most spiritual and moving thing we've done as a group. I also liked how we accomplished it—my idea, Jack's implementation. Good teamwork. I have this in my schedule book again for sometime in late June—we'll let you know in case you want to attend!

I have just submitted requests for our group to assemble on Good Friday, hopefully in the gym where there is lots of room, and enact the Stations of the Cross. That would be wonderful . . . we'll see what they say. I would also like to invite our good bishop here to hold Mass, or just visit. I'll get with Father first on that, though—"chain of command" and all that. Hey, I liked your letter to the editor. Very nice. Hopefully it and the bishop's letter and survey will result in a greater awareness of the needs of Catholic inmates.

I've enclosed a recommendation form for Franciscan University—finally! I ran out of stamps for about ten days and so the whole project was delayed a bit. Nevertheless, I'm on track now. Hopefully I'll be accepted and then I'll begin phase two—the search for funding. That will probably prove more difficult than getting in! For starters, we'll see how much the school itself will knock off the tuition rate. Anyway, I think the recommendation forms are primarily for the question of whether I'll be academically able to handle the work. That should be no problem; my credentials attest to that. My grades in law school were mediocre, but part of that was because I was working forty hours a week the whole time (in violation of ABA rules for students). Hey—I had to support myself and pay child support.

Go ahead and tout my BA from the U. of Maryland (1995—in government and politics) and my Juris Doctor (law degree) from Catholic U. (1998). My Marine Corps service and leadership of our Catholic group might be selling points as well. When you're done, send it directly to Franciscan U. (address is on the form). I very much appreciate this, Chuck. Thanks a bunch, buddy!

Dear Chuck,

I'm very sorry for not having written to you in so long. You have certainly been on my mind often. This past month or so has been extremely difficult for me, for many different stressors have formulated—in particular, as you know, my parole situation. I was going to wait until I actually heard something, but as I'll mention later, I do have an ulterior motive for writing now as well.

So of course, no, I haven't heard anything as of yet. I haven't because we've asked them to hold off on a decision until the fifth board member came in—which he did—so I might get an answer anytime soon. I won't speculate!

Enclosed are copies of the letters my attorney submitted on my behalf—three years ago and just recently. You are free to keep them or "properly" dispose of them. My attorney has been trying to help me now for a number of years, and frankly, I'm astounded as to how much time, effort, and money has been expended on my behalf. I feel so undeserving and can only hope that if in some way I haven't already paid them back for all their generosity, that I would be worthy and capable upon my release. My attorney and his firm are truly special people to say the least.

I've been distraught lately because my attorney and my family members all met with one of the parole board members, and I'm told the meeting went well. Then my attorney told me the chairperson of the parole board called him twice and expressed her personal feelings in my regard. She said, in essence, that she wasn't moved by anything I'd done in my life except that my crime was premeditated. It was—as to breaking into the home where my victim lived—but not in attacking her, because I understood she wouldn't be home, and then she came home. The chairperson also made note of a few other details, which really bothered me. I say this because a third of the information in my pre-sentence report—upon which the chairperson depended in making her decision—contains false information, fabricated to secure a conviction at best. The attorney who represented me at trial knew this, and yet it was entered anyway. He has since passed away and so I cannot challenge any of it against him. I'm cursed now with this pre-sentence report compiled from the police report—and all highly suspect.

The chairperson said I should do the high end of my sentence, the average being sixteen years, which I've done, and with a life sentence that could mean for me up to thirty years. So I'm really just sick over all this right now.

Dear Chuck,

I am happy for all the response that you received from the letter and saddened that no priest had anything to say. I can only hope that in the future, it will get better. I made mention in my letter to the advisory committee about the lack of local support from our county or the Charlottesville Catholic communities.

At least someone cares. That is what I say about your activism. WE NEED PEOPLE TO BE ACTIVE IN PRISON MINISTRY AND IN REENTRY PROGRAMS FOR THOSE WHO ARE GETTING OUT. I like the idea of your parish and the Staunton one combining ministry. That may help.

The members will always be in flux in the group. That is the nature of the beast. With all the transfers, we have been hit pretty hard. These men don't realize that we can help them and they can take their problems to us and we can be there for them. It is sad, but again, there are control issues and trust issues. Our ministry leader has an idea to recruit new members. We'll see if it works.

Chuck, I am enclosing a letter generated by an inmate's family about three issues we face here that affect both the inmate and his or her family. If you would please copy it, along with the list of people to send it to, and send it to as many people as you can who are willing to send it in. The goal is to have 100,000 of these letters on the governor's desk by next month. The issues are real, and we hope to get as much support as we can. Richmond listens to voters, so please send this to as many people as you can who will send it to the six people listed. Thanks.

Okay, I will close here. God bless you and God love you. Peace and Love.

Enclosed Letter:

I am writing you on behalf of concerns that my family and I share regarding the Virginia Department of Corrections (VDOC) and the services and programs that have been instituted in dealing with those we love who are behind bars. I realize that your time is valuable, so I shall make this as clear and concise as possible.

There are three areas of accountability where we have questions. The areas of concern are the VDOC medical treatment and services; MCI and the services they provide; and finally, Keefe and the items they sell throughout the VDOC.

First, inmates are often informed that their medical treatment and bills for services are out of the hands of those who provide them treatment. The lack of responsiveness on behalf of staff members ensures that inmates are often turned away without a proper avenue for redress. Who is accountable for the medical services offered by the VDOC?

Second, MCI maintains a stranglehold over the telecommunications system throughout the VDOC. They were recently expelled from the New York DOC for bilking inmate families for hundreds of millions of dollars. Who is accountable for ensuring that our best interests are being met?

Third, a monopoly is maintained over VDOC commissary and property expenditures. Every few months the prison population's buying power decreases due to ever-increasing prices and their stagnant inmate pay. Who is held accountable for ensuring that Keefe offers fair and affordable prices?

My family and I are also concerned with the 85 percent system as it exists today throughout the VDOC. The amount of time that convicted felons are being required to serve is ensuring that in the not-too-distant future, we will have a generation of geriatric prisoners released into society. There is nothing as sad as a hopeless spirit denied the tools and opportunity to adequately prepare for reentry into society as a viable participant.

Lastly, discretionary parole appears to be virtually nonexistent for the more than 5,000 old-law inmates still in the VDOC.

The seated members of the Virginia parole board are the sole determining body for whether a prisoner is granted discretionary parole or not. A rational person would believe that a conflict of interest exists between the parole board and their appointed duties. Their very livelihood is only ensured by continuing to deny old-law inmates discretionary parole. Each old-law inmate that is released from confinement brings the Virginia parole board one person closer to unemployment; hence, the conflict of interest.

I am writing you because we would like to see progressive and forward-thinking changes within the VDOC as it exists today. Thank you for your time and consideration, and I look forward to hearing from you and witnessing some changes in the not-too-distant future.

Dear Chuck,

Thank you for those articles off the Internet about the sex offenders in Miami. It was not pleasant to read, but it shows the problems and issues of the inane laws being passed and the stupidity of the city councilman who thinks he is doing nothing wrong. I wonder how he will be judged at the end times? I'll leave that one up to God.

I shared the articles with my treatment group. For the first time, I got some reaction out of the psychologist. The week I shared with the group, Don Imus had been fired for his "nappy-headed hos" comment. The psychologist rather forcefully said, "Where are Sharpton and Jackson on this issue? Why don't they speak about this?" I could not agree more. I got my last Sunday *Washington Post*

(15 April) and the "Outlook" section had excellent pieces on the Imus issue and how Sharpton and Jackson actually help to keep the blacks down. Having lived on Long Island and growing up in that area, as you know, Sharpton and Jackson are frequently in the media on racial issues. It never occurred to me that they make their money on the backs of the poor blacks—something to consider.

Anyway, I wanted to thank you for sending that. There were things there that were just not in the *Post*, and while USA Today.com had it, the *USA Today* paper did not. Goes to show you how much I miss by not having access to the online versions of things. Oh well, it will be twenty-one more years until I have to worry about that.

I heard you were at the parole board forum. Can't wait to hear about it and how you felt about what went on. Even though I am not eligible for parole, they still, in a way, affect what goes on with all of us. Again, the "serious nature of the crime" was the reason combined with an "unofficial" you haven't served enough time yet for your crime response.

Okay, Chuck, let me get going. Thanks again for your support of us and for being a good friend. God bless ya and God love ya! See you in a couple of weeks.

Dear Chuck,

I got your letter last night. I agree with you: The Tech tragedy has no more words to say. What gets me is the incessant quest to pin the blame on someone—someone OTHER than Mr. Cho. The media went after President Steger, his instruction, etc. I read an article where someone in the dorm, maybe his ex-roomy, was blaming himself for "not doing something." At least some in the media have it right in a few editorials I've read, that NOTHING could have been done to prevent Cho from doing this—NOTHING. No one person is responsible for the behavior of another. The video showed the sickness of Mr. Cho and I am glad it was aired. We won't know why he did what he did, but we do know that he was seriously ill, and on 14 April, Mr. Cho "snapped," and we know the result.

This "the campus should have been locked down" idea is ridiculous. A university is not a prison. If they want a lockdown, come down here on one of our lockdowns. I'll show them what a real lockdown is. All "shutting down" would have done is move Cho to his dorm where he would have shot it up.

Why not add to the "blame list" the students in the classrooms or the teachers at Morris Hall—couldn't someone have tackled him? Or a group of people stopped him? We need to leave the "blame game" alone.

Re: Parole Forum. Glad you went. I am not surprised that things went as you found. I am also happy that Bishop Sullivan was there. We need that kind of support. What I want to know is that with changes in administrations, usually all the appointers leave because they served at the bequest of the leader, i.e., president, governor, mayor, etc. Yet the parole chair has been on the parole board for a long time now, under multiple governors, so why isn't she "fired" by a new administration? Other than Alan Greenspan, and occasionally an FBI or CIA director, all appointees go. There is or seems to be no accountability of the parole board, who are acting unlawfully by not putting forth parole guidelines and publishing them as a 2006 Supreme Court decision required that all states do. "Serious nature of the crime" is supposed to no longer be a criterion for denying parole as the only decision for refusal. I guess Virginia feels that it can operate above the established law of the country.

Re: Your Article. You hit the nail on the head, Chuck, with your letter. The sex offender residency laws do nothing to protect children. Since 90 percent of children are abused by people they know, these inane laws affect only 10 percent of all sex offenders, and not really all offenders, because greater than 95 percent do not hang out at schools, day-care centers, libraries, bus stops, etc. They live next door to you, teach your children, coach your children, are Boy or Girl Scout fathers or mothers, soccer moms, baseball dads, and sadly, even clergy. Should we not let a rapist live near a bar or a nightclub because scantily clad women may be raped?

To me, the correction departments and the psychological/ psychiatry fields need to link in collaboration with each other to find ways of dealing with criminal behavior, and we need to make it attractive both financially *and* professionally for *good* people in their fields to want to research in the area.

What we need are restorative-justice models of incarceration that help *both* victim and perpetrator. I just had lunch with a friend who told me that a DOC psychologist told him one time that he felt no one in prison could be rehabilitated, and that fools worked with prisoners! Is it any wonder why there is so little rehab in prison?

Chuck, I could go on and on, but I feel I am preaching to the choir. You "get" this more than many others I talk to. You are in a position and have "clout" to do something about it.

We are indeed a punishment society that is reactive rather than proactive. It is fear-driven to propel politicians to higher offices based on how "tough" one is on crime. Don't let those bad boys go, they will come after your kids, sister, momma, grandma, aunt, niece, etc. No one listens to this data, but put the latest medical study on the TV and people demand that treatment. It is not "politically correct" to defend prisoners or to humanize those behind bars.

Maybe that is why I have an ex-wife and am estranged from my brother and other family. If they look past the crime, I am still the person who they knew and loved and married. But to distance oneself, to not communicate, to divorce and annul, to shun, easier to put me out of mind, easier to just "go on with life" and not worry or concern yourself with that person anymore. It's a theory.

Okay, Chuck, let me get this off to you. Take care and God bless you. Thanks for all of your support, love, and fellowship. See ya soon.

P.S. A great mentor of mine in ethics at UVA used to say, and I'm sure it is not his quote, "What is ethical is not always legal, and what is legal is not always ethical." Boy, in the case of prisoners, sex offenders, and corrections departments, ain't this the truth?

Another tidbit—I saw on NBC-29 news that one of our state representatives who is running for reelection wants to castrate sex offenders for reduced sentences. Obviously, this idiot has no idea about what drives sex offenders or sex addictions. Maybe we should castrate his brain for lack of common sense? What do you think?

Dear Chuck,

From my many years of managing campaigns in North Carolina and Virginia, I always stressed the importance of face-to-face media contact with local and regional newspaper editors. Before we would even ramp up an earned media campaign, I'd make arrangements for my candidate to have "sit-downs" with every single agreeable editor or publisher in the district. It's amazing how far a personal greeting and introduction will go in the effort to garner media exposure. I look at all the efforts afoot to get this kind of exposure for prison issues and I wonder how much "flesh" time is involved. I, of course, understand that volunteers are already maxing out their available time in the trenches. And, God bless them for all that they do. But it would be a mistake for those of us intimately involved in the business of prison/justice advocacy not to realize how much the battle occurs through the channels of public communication. Between the reality of current policy related to penology and criminal justice and the perception created by policy works and expositors (politicians and media) is an enormous gulf of accurate knowledge. Simply put, modern media is obsessed with profit, and news about advocacy doesn't do a thing for the bottom line. People want pluck and pizzazz neatly wrapped in the comfort of their own stereotypes. It takes superior organization and aggressive marketing to overcome these obstacles for people who want to "sell" the Gospel approach to human dignity and justice.

One can more or less forget about the six o'clock news broadcasts—they are entirely sold out to corporate America, and corporate America couldn't give a hoot about reforming anything that doesn't make it look good. Prison and criminal justice do not rank high on the list. Nothing would be more crippling to the image of, say, General Electric, than to have supported—even indirectly—the early release of a convict who re-offends. It's got "Willie Horton" written all over it. On top of that, the six o'clock crowd has become lapdogs of local and state government. If it comes across the fax machine from the county law enforcement office, it might as well have the indicia of heaven stamped on it: It's *going* to be on the news, no matter how invidious it may be! However, print media outlets are not as intractable, and are often prone to the sort of cajoling and massaging that broadcast media resist. It seems to me that what is greatly needed are organized campaigns to increase the overall level of awareness about prison and justice issues among the intelligentsia of newspapers, news journals, and nationally syndicated magazines. This is where the face-to-face, flesh-pressing techniques have the most to offer. What needs to happen is for right-minded, reform-oriented, social justice advocates to make as many pilgrimages into the editorial boardrooms of as many American publications as possible. Far too many people are locked up to begin with. Far too many people are forced into pleas by unscrupulous (scandalizing) tactics. Far too few alternatives to prison are available. Far too many people have been wrongly convicted.

(As an aside, when one considers the number of people who have been released based exclusively on DNA evidence—and these are normally people with quite lengthy sentences—has anyone stopped to consider the statistical probability of wrongful convictions in cases where the stakes were much lower and the evidence was not biologically supported? It is quite reasonable to suggest that thousands of innocent people sit in American prisons today.)

In sum, something is seriously awry in our entire approach to criminal liability, and the United States is quickly becoming the laughingstock of the civilized world and the greatest judicial hypocrite since Soviet Russia. This is the message that ought to be conveyed to editors, along with supplications that they turn their rhetorical guns on a common American enemy: injustice in any and all forms. Throw an MLK quote at them and watch their sympathetic countenances take shape with something like: "Injustice anywhere is a threat to justice everywhere . . . Whatever affects one directly, affects all indirectly . . . There comes a time when the cup of endurance runs over, and men are no longer willing to be plunged into the abyss of despair" (Martin Luther King Jr., *Letter from a Birmingham Jail*). These are not slogans. These are Truths. What we have in America is nothing short of the institutionalized oppression of the poor before, during, and after the trial, and the ultimate betrayal in consigning that person to a life of perpetual groveling after prison. This is an injustice that cries out to heaven because it diminishes and disregards the essence of Christ in every man: the Image of his Creator.

In closing, please allow me to plant a seed about what I perceive as the deeper dilemma with regard to crime and punishment. The moorings of our republic have largely slipped loose. We hear and speak so often these days about being a democracy that we've all but forgotten that it was precisely the latter form of political system our framers sought to avoid. As a fellow Catholic, you undoubtedly recognize the subtle dangers of too much democratization. Let me give you a couple of quotes to treasure in your heart: James Madison opposed too much democratization because "there is nothing to check the inducement to sacrifice the weaker party or the obnoxious individual." In Federalist No. 10, Madison wrote, "Measures are too often decided, not according to the rules of justice and the rights of the minor party, but by superior force of an interested and overbearing majority." John Adams, Thomas Jefferson, and John Marshall each shared similar opinions which, for the sake of brevity, I'll not include herein.

What, you may ask, has this got to do with prisons, prisoners, justice, or recidivism? A whole heap of a lot! The fact is that our politicians will more or less oppress anyone so long as it will translate into votes. You can see the symptom of this phenomenon playing itself out in the ever-increasing absurdities regarding sex offenders. You see it playing out on a broader scale in the always-escalating number of criminal statutes added to the code. There is nothing, other than financial constraints, to stem this tide. There is no incentive for politicians or judges to stop locking more and more people up because, quite simply, the majority of people demand it. So all the dangers warned about can be witnessed close-up in our present culture's obsession with incarceration and institutionalized "vengeance justice." (The "victim justice" mantra has literally destroyed the intent of the Bill of Rights—our system of legal protection was designed to protect a citizen put in jeopardy against the enormous plenary power of government. It was not designed to protect victims, no matter how noble—or democratic—such a notion sounds.)

Now, please don't misunderstand me. I am not suggesting that we ought to stop punishing crimes that require it. What I *am* suggesting is that the use of criminal laws to impose social and moral constructs that not everyone agrees with is a violation of human rights—rights that one holds from heaven. We were never "delegated" as "subjects" of the state or nation. There ought not be "subjects" in America. We are citizens and free men, by God! Sovereigns in our own right.

The "war" on drugs is an absolute failure. Over 500,000 Americans are in prison for this alone. It is true that many of them were potentially dangerous to society because of the milieu in which the drug industry operates. But anyone with a modicum of rational sense can clearly see that if you legalize many illicit drugs, the milieu evaporates and the incentive to pushers and thugs no longer exists. You don't see many bootleggers running around causing mayhem anymore. For obvious reasons; there's an efficient, free-market relationship between the demand for alcohol and its supply. The demand for drugs is high and is not likely to dissipate. We are ignoring the inevitable and choosing—quite deliberately—to prolong the current nonsense of a "drug war" that cannot, and will not, be won. In the meantime, 500,000 Americans are felons, which virtually eliminates their long-term opportunities for personal growth and productive citizenship. What objective reason do any of them have to seek after the best in this world when they have been systemically oppressed for either using or supplying a product that millions of their fellow citizens obviously want? This is an injustice wrapped in plain stupidity.

I am not a user. I am not a pusher. I frankly believe that anyone who uses drugs is very unwise. By the grace of God, I have never been induced to join in with those who participate in the use or trafficking of drugs. Morally, I strongly advise against it, and I will not befriend anyone I know to be a user. But, none of this has anything to do with the larger issue over drugs and the culture which supports them. It's legal to jump out of a perfectly fine airplane. Yet, I don't advise anyone to do it. It's legal to drink yourself into a coma in your own home. I don't encourage this either. We are surrounded in life by activities which others do that we find offensive or distasteful.

Nevertheless, it is not reasonable for us to use government as a tool to suppress others from doing things that may offend us. This is the wrong use of government, and, I believe, not a particularly Christian approach to government, either.

The drug war is merely one example of the revolving door of direct democracy imposing its will on a substantial minority. A growing phenomenon that ought to scare the hell out of thinking men everywhere is the prosecution of pure speech. The rise of the Internet has given renewed life to oppressors of speech and expression. The criminal prosecution of a human being based exclusively on the content of his speech—especially in circumstances where there is absolutely no objective measure of his criminal intent—is anathema. It is so contrary to the values encoded by the Bill of Rights (Congress shall make NO law) that it is nearly impossible for many people to believe that it happens. But, it IS happening, and on a more-frequent basis than is presently apparent. The reasons it's happening are multitudinal. But, the chief reason is that courts have somehow or another grafted exceptions on to the legal rules related to the First Amendment jurisprudence. Being a strict constructionist myself, I have no idea what cogent mortal could possibly read "Congress shall make no law" as allowing room for the control and punishment of speech. It is quite beyond me to comprehend it . . . and I comprehend a fair amount of things.

The advent of a "presumptive strike" in warfare was preceded by the advent of a "presumptive strike" in criminology. The entire approach to modern police power is prepossessed of the idea that it's better to stop crime before it happens than to punish crime after it happens. This is a *flawed* postulate that threatens the very foundations of liberty and justice because it obviates the Divine Law of God. We ought not punish the germ of sin. We should punish its manifestation. God did not throw Adam and Eve out of the Garden because they walked near the Tree of Knowledge. He did not even punish them because Eve had a conversation with the serpent. He did not punish them for the contemplation or preparation of their crime. Indeed, it might even be said that God fully expected all these things to occur, by virtue of the fact that He placed the Tree of Knowledge within the Garden to begin with. God punished the act of *completed* sin. To have done anything less would have placed God in contradiction to His own Righteousness. However, had God punished Adam and Eve for merely making preparations to sin, He would have shown Himself to be quite an unjust Creator for having allowed the temptation to exist in the first instance. I do not charge God with sin; such would be openly heretical. But I believe it is obvious and implicit that God allows evil to run its natural course . . . all to His ultimate glory.

Having made this theological link, let me fall back to my premise. Our "system" is built on a house of cards because it has distorted the very purpose of temporal power and the "sword-wielding" state. The judicial system and all its appurtenances are used for social construction rather than the perpetration of social order, for which its noble progenitors created it. When a man is made to answer for a crime that never occurred, it is unjust. When a man is made to answer for a crime in which the state participated, it is unjust. When a man is made to answer for a crime for which he had merely given consideration, it is unjust. When a man is made to answer for a crime that does not *directly* impact the good of society, it is unjust. When a man is made to answer for a crime for which there is but one accuser (except for the biblical insults for rape provided in Deuteronomy, chapter 23, and is elsewhere expressed in Church law, since, by its very nature, there is only one witness to rape), it is unjust. Yet we in America practice these injustices with pitched fervor—believing somehow or another that by doing so we honor God. The rest of the public, fueled as it is by its lust for sin and vengeance, simply don't give a damn. Politicians, in responding to a sinful public's lust for vengeance justice, have increasingly thrown wider and wider the nets of criminal liability to ensure that more and more people are made to answer for what they "might be doing" or "might have done." This cannot last before it boils over and into a cauldron of revolution. Let history be our guide for this. We are quite literally witnessing the systematic erection of a rebellious class of oppressed Americans (numbering now in the millions and predicted to soon number in the tens of millions) who have been so mercilessly objectified that they cannot but consider themselves at war with their own neighbors. Is it possible even to imagine the chaos that would ensue if a match was ever struck to light the fires of this nascent combustion?

We have been warned to avoid these roads. As a culture, we have nevertheless chosen to march down them. I realize you may think me a little mad in my portrayal of the crisis. And, if I sound it, I will admit to you that I am a bit disappointed in what I view as the absurdity behind the reasons I sit in a cinder-block cell in the armpit of Virginia. I have been violated. I continue to be violated. This naturally angers me . . . though I am well in control of that anger, by the Grace of God. But the circumstances cannot fail to incense me because they do not fail to incense God . . . who has created me in His image and imparted to me something of His spirit.

I can see hope, however. If we could only awaken the body of Christ from its slumber. If we could somehow seize the churches in America back from the grip of the Pharisees on one side (radical right-wingers) and the Corinthians on the other (those who would have God's church sanction filth). Maybe then the true Christians, the elect of God, could give voice to the full spectrum of moral challenges. As regards crime and punishment, this voice would sound the eternal themes of hope, redemption, reconciliation, restoration, and resurrection. Enough already of the doom and gloom of judgment! Let us have judgment tempered with mercy. For without it, there is no such thing as justice.

Once again, I thank you for the work that you do. I pray God's strength for you in your lonely advocacy. I wish there was more that I could do to assist you in your efforts. I would just encourage you to proclaim the Gospel of Jesus Christ boldly both in season and out. Remember always the great resistance so often met by the doctors and saints of the Church throughout the ages (to include the prophets of old). Remember as well the suffering of our Lord and Savior: "They watched him closely and sent agents pretending to be righteous who were to trap him in speech, in order to hand him over to the authority and power of the governor" (Luke 20:20). Nothing has ever so riled the world than the sound of the truth. Even good men condemn it!

Forgive the length of this letter. Be blessed.

Dear Chuck,

Hello. Hope this finds you doing well. Thank you for your letter and articles, especially "Everyone Has a Pet Peeve" (I've wondered the same things about my phone bills!). I found your article quite hilarious. Wit is a tough technique for a writer, and most people are pretenders, but your article was genuinely funny and well thought out.

I had a $27/month home phone plan and a $70/month unlimited cell phone plan. As long as my bill didn't exceed that, I figured that's what I agreed to, and stroked them a check. Insurance is what used to rattle my cage. Auto, homeowners, health, business liability, workman's comp, life, etc. . . . Workman's comp was 11.4 percent of my gross payroll—ouch! That used to really ruffle my feathers. But the Lord always provided. I always had more than enough. When I was in college, several professors encouraged me to become a writer. Alas, I'm just an ol' construction Bubba at heart. The advice they gave was to write about what you know, or write about what you're passionate about. Personally, I believe people should follow their heart and try to keep an eye out for the doors God is opening for them.

You are so right about the parole board, and the injustices brought about by our current political structure. For all the old-law (pre-1995) inmates, there is a formula the judges and Commonwealth Attorneys used to use. A person would, contingent upon their good behavior, become eligible for parole in one-sixth of their time. So if the court wanted someone to do a minimum of five years, they would say 5 x 6 = 30, and give a thirty-year sentence. It was assumed that, again, contingent upon good behavior, one would make first, second, or third parole. That was a valid assumption. When Doug Wilder was governor, the parole grant rate was almost 40 percent. But things changed. It became a vote-getter for politicians to bill themselves as tough on crime, and being "soft" on crime became political (and, thus, career) suicide. All the hype in doing this created an irrational public fear that did not previously exist.

Take my friend Jack, for example. No court ever intended he do as much time as he has done. John Q. Public has been duped into fearing him. But if Jack moved in next door to John, and John got to know Greg and then found out about his criminal past, ol' John would say Jack is obviously a good person. Not like the rest of'em, an exception, if you will. Little does Mr. Public realize that Jack is not the exception; Ted Bundy is the exception! But Mr. Public has been virtually brainwashed into believing "they're all alike."

Personally, I believe the parole board should be abolished and old-law inmates should be taken before a judge for parole consideration. At least they would get a fair hearing. Second best—put five doctors of sociology on the parole board. Sociologists are better than anyone else at predicting human behavior. Of course, a little known fact is that Virginia has turned prisons into a money-making enterprise. The Department of Corrections is one of the top moneymakers for the state, according to one of my uncles who looked it up on the computer in 2005, after the parole board imprisoned me in spite of what the judge had said. Who knows for sure, and who knows if anyone actually has conceptual oversight of the whole ball of wax. I would guess not. I would say the parole board is letting their own personal biases dictate their professional opinions; most politicians will take votes over fairness and justice, and the governors just kinda want to keep it all under the rug because it has political-disaster potential. I have often said in jest that we need Grant to march on Richmond again. And I have often wondered what Thomas Jefferson, Patrick Henry, John Hancock, and the like would say and do if they were alive today.

I think therein lies a wisdom lost that is so sorely needed today. Now wouldn't that be interesting if our founding fathers were in charge again. I'll bet the Ten Commandments and prayer would be back in our public schools, and evolution out. Abortion clinics would be no more, along with pornography shops and head shops, and all the Internet filth. The most risqué thing on TV would be the six o'clock news. Our Supreme Court might be in prison for high treason. We'd better get them back in stages, though. I think there's more to fix than can be fixed in one lifetime. Maybe not . . . I think the roots of Sodom-and-Gomorrah America can be traced back to the removal of the Ten Commandments from our schools. As you said, people will become what they think. When people are taught they came from animals . . .

Well, I could go on and on, but you never said you wanted to read a book. Thank you again, take care, and God bless.

Dear Chuck,

I am a close friend of an inmate, and he has stated that I ought to write to you. He believes that my case may be of interest to you for your writings. I hope you don't mind, which I am sure you don't, but he gave me your letters to read so I can get a feeling for who you are.

To write is not one of my best features. I enjoy writing, but my spelling and grammar is not the greatest. Through school I suffered from dyslexia, and this really hurt me in the areas of English and math. When I saw your letter in the *Catholic Virginian*, I was going to write, thanking you for speaking about the unspeakable—prisons and prisoners. I was also going to mention some ideas to help reformation and some of the problems with the prison/justice system. When I found out my friend was writing to you, I refrained, as our ideas would probably be the same or close to the same, since we spend so much time speaking of the situation. Besides, his writing is much more eloquent than mine.

I have enclosed a form letter I wrote, as it is the whole of my case with many of its twists and turns. In it I state that I have applied for a conditional pardon. This has since been denied. My mother, who lives in Florida, had extensive contact with the investigator for pardons at probation/parole. While speaking with my mother, the investigator stated she could not believe I was charged with these charges or that I got so much time, and that she was "truly very, very sorry for all my mother and I were going through," but it was unlikely that I would get my conditional pardon as "they don't like to give pardons to sex offenders no matter how meritorious our claims were." But she would try all she could. I state this just to show you how bad our justice system really is.

Just to give you an idea who I am, I will give you some of my life history. I hope I don't bore you with it.

I am thirty-six years old, born in Lewiston, Maine, and raised just outside of Lewiston and a small town called Hebron, until I left for the service at nineteen. I entered the army in '90 as a radio equipment repairer. After AIT I was sent to Schweinfurt, Germany, for two years with the third I.D. There I met my first wife, a German citizen. We were married in '93 just before I transferred to Fort Bragg, NC. There I was with the 4th Psychological Operations Group as a loudspeaker repair man. Two years after being in the U.S., the day she got her permanent green card, my wife left me. I was with the 4th POG for four years (I reenlisted). While there I spent six to nine months out of a year deployed. I was on one of the first planes into Haiti and was one of the first of my unit into Bosnia, as well as many other operations, both training and otherwise. I was honorably discharged in '97.

Prior to my release, I met my second wife. She was with military intelligence. We were married just after my release from the military, and just over a year later we had a beautiful daughter together. She then decided to get out of the military herself and we moved to Virginia, just outside of Lexington. This was where her parents lived, and also the biggest mistake of my life.

Her parents were controlling, and she would not go against their wishes. I would fight them and this created more problems. I think they would go against me just for spite. I come from a middle- to upper-class family. I wanted to make something of ourselves, not rich, but at least financially sound. They wanted us to be dirt-poor farmers like themselves. Oh, they had some nice assets and put on a big show—Cadillacs, and country club memberships—but they were so far in debt that their assets probably would never pull them out. My father-in-law would borrow money from me to buy birthday and anniversary gifts for his wife. They even convinced her (my wife) that I was the man and thus she should not have to work, so she didn't.

When I met her, she had two kids from a previous marriage of which she had lost custody. I had one child born out of wedlock and for whom I was paying child support. We had one child together. One year later, after moving to Lexington, she regained custody of her two other children after her first husband divorced, making us the more stable household. Here we were, living in Lexington, a family of five, paying child support of $200 a month (she declined child support for her children). Me, the only breadwinner in an area where my trade—electronics—was of no use. She wanted still to live the big life: eat out, new cars—at least for her, anyway. I had to drive a ten-year-old junker. If I said no, her parents would convince her to go ahead. She had her hobbies: horses, movies, etc. . . . all costing lots of money. I had mine: kayaking (costing little money, yet it was always a fight to go kayaking).

As you can imagine, I became miserably depressed and a workaholic. Of course, I knew of the Lord but did not believe in the Lord. God to me was a myth. My mom and dad were believers but had stopped attending church when I was twelve, and were more interested in "the world." They divorced when I was sixteen and my mom started dating a Catholic (now my stepfather), but he was not practicing except going to Mass at Easter (my first of a couple Catholic experiences). Well, as years went on with my wife, I got more and more depressed. Some people resort to drinking or drugs. For me, in the summer I worked outside around the house until late. Late enough that many times I would come in, take a shower, and go to sleep. The winter was different. Cold and dark early so I couldn't stay outside. All my wife wanted to do was watch TV, and God forbid if the show was interrupted with talk. So I resorted to the cave. You know the cave? A place you go to get away from it all. Mine was a spare room. (Yeah, imagine that, a spare room with three children and two adults living on $500 a week.) This had a sofa, a desk with a computer, and a second television for the kids. In the winter it became mine.

At first I would go in there and play video games on the computer. Then it became surfing the Internet, then Internet porn. I am not convinced that the Internet is Satan's tool. First he entices you in with the useful information, but look how porn finds you on the Internet. You don't even have to be looking for porn, then bam, there it is.

My wife found out about the porn and put a block on the computer (password). By then I was a winter addict with my electronics background, so I overcame the block. She blocked it again and again until I could not find a way around the lock. But I wanted the nude pictures; somehow in my mind, I thought that they made me a little happier. But, I couldn't get them.

In walks my wife's best friend from Northern Virginia. She was having marital problems and started to visit once or twice a month. Every time she would stay in my sixteen-year-old stepdaughter's room, and the stepdaughter would stay at her grandmother's a mile way. On one of her visits, my wife, her best friend, and I went kayaking together. At the end of our kayaking trip she "swam." A term used when you cannot roll your kayak back up so you have to get out and swim for shore. When we got to my truck, while I was loading the kayaks, she changed right next to the truck. White panties and bra—wet, so of course, one could see through them.

This piqued my nudity interest and brought back the memory of a website where hidden cameras were put into rooms of unsuspecting women. I went out and purchased a security camera (wireless) and placed it in my stepdaughter's room in hopes of capturing my wife's friend nude on her visits.

A couple of months later, late at night, my stepdaughter's father called. I answered the phone and called to her that she had a phone call. I guess thinking I was in bed, she came running down the stairs topless and in thong underwear. It was then that I saw her not as a child but as a woman, with all her womanly features. I remembered the security camera already in her room. On several occasions I turned the camera on and let it run, capturing whatever it captured in hopes of seeing her nude again. I didn't want to see her doing anything sexually explicit. Just a nude young body of a woman, the beauty God created that we men, unfortunately, look to for our own pleasure sometimes.

The video was about four hours long. Of that four hours there was fifteen to twenty minutes of partial nudity. The rest was either no one in the room or her doing normal stuff while clothed. The tape found through illegal search (warrantless, without my consent, only my wife's, which is now found unconstitutional by the U.S. Supreme Court) was partially destroyed, and pulled from the case. It was sent to the crime lab in Richmond and repaired, and an edited tape made removing all cases where the victim is not nude/partially nude. That is the tape used in court, which takes things a little more out of context.

The rest is explained in my attached form letter. Throughout my marriage, especially after regaining custody of my wife's kids, her parents would state that they would never let someone take their grandchildren again and would do whatever they had to do to make sure that didn't happen. I now see what they meant.

You may ask, "If you were so depressed, why didn't you leave her?" All I could say is pride and love of my daughter. I could never get ahead enough monetarily to leave her, and I was too proud to ask my family, who would have helped me. Furthermore, when we would fight and I would get up the nerve to leave her, she would throw my daughter at me. "Oh, you are just going to leave and do that to your daughter." I couldn't bring myself to do that to her. Her mom would spend very little time with her except to watch a movie. Now I wish I had, as my daughter is now without me, hasn't heard from me or seen me in over two and a half years, and her mom won't even let me send a letter. Furthermore, the money spent by my family for a bogus lawyer far exceeds what I ever would have needed to reestablish myself.

Even with all of this, I give praise to God. Through this I have come to know and love Him. Through research and reading I have come to know the true church instituted by our Lord Jesus. My father has started to get involved with church again. My mother and stepfather still are not attending, but look forward to the day I am released and can help them find a Catholic church they will enjoy and can attend with me. I have given my father and the rest of my family better knowledge about the Catholic faith so that they do not look badly at Catholics anymore. I was baptized on October 31, 2006, and confirmed January 16, 2007. Believe it or not, my depression while married was so bad that I am much happier now even while in prison. I have found new friends both inside and out of the prison, some of whom, on the outside, I am helping with their spiritual walk. My future is unknown, and is probably going to be tough, but it is bright.

Well, now that I have totally bored you, on to something else. Mr. Brown, keep up your work both in the prison and in your writings. There will always be people who are against humanizing a criminal. Media conditions them so. Even Christian literature, and even more so, advertising. Recently, I had to write *Partners in Evangelism*, the providers of "the word among us," because their advertisement with a picture of a prisoner with an angry or fierce face so disturbed me. They had not even realized what "image" they may be endorsing. In all our movies and television shows, all you see are the fights and scheming. What do you expect a populace to think? It is people like you and Mark Early, former state senator and former attorney general of Virginia, who can make a difference.

Oh, in addition to all I told you before, I wish to add one more thing, as it shows why we need alternative sentences. In my pre-sentence report done by a parole officer, it is stated that there was no harm done to the victim, neither physical, mental, or emotional, that I am not a threat to society as it was an isolated incident taking place in my own room, and his sole recommendation for sentence was that I maintain seeing the counselor I was seeing for addiction to pornography. I was sentenced to five years in prison.

We need people like you! God bless you and all you do.

Dear Chuck,

No, you have not lost touch with me. I'm just having a tough time in finding a job that pays enough for me to go on my own. The folks whom I'm living with at this time would like me to go on my own by August, but until I find a good-paying job, I can't afford to go on my own. And I have a car that is dying on me. Not very good times right now. Sorry if my mind has been elsewhere.

I'm not giving up, Chuck, but my life is not going exactly the way I thought it would be. My pet peeve is this: I don't like other people who judge other people without knowing them. The folks I am living with are great people who love the Lord, but they want their house back to themselves! I can really understand that.

Thanks so much for your letters and friendship, my brother in Christ Jesus. Pray for me as I will pray for you, Chuck. I will write back again when I have some good news. God bless you now and always.

Dear Chuck,

I got your letter and enclosure the other day. Thanks for writing and responding. Allow me to respond to your "global" letter first. I am glad that you have more men to write to from other institutions. That means that there are Catholic groups out there and there is prison ministry happening.

As for your recent byline in the *Catholic Virginian*, thanks for the encouragement you gave and the support that you show us. We are blessed to have a friend and advocate like you.

Okay, now to your letter to me. Yes, it is unfortunate that we can't sit and talk at length, and rules against you visiting on a Saturday or Sunday don't make much sense, but are there to "protect" you from us and the "extortion" we may try to do to you. I know from your background that you are aware of this. Maybe one day that can change. Even Kairos volunteers can't visit unless it is part of a Kairos event.

I think my letter was too long and too controversial for the *Catholic Virginian* to print. That is okay; I figured not all of mine would get published. It is an honor to get one in at all. I do have a copy of my rough draft that I used to compare the letter. I will write it out for you and include it in this letter. It will not be 100 percent word for word what was sent, but the main points and arguments will be the same.

What I wrote is the tip of the iceberg. As a sex offender, I am a "leper" of society. No one wants me out and living near them for fear I will sexually offend with a child. They have no idea of my treatment or what a sexual addiction is, and that I am not a true pedophile who needs to have sex with children. My crime was a result of opportunity that my addiction thought was okay. My thought processes are undergoing changes and I am working on myself so I don't offend again, and to control my sexual behaviors to appropriate relationships. So my treatment is working because I am open to it and want to get better. Many don't, but there are ways to treat us all. It is a very complex issue.

Actually, my political article has nothing to do with prisoners, prisons, etc. It will be about the issue of certain bishops who say they would refuse to give the Eucharist to politicians who support abortion rights, contraceptives, stem-cell research, etc. . . . It will ask these same bishops if they will refuse the Eucharist to Catholic politicians who vote to cut funding to food stamp programs; who refuse to support a universal health-care package so all Americans are covered; who vote to reduce taxes on the wealthiest among us while the poor are taxed beyond their means; who vote not to increase the minimum wage or institute a living wage; who continue to support legislation that keeps people in poverty; who won't increase support to the mentally ill; and so on. These bishops have no business refusing the Eucharist to a John Kerry or a Ted Kennedy, and not to other politicians (i.e., Republicans) who support oppressing people in other ways and do not follow Catholic social teaching. Or a governor who allows inmates to be put to death when the Church doesn't support that. Or an attorney general who oppresses Virginians with legislation and prosecution that doesn't take into account Catholic principles. It is not a one-way street, and I am sick and tired of the Church preaching against abortion, stem-cell research, and euthanasia issues that affect only small percentages of people and seemingly ignoring publicly the needs of those whose numbers are larger and situations more dire. If the bishops want to stand on principle, stand on *all* principles and stop being a "cafeteria Catholic" who speaks out about only certain issues.

I need the right timing and the right forum for it. I would love to send it to *The Washington Post* or *USA Today* to see if they would pick it up. I could try something for the *Catholic Virginian*, but the impact would be less. I have to see what it looks like.

The inmate's letter to the **Catholic Virginian:**

As I read Mr. H's critique ("Criminals Need Change of Heart") of Chuck Brown's column ("Whatever Happened to Rehabilitation and Restoration"), I found a major misunderstanding of

prisons and prisoners. Please allow me to address Mr. H's "flawed premises" from an inmate's perspective.

Incarceration does not equal crime prevention. Incarceration only isolates those who have been caught; it is not a deterrent to crime. I agree that we who commit egregious crimes need to be incarcerated. The criminal justice system is man's idea of vengeance, yet vengeance is supposed to be the Lord's purview; the two are not equal. Restorative justice programs focusing on community healing and personal accountability does decrease crime rates, as research shows.

Treatment programs and rehabilitation do work if done correctly, but methods vary, as do a person's response to a particular treatment modality. They are not a "one size fits all" approach that we often see. Statistics clearly support the success of rehabilitation programs, but they are expensive and require a long-term commitment to show results. These are not your "one month and you're out" type of rehab programs so popular with celebrities. The poor performance of current rehab programs lies with the individual programs and use of approaches that are not supported by research.

As an example, the sex offender recidivism rate is 10 to 17 percent nationally. With treatment, this rate decreases to 5 to 7 percent. Does treatment work? Yes! Education of any inmate has been shown to decrease recidivism rate of less than 1 percent for any crime.

The problem is that the Virginian Department of Corrections is mostly about punishment. Prisons and prisoners are promoted as "economic opportunities" for depressed rural areas whose industry has dried up or relocated. The "new" industry is warehousing human beings. The programs that Mr. H wrote about simply do not last in our prison system.

The idea that behavior is what lands someone in prison is only a partial truth. Denying one his liberty is not a deterrent to criminal activity. It is a multi-factorial problem with societal, individual, and cultural components. It is not a heart issue; it is a brain issue. Criminal activity comes from faulty thought processes and poor decision making—not to mention that approximately 30 percent of inmates are mentally ill. I live with and listen to these faulty thought processes and observe the poor decision-making skills daily. Fix these, provide hope, opportunity, employment, and housing, and crime will decrease. If incarceration is a deterrent, why does the nation's incarceration rate continually increase, and why do we have the highest incarceration rate in the world?

What is needed is better and more coordinated efforts between criminal psychologists/psychiatrists, the Department of Corrections, and the courts to perform and follow research recommendations that are proven to work. These programs need to be funded adequately, staffed, and benchmarked. Helping inmates upon transition back into society with employment, support, and affordable housing is also needed.

We did not give up on finding cures or vaccinations for deadly diseases; we should not give up on humans. As Christians, we have a responsibility to help those in prison, not to condemn, but to live Jesus's commandment to love one another, including our enemies, and yes, even prisoners.

Unfortunately, Mr. H could only critique Mr.

> **Brown's article without offering any solutions other than admitting and agreeing to continued incarcerations at over $30,000 per year per inmate. Is this really the best, most cost-effective solution? I invite Mr. H and others to visit their local jail or prison as a Catholic volunteer; they may be surprised at what they find.**

Dear Chuck,

I want to begin with an apology for not responding to your letters and for not showing up at the meetings. I have had a tough time these past couple of months. You are already aware of my mother's health problems, and just last month she was rushed to the emergency room due to severe abdominal pains. She had to have an emergency gall bladder (removal) surgery. But right now she is doing fine. All that plus my depression and anxiety problems lead me in a bad direction, gambling and overeating mostly; I am a very compulsive man when I am down.

I am tired, Chuck, of everything. The more I try to stay positive, the worse things seem to get. I am very lonely, and I can't seem to find a woman around my age to write to as a friend and/or pen pal. I have begun to think a lot about an ex-girlfriend, and I would like to get in touch with her again, but no one I know seems willing to go on the Internet and find her address for me. I have no doubt that she'd be happy to hear from me and be willing to write to me.

In five months, I will be twenty-nine years old and it will be my tenth year in prison. Time is passing me by at a frighteningly high speed. Everyone is building a life for themselves, and I feel I am frozen in place and being left behind while the world moves on.

I have not heard from my little brother or my sister now for ten years, and as I get older I miss them more than ever. I won't lie to you, Chuck—I feel lost, and I don't feel like God even knows I exist any longer, or else he is testing and preparing me for a nastier surprise than I can imagine.

I did not write because I hate to be a burden and dump my problems on others, but at the same time, I wanted to let you know I am okay. I promise to write more often and have my name placed back on the list by the chaplain. I will close for now. Take care of yourself and God bless.

Dear Chuck,

I received your July 4 letter thanking me for the *Virginian-Pilot* article. It was nice to have found such a positive call for reform in a newspaper the size of the *V-P*. You're not alone in the injustice you see.

Re: transfer. No idea why! But I'm looking forward to the adventure. The transfer probably won't materialize for six to eight months, but one never really knows. Shucks, I'm not even supposed to know I'm pending a transfer, let alone where.

As for any mail you might send that arrives after my departure, it will be forwarded to me. The Department of Corrections policy is to forward all mail for two months.

As for getting settled in, I started doing that the first week of my arrival. As for the recent update on my room location, it was a reminder of my March 27 notice of my room change.

By now you have received the letter I asked you to forward to the *Catholic Virginian*—needlessly to say "Hi!" After I finished up the letter, I spent the remainder of the day and evening laying out a crossword puzzle for my class. Something that I should have been able to do at work—especially since it was supposed to have been created for the course years ago.

My boss was asked how much chemical would be added to thirty gallons of water at a 1:4 ratio. He told the student six cups. After I told the student that six cups was wrong, he went running to my boss's office. Needless to say, I had to explain to him very slowly the way I came to seven and a half gallons. Even going step by step, he seemed clueless. Think I know why he doesn't measure chemicals. Anyway, my boss seems to be staying out of my way and allowing me to do his job. In fact, he sent a building manager to me to schedule and plan the work the office needs done next week.

I thought my boss understood that I was pending transfer, but that doesn't seem the case. He is trying to hire another guy to assist me. With one more guy, I'll be able to get all the forms and worksheets done before I transfer—hopefully.

Dear Chuck,

Howdy there. Got your letter; good to hear from you. Hope this finds you and yours doing well. All goes well enough here. I think your book idea, using the words of inmates, is a good idea. I believe people will still want to hear what you have to say, your principles, your points, your take on it. Using inmates' statements, as well as your own experiences with the incarcerated and recently released, to illustrate how you came to your stated principles is good as well.

As for needing to learn a skilled trade while incarcerated to enable one to be successful upon release, I must disagree with you on that one. One of my favorite quotes is from Henry Ford: "Success is 90 percent attitude." Millions of people make a go of it all their life without a skilled trade. When I got out in 2001, the first electrical company I went to hired me at $12 an hour. I could have made more driving a delivery truck or working in some factory, but my original goal upon release was to one day have my own electrical company. God opened different doors. I was flexible, and ended up with a very successful home improvement company. I worked for eight months at $12 an hour, and brought home $375 a week. During that time I qualified for a 90K mortgage and bought a three-bedroom house in need of much repair.

Chuck, I wasn't successful because I had work skills. I was successful because of my mind-set. That mind-set was "I will succeed!" No matter what the cost, no matter what I have to do. Everyone, and Chuck, I mean every single person, family included, told me how difficult it was going to be for me to readjust to living in society. I never believed that, never accepted that, and I had no problem. I would have, though, if I had believed that I was going to. It's a self-fulfilling prophecy.

Chuck, the prison experience subtly incorporates into people a very self-detrimental mind-set. One reason is because there is positive reinforcement in here for breaking rules, lying, manipulating, etc. . . . Another one is people are leaving out of here with a deep-seated sense of shame for the crime they committed. Let me pose a question to you: If a person commits a shameful, dishonorable act, how do they regain their honor and dignity? Paying your debt to society, as the judge has assessed your debt to be—would that do it? If not, how about now (that one is living in society), living a law-abiding life? What if we throw in some service work? Tell me, would you rather have a next-door neighbor who believes he lives with honor, integrity, and dignity, or one who believes he lives in shame? Which one do you think would more easily begin traveling down a wrong path?

For the vast majority of inmates reentering society, the concepts of honor, integrity, and dignity are as far from them as speaking Chinese is. And for the sex offender, our laws have created an umbrella of shame they cannot get out from under. Again, though, accept it and it is yours! Virginia CURE (Citizens United for Rehabilitation of Errants) introduced a tiered proposal for dealing with this issue. It was an excellent idea and would have made a big improvement to the current system, but was rejected. Personally, I think after a person has done his time, he has paid his debt. Once you've paid for something, it's yours. I think the only ones that should be able to find out about a person's criminal record is a judge and prosecuting attorney, or for a federal security reason. I believe in the "three strikes and you're out" law. Actually, I think it should be two strikes for committing the same violent act! But as it stands now, our society, our politicians, our laws, are stacking the deck against us, making it very difficult for first-time offenders to even get past their past.

You said you were concerned about how we would be accepted by the outside world. Here is a great irony. By society as a whole, not really so well. But by an individual John Doe, it all depends on the person I am—my personality, the context of my character, etc. Me personally, I had no problems whatsoever, but I know others that did. Because I was in a treatment program for two years with other ex-offenders, and then an aftercare program facilitated by the parole officers, I have closely known thirty or forty people recently released, their hopes, struggles, etc. . . . This would be one of my conclusions: If society has a vested interest in these people going straight, becoming productive members of society, not having any more victims or committing any more crimes, then people must understand that prison has not prepared them for this. Society's structures and mind-sets are designed to make their past inhibit their future success. The deck is stacked against them. Herein lies the brilliance of CURE's slogan: "Today's prisoners are tomorrow's neighbors."

One of the major issues that needs to be addressed for your book, I believe, is a restructuring of the prison system and of sentencing guidelines. I would make a progressive system, to reward positive change and identify and penalize the old negative behavior. Everyone would get work release before they got out of prison. But here, Chuck, is the heart of the issue: Everyone incarcerated must learn not to break the law or break the rules. I did not learn that my fist time in. No matter how mild or compelling the circumstances, or my not intending any harm, nor doing anything that endangered others, etc., I used cocaine. That is against the law, and that alone should have been enough to automatically make the very idea and notion out of the question! It should have brought an automatic and immediate "NO" to my mind, but it didn't. And I was able to rationalize and convince myself that it was okay. Wrong is wrong, Chuck—period! And breaking the law is always wrong. No matter how much "right" you can heap on the other side of the scale, you can never make it right to break the law. It should never be a thought I would even have, much less entertain. That is what I have learned from this incarceration, and that is what I was lacking.

You see, I would *never* commit another violent crime, or steal, or anything like that. But I *would* drive 65 in a 55-mph zone, or get high with my fiancée in the privacy of my own home. A "minor" infraction is just as much breaking the law as a "major" infraction, especially for those on parole or probation. And the rules of supervised release actually become laws, because it is a felony if convicted of violating these rules. It has been extremely costly for me to learn this.

The losses I have incurred for this are unbelievable: A remodeled, very nicely furnished three-bedroom house, my business (vans, tools, etc.), my money, my fiancée, my puppy, my freedom, social status, retirement plan, self-respect—the list goes on and on. And on top of it all, the parole board overrides the court's ruling and gives me eighteen years in prison. Ergo, my current dilemma.

Thank you for contacting the director of Virginia CURE on my behalf, and please extend my appreciation to her for her time and efforts. With election time so near, I must wonder if any politician would be willing to act upon such a matter right now. The prospect certainly is exciting, though, and I wholeheartedly thank all who are trying to help me with this. As I said earlier, wrong is wrong! But I'm praying for a miracle. I believe in those things, ya know!

Anyway, back to your vocational training issue. I do agree that it would benefit one to know a skilled trade upon release. I would not say it's vital for post-release success, though. But keep this in mind: A person is only going to learn so much in one of these classes. They'll probably learn enough to be a grade-A helper. But if they take one of these schools' years before their release, then don't use their newly acquired skills until released, they will have forgotten much of what they learned. On the job, I could teach a man what he learns in most of these vocational schools in about a month. These men need to learn how to sell themselves to potential employers. They need to understand what an employer is looking for. Because their experience and knowledge would be minimal, that is not their strong selling point to an employer. Unfortunately, the Department of Corrections doesn't teach these men things like this.

Well, my friend, I'd love to keep chatting on here, but it's off to work with me. Thank you for your letter and all your help. May the Lord keep you and bless you always.

Mr. Brown,

I hope you are well. I am keeping busy with this and that. Besides work I am carving a kayak and kayaker from soap. The kayak is done but the kayaker needs some more work. Soap is too fragile to carve on when it comes to small body parts like arms. I have one arm that keeps detaching and when it does I have to wet it and stick it back together. This costs me twelve to twenty-four hours for drying time. It is very relaxing as I get lost in my work, listening to some good music.

You are welcome to that copy of *Prison Legal News*. It is wonderful how God works. I randomly selected an issue. I say randomly because I did not look at issue dates. I chose by content and figured you could use some of the population statistics. Two days later the publisher either screwed up or is trying to gain extra subscriptions by sending extra copies. Anyhow I was sent a duplicate of the issue I sent you.

My daughter, who is nine years old, is starting to call my parents on her own accord. Before my parents would have to call her and the conversations were pretty much one-sided; them asking questions and her giving short answers. Now she is talking like crazy and about all kinds of things. This gives me much hope for the future. Through the form letter I sent, you know my case. You also know my trial was more about getting me and consequently my family away from my daughter. What wasn't in there was that during sentencing, they put my wife on the stand and asked her about the effects of my crime on the victim: my stepdaughter. The answer in the transcript shows ten lines about the effect on the victim, and thirty lines about the effect on my six-year-old daughter, who quite frankly was too young to realize what was all that wrong with what I had done. As I said, this is all about my daughter and custody.

Prior to this summer, the sole contact my family had with my daughter was when they telephoned her. My ex was always there. The victim is home for the summer, and when my daughter called, my ex was not home. This means the victim, my stepdaughter, is more than likely helping my daughter contact my family. I don't know if it was in the letter, but the day after everything came to light, my stepdaughter saw me crying, came up to me, hugged me, and gave me a kiss on the cheek, saying "Everything will be all right."

This is all more hope for the future as far as the relationship with my daughter is concerned. I haven't heard from her or been able to contact her since mid-2004. At first my dad set it up that I could write him a letter for my daughter and he would then send it to my ex, who would decide to give it to her or not. I wrote a few times but then received a threatening letter from the Commonwealth Attorney about my contact with her. Seems that in this same sentencing order—that had an error of an extra three months—there is also an error regarding "no contact with the victims or their family."

On sentencing transcripts the judge does not make a non-contact order. Once we appealed or noted our intent, the Commonwealth Attorney asked that there be no contact with the victims or their family until the time of the case before the circuit court, at which the judge says she will "note his request." Amazingly, like the extra three months, it ended up in the sentencing order. Unfortunately a habeas corpus only deals with prison time, so I could not bring up this error to be fixed. I have to wait for my release, then find a lawyer who is willing to work to correct this error in court. Just another of the many injustices done to me by the County.

Dear Chuck,

Yes, I believe we crossed letters in the mail, but that's okay.

Let me pick up a discussion on drugs. You may not agree with my position on drugs, but I believe (and have long argued) that the recreational use of "low-impact" drugs ought to be legalized. I am not now, nor have I ever been, a drug user. Yet I have studied the economics of the present policies quite a bit, and am fully convinced that the demand is so high that our nation would benefit by bringing at least a portion of the drug industry into the white (normalized) marketplace. We are waging an impossible "war" on marijuana that will never be won. It is simply too big.

I do not believe, however, that we ought to legalize high-end drugs such as crack-cocaine, LSD, or methamphetamines—these drugs produce such deleterious effects on the minds, bodies, and souls of their users that we ought to focus heavily on the containment of *supply*. Nevertheless, I still believe that the vast majority of the laws criminalizing usage ought to be rolled back. Punishment has been a disastrous failure in the treatment of users and addicts. The major-and middle-level pushers often go unscathed for many years before the long arm of justice has its way with them. It's the smaller guys who get caught up in the criminal justice machinery, and that's a basic unfairness because of its disproportionate impact on the poor and minorities.

People seem to have the wrong impression about the relationship between a legalized substance and the government's official policies regarding the same substance. It is simply not reasonable to believe that what the government makes legal it thereby endorses. Alcohol is legal, yet the government certainly doesn't promote its use. Tobacco is legal, yet the government has damn near destroyed it (and unwittingly transferred the majority of its economic benefits to growing markets overseas). And there are copious arguments in favor of legalizing certain categories of drug use because of the better ability government would have to control it—not to mention the degree to which competitive market players would seek to protect their turf from illegal growers, manufacturers, and distributors. Try growing some tobacco in the backyard and see how fast someone from Philip Morris gets to your front door. The marketplace protects its own.

Finally, just imagine the massive reservoir of untapped revenue in the form of a traditional "sin" tax. If certain drugs were legalized, if possession and usage of many other drugs carried lighter penalties, the prison population could be cut down in size by a considerable margin. Moreover, the shooting and killing associated with drug use would be minimized because the entire drug-pushing apparatus would be cut off at the knees. There's no use in fighting over a street corner that's owned by Philip Morris and R. J. Reynolds Tobacco Co. Legalizing drugs shuts down the turf wars. When's the last time you heard anybody being killed in a shootout over liquor sales? Yet, you heard it all the time during Prohibition (well, we read about it in the textbooks, anyway). When substantial economic markets are black (illegal), they create havoc and the opportunity for thugs to extract a financial gain in transaction costs. When substantial economic markets are white (legal), everyone gets his fair share of the available wealth—and the consumer gets a dependable product sold according to fair weights and measures.

There are, of course, moral questions to consider. But, I believe it's preferable for people to be allowed to exercise morality without interfering with the other guy's privilege to exercise profligacy. Government has a responsibility to protect people from the harmful acts of others. I do not agree with the modern use of government to protect people from themselves. That is tyranny. As an Augustinian through and through, there is a right use of everything God has made. Nothing is, by its nature, bad or evil. The marijuana plant was made by God and is disposed to burn just like any other plant made by God. The idea that it ought to be banished from God's earth seems to me a greater sin than the use of it. What right have we to chastise a thing God has made? Is it not worth considering that He may have made it for a right and proper use?

As for sex offenders, I have much to say, of course. I don't see how it's possible to have productive dialogue about sex offenders until people are first willing to come to some agreeable definitions about the diversity of sex offenses. It is wholly insufficient to suppose that all sex offenders fit into the image that's been constructed by politicians and the sensationalized news reports about the most horrendous of sexual offenses. It's akin to using Jeffrey Dahmer as the standard measure of all murderers; Hitler as the standard measure of all Germans; or bin Laden as the standard measure of all Muslims. Sooner or later, someone has got to take the initiative to say, "Hey, you know what—the guy who's doing two or three years for having sex with a willing minor is just not the same as the guy who's doing forty years for luring an eight-year-old boy into his van and driving off into the woods to force him to perform sexual acts." Lumping these two guys together is simply wrong. Everybody ought to see that.

Likewise, the guy who's doing five to fifteen for the simple possession of child pornography (especially since the damn stuff is ubiquitous now) is not exactly your prototypical pervert who hangs out by the schoolyard. The vast majority of child pornography is images of developed, post-pubescent girls and boys—they often cannot be distinguished from nineteen- and twenty-year-olds. And the people making the decisions as to what is and what isn't child pornography have gradually stretched the criteria for the types of images so defined. (You may recall that when attorney general John Ashcroft first took office, he ordered all the nude statuary at the Justice Department covered—these people are just prudes!)

Another serious problem for sex offenders is that there are no national standards governing the distinction between those who are "violent" and those who aren't. In Virginia, for instance, it is a violent offense merely to propose a sexual act to a person fourteen years or younger. I can sympathize with the belief most have that proposing a sexual act to someone that young is inappropriate. But at the same time, I do not see what is so particularly volatile about it that the person proposing should be labeled violent. Where's the violence? People scold me for it when I remind them that it was not too many years ago that a twenty-seven-year-old Elvis began to "court" a thirteen-year-old Priscilla—do we really believe Elvis was a saint? Assuming that he was not, do we regard his dalliance as violent? Why does Elvis get a pass? "That was then; this is now?" How comes this? Who made these rules? And Elvis is just one example of a great many. Something happened in this culture somewhere along the way—cultural mores made a sharp shift, and it would be interesting for someone to do the research into what, where, when, and why. What passed as acceptable fifty years ago has all of the sudden become the cause of unbounded, vitriolic hate and public castigation.

While I'm on the subject, I might as well venture further into the taboo, for I believe there are a lot of men (and now women) who are getting caught in the crossfire of an unresolved debate about consent. We hold this age of eighteen with such a rigid regard that we have forgotten that it is a *legal* line, not a cultural and moral absolute. You will search the Bible and the Quran in vain to find any moral basis to the notion that the age of eighteen is the acceptable age of majority in matters of sexuality. It is, in fact, a quite recent development in the whole of human history. There is no biological basis for it either. Through most of human history, the age of consent was generally commensurate with the age of reproductive capacity. That is why we continue to see much younger ages of consent accepted throughout much of the "less-civilized" world. Heck, even the Vatican views this issue with less rigidity than the American people, favoring sixteen as the age of majority in this issue of sexuality. So we have to begin to be *honest* with ourselves and at least allow for the possibility that people younger than eighteen are in some, maybe many, cases capable of determining for themselves what is agreeable in the area of sexuality.

This is hard to do when so many people are irresponsibly perpetuating the idea that a man who happens to lust after a sixteen-year-old he spies at the beach is a certifiable pedophile. That is an absolute untruth, and not a single respected psychologist in the country will attest to it. They will say—and often do whenever their views aren't for the television audience—that it's quite normal for men to find young, beautiful women attractive and sexually alluring. Yes, lines have to be drawn someplace . . . but the lines ought to reflect what is reasonable, and it is, I believe, unreasonable to continue prosecuting consensual sex as if it were rape or child molestation—especially in cases where there does not appear to be anything but a strong attraction between an older man or woman and a younger adolescent. This is my opinion, has always been my opinion, and by God in heaven, I can have no other—my conscience will not allow it. I will not lie to myself to make the world feel better about something it would rather hold irrational (and, as I say, quite new and novel) opinions about.

I tend to agree with the prevalent opinion that it is hard to "cure" someone of the fixation on children as a target of sexual lust and conquest. *Real* pedophilia is difficult for me to comprehend. I cannot even fathom what is traversing the mind of a man who has a desire to fulfill his sexual urges with an innocent child. I do not understand the attraction anymore than I understand bestiality. In fact, it is so far outside the range of normality that it is plainly neurotic and may only lend itself in the long run to a spiritual analysis. I can, in fact, fully comprehend the claim of demonic possession by one who happens to have been freed from the malignancy of pedophilia. Frankly, I cannot think of any other reasonable explanation. And you must admit the incredible power of Satan to seduce and enslave the minds of men. It is one of the more remarkable powers of Satan that he can invade a man's mind and body and produce in him certain effects, the likes of which the man so possessed has no rational understanding of. In this state of being, the man possessed of evil may very well believe that he's perfectly okay. Indeed, that is the Vatican's chief exorcist's professional, theological diagnosis of Hitler. Those who scoff at such things are so carnally minded that they have no respect for the forces of darkness—and, as such, they are really worse off than the man who has been redeemed from pedophilia. "The devil made me do it" is no defense, but it *is* an explanation worthy of greater respect than it receives in a postmodern world.

Anyone who is so numb and dead to matters of the spiritual world that he cannot look upon incidents like the one at Virginia Tech, or the Amish community, or the destruction of the Twin Towers, or the shootings at Columbine, or the rape and murder of a little girl in Florida, or the use of a three-year-old in the production of pornography—*anyone* who can look on these things and then suggest that the devil has nothing to do with it, is either deliberately ignoring the obvious or is a complete and utter imbecile.

For the Christian, we have plenty of Gospel accounts wherein Christ freed people from the oppression of demonic spirits: the story of the man at Gerasenes/Gadarenes comes to mind (Luke 8:26–39; Matthew 8:28–34; Michael 5:1–20). To quote C. S. Lewis, "It's a kind of modern, chronological snobbishness to dismiss these stories as mythological when we have no reason to believe they were recorded as anything other than historical truths." Just because we can't bring ourselves to believe in demonic possession (or delivery therefrom) is no valid proof of their impossibility. So when a man claims to have been delivered from possession, who are we to deny him? His fruits (after delivery) ought to speak for themselves—which brings me to another point I'd like to make.

In the high Middle Ages/early Age of Reason, there developed in English law a new tool in the arsenal of police powers: perpetual stigmatization. It mostly affected people of a noble peerage who had been convicted of a high crime. It started out as a way of shaming the treasonous. What it essentially entailed was the perpetual punishment of an entire family because of the ignominious deeds of a single person. The nobleman would be divested of all his worldly possessions and claims and publicly dispossessed of his title to nobility forever (which meant that his wife and children suffered the same designation as "déclassé"). Eventually, more and more types of crimes and kinds of classes were subjected to the same post-conviction treatment. There began to be a term of art associated with this form of punishment extending beyond the prescribed sentence: "attainting." The root of the word is "taint," from which we derive also the word "tint," both of which convey a similar meaning in the alteration of a thing's color in the case of a human being. It was the legal act of "coloring" one's reputation in the public eye. This practice remained popular well into the nineteenth century, when, due to a resurgence of Christian values in Great Britain, the act of attainting was abolished.

Our own forefathers actually got a head start on our English progenitors and were so opposed to "attainting" as an acceptable use of criminal and civil laws that a provision forbidding the use of "Bills of Attainder" made its way into the Constitution proper. You don't hear much discussion of Bills of Attainder anymore. That's for two reasons: Modern legislators have practiced a wise restraint in attempting to impose them, and the U.S. Supreme Court has eked out an interesting dichotomy between civil and criminal law. In effect, so long as a condition or consequence of one's punishment for a criminal offense arises exclusively from the publicizing of his conviction for the offense, the prohibition on Bills of Attainder does not attach. However, whenever a legislature imposes additional restrictions on a class of people that is either intended to serve as punishment or is, in effect, punitive, the Constitution's restriction on such Bills of Attainder holds sway.

As the United States erodes further and further into a pagan nation, the idea behind tainting people perpetually for the commission of a crime is gaining new currency. You see it all around. Look at the recent spate of new laws regarding sex offenders. Recently in New Jersey, the Gannet Publishing Co. completed a survey of all the state employees and publicized that 1,800 of them had criminal records. Many of these state employees committed their crimes years ago.

Nevertheless, there is enormous pressure on the state to fire all of these people, and Gannet is catching hell for "outing" them. The average salary of all 1,800 employees was $68,400—which should give you some idea as to the caliber of person affected by this calumny. The common perception of anyone who has ever been convicted of a crime is so bad that felons are literally shut out of consideration for jobs, mortgages, college admission (in some instances), and other essential areas of productive life. This is a major problem that reveals an American culture altogether different from the fair-minded, forgiving, second-chance-oriented culture we've always read and heard about. This new America is heartless, cold, uncaring, self-absorbed, and allows for one strike before the game is over. I think it was F. Scott Fitzgerald who quipped, "There are no second acts in American lives." Sadly, this appears to be truer all the time.

We must figure out a way to move the culture away from this idea that the commission of a felonious crime ought to mean a lifetime of third-class social status. We do not *have* to think like this. We as a people simply enjoy thinking like this because we are so driven by the ambition to succeed, we will do anything to make sure the other guy is kept out of the running. Felons are simply easy pickings. Everybody piles on because it's so easy to do. But clearly this is wrong. Everybody deserves a chance to recover from the challenge of person failure, even the person whose failure may have impacted the lives of others in a negative way. Perpetual stigmatization is a crime against the dignity of mankind because it is ultimately a crime against the image of God in every man. Once a man has completed his duty in service to the community for the crime he committed against that community, it is incumbent upon the community to embrace him and restore him to his proper place as a fellow workman in the social enterprise. This is not what the United States does. It does exactly the opposite and makes nonsense of all its nobler ideals in the process.

Therefore, I propose the formation of a national task force to study the ways in which legislation could be passed at the federal level aimed at doing the following things to improve the conditions of the entire criminal justice system as it affects the lives of defendants, prisoners, and ex-felons:

1. Adopt national standards for sentencing to guard against wild disparities from state to state, and create a compact to which the stages could sign on in exchange for various economic stimuli in the form of federal funding. It's time the individual states treat their citizens as Americans, first and foremost.
2. Adopt national standards to regulate the distinctions between violent and nonviolent crimes so that the states are in substantial agreement about what constitutes a violent crime.
3. Impose upon all states the federal rules of criminal procedure so that everyone involved is held to the same measure of evidentiary accountability.
4. Amend 42 U.S.C. § 1983 so that "any person" specifically references law enforcement personnel, prosecutors, and judges (the Supreme Court has explicitly excluded the latter two by judicial fiat).
5. Create and empower a national board with the authority to review every single prisoner in the United States who has been in prison longer than twenty years and to recommend release on a case-by-case basis. This board could be given the additional authority to trump state sentencing decisions, thereby taking the political heat off of state and local officials who are reticent to disturb unfair and disproportionate sentences.
6. Recommend that Congress pass a "Full Restoration Act" with attending criteria and with the goal of making it possible for an ex-felon to be completely "washed" of his criminal record after a set number of years and based upon the additional stipulations of the law.
7. Recommend the addition of a Justice Reform amendment to the Bill of Rights, which would accomplish the following:
   a. Guarantee the right to vote to every American, including incarcerated Americans.
   b. Strengthen the Fourth Amendment by grafting onto it the exclusionary rule and adding a reference to "communications."

c. Strengthen the Fifth Amendment by requiring all its elements be applied to the states (there are provisions not yet fully incorporated).
d. Outlaw the death penalty at every level.
e. Forbid the compulsion of giving any evidence against one's self (so that it includes biological and other identifying evidence).

8. Re-sign the "Optional Protocol" of the United Nations Human Rights Commission from which President Bush had us withdraw in 2001—that was a HUGE step backwards for civil rights in this country.

Well, Chuck, that just about covers it, I think. Once again, I've written far and away more than you had asked for. I thank you for the invitation to proffer my thoughts and I stand ready to be useful if you have additional requests.

I leave you with a quote from St. Thomas More, whom I hold in great esteem and affection: ". . . [A] very good man can at times happen, in the indiscretion of fervor, to say something, and write it too, which when he later considers more carefully he would very much like to change" (from *Dialogue Concerning Heresies*).

God bless you and keep you!

Memento Hagia Sophia!

Dear Chuck,

Sometime ago we had a discussion about what it is truly like on the inside. What follows is a follow-up on that discussion, as well as another discussion on the potential for rehabilitation of prisoners, and sex offenders in particular, of which I am one, and how spirituality fits in with "doing time."

"Prisoners cannot be rehabilitated" (from a prison psychologist to an inmate in the Virginia prison system, Department of Corrections).

In a 2007 poll of Americans measuring attitudes about freedom of religion, speech, and the press, 55 percent believe the country's founders wrote Christianity into the U.S. Constitution (*Chicago*

Sun-Times, 12 September 2007).

Recent (2007) Bureau of Justice statistics estimate the prison population of the United States at over 2 million people, the highest incarceration rate of any country in the world.

Do you see a disconnection, Chuck? We are a "Christian" nation, yet we have the most people in prisons. Many states have abolished parole, sentences are increasing, new prisons are being built, and the U.S. has a *private* industry devoted to incarcerating humans—Correction Corporation of America. Is this how a "Christian" nation should behave?

I can only speak to the Virginia system because that is where I am, but others who have spent time in federal or other state prisons report similar situations as I will describe.

A June 11, 2006, *Washington Post* article (p. A3: "California's Crisis in Prison Systems a Threat to Public") summed up the problem most states have: From the 1950s through the 1970s, prisons used rehabilitation as a focus for convicts, using education and psychotherapy with qualified therapists to treat inmates. California was a leader in the field. But in the late 1970s, crime rates increased and states "got tough on crime." Punishment alone became the model. Laws were passed increasing sentencing. Judges no longer had discretion in sentencing. Parole was abolished in many states. Prison populations grew and departments of corrections became human warehouses, what we call modern-day slavery amongst ourselves.

A fact most people do not know: 95 percent of all inmates will be released at some time (*USA Today*, June 12, 2006, p. 12A editorial, "Rising Prison Problems Begin to Trickle into Society"). The op-ed piece focused on violence, rehabilitation, medical care, and accountability as areas for improvement in prisons.

I am incarcerated in the Virginia Department of Corrections. The implication is that I will be "corrected"; in my mind, that means rehabilitation.

How do you correct when the recidivism rate for all ex-offenders is approximately 66 percent? If you ran a business with a two-thirds failure rate, you wouldn't be in business long, but Corrections *stays* in business because of a two-thirds failure rate. I do not know all the answers. I am not an expert in the field. To me, it seems that the prison system and the criminal justice system do not follow psychiatric and psychological research on their respective systems. Any behavioral psychologist will tell you that punishment does not work. It is a deterrent to nothing, and teaches no lesson. This is why grounding your teenager has no impact on his or her future behavior. One needs to replace destructive behavior with constructive behavior for treatment /rehabilitation to work. Prisons do not do this anymore.

Prisons actually encourage continued criminality. Here is an example: I get only three pairs of boxer underwear and T-shirts and socks. Also, three pair of jeans and three shirts. Laundry is done twice a week (it used to be *once* a week). Do the math. Seven days, or now, three days and four days, between laundry, and if you have to wear a set of clothes in between, you have to wash some things yourself. Or you go this route: You "hire" a laundry worker for 8 stamps or 10 stamps a month to do your laundry. He then steals for you three or four extra sets of underwear or towels, or jeans, etc., so you can wear clean clothes.

Another example is food: Prison food is notoriously atrocious. They cook it to death, so it loses nutritional value. In order to get some nutrition, you find a kitchen worker who will steal eggs, fruit, vegetables, etc. for you, at a price.

I am only allowed twelve books and a Bible. But I have twenty-five books in my cell. I "bought" what are called "turn-in" books that I give to the property officer to throw out, and I keep my "good" books in my cell. I have contraband and could be charged. Luckily, this institution is not big on counting books. But I am "breaking the law" of the prison.

The rules are for our safety, but many are so inane that in order to have some kind of life, you have to break many of them. I was not really a criminal when I came in here. I am learning to be a competent one, though, due to my "education" in prison living.

Prison is a very violent milieu. No one is taught how to deal with their emotions or anger, so it manifests itself in violence. Fights occur on a regular basis. Gang activity is on the rise. You have to always be on the lookout and ready. Some men will not sleep with their face toward the wall for fear of someone running in on them. Many lock their cell to take a nap.

Stories abound about past riots, stabbings, raping, fighting, etc. You are accepted as "cool" by having been in the "hole" for anything. Fighting earns respect in prison.

One program offered to us is Kairos prison ministry. This is a Christian-based ministry, but it welcomes anyone. The message is that Christ died for us and prison can free us if we let God into our lives. Kairos means "God's special time." Men from all denominations come together in fellowship to come into the prison and minister to us. This is the spiritual help many of us need beyond our specific denominations or churches. It is by far one of the best things to offer prisons. It is a community. The monthly reunions are follow-ups to the three-and-a-half-day retreat, and they keep the movement going. Weekly "prayer and share" groups are supposed to take place to reflect on how God is working in your life, and to identify any struggles. I am in a development group where we are using the monastic rule of St. Benedict, developing a "rule of prisoners" that we can hand Kairos graduates or anyone who wants to live a Christ-like life in prison. This is an exciting opportunity and we hope it will be fruitful and useful to many inmates.

Other programs include Anger Management and Breaking Barriers. They are all designed to help us manage our emotions, but they are forced upon you, and if you are in denial or just "have" to be there, what can you really get out of it? These are actually good programs with good information, but the lessons are not carried out in prison life.

Let me continue with rehab and programs. We have AA and NA here. I do not know much about either, but I do know they have outside support volunteers that come in, as well as in-prison support via counselors. There is also a program called "Phase IV" that is for inmates who complete earlier education programs and who want to "take it further" and "get real" about recovery. I know nothing about this program, nor do I know anyone who has been in it.

A pre-parole class known as Preps can be taken by anyone, but is geared to those who will be on parole, or "old-law" (pre-1995) inmates. This is supposed to be a good program to prepare you for being released and what you will face.

There is a program for men who have children and want to parent from prison. I knew one man in it, about three years ago, and he said it was excellent.

Youth outreach is a predominantly black program that invites young black men (or any young man) and uses older inmates to act as teachers and mentors to help them gain maturity. I do not know much else about it.

There is also the "Alternative Therapy" group, which is a code name for the sex offender treatment group. This is what I am in. It is a voluntary program, and you must complete an education class about sex offenses and sexuality to be eligible for the group. As of now, we have one group of ten men, a psychologist, and a sex-offender treatment provider/prison counselor. We meet weekly, go over our sexual histories and crimes. The focus is to stop victimization of *any* kind, but especially sexual.

This program has helped me tremendously. I can see how I got to this point, and am integrating my past with my present. I am confronting my faulty thought processes regarding sex and women, and learning healthy thinking and tools to use so I can stop victimizing. I have taken responsibility for my crimes.

Some say that sex offenders can never be rehabilitated. To some extent, this statement *is* true. Those pedophiles that can only become sexual in the presence of children and have failed attempts at therapy may truly be impossible to rehabilitate. Civil commitment would be acceptable when all else has failed, but treatment should not cease.

I would say sex offenders, like alcoholics, drug abusers, compulsive gamblers, shoppers, overeaters, etc., are in recovery. Insofar as these groups "cure" their members, sex-offender treatment "cures" the offender. Many sex offenders are sex addicts, manage the addiction, then stop the sexual acting out.

Allow me to clear up some misconceptions about sex offenders. According to *USA Today* (August 25, 2005, pp. 1A and 4A, "Despite High-Profile Cases, Sex-Offense Crimes Decline), from 1993 to 2003, sexual assaults decreased 79 percent against adolescents aged twelve to seventeen. The number of substantiated sex-abuse cases involving kids of all ages fell 39 percent.

Canadian psychologist and sex offender Karl Hanson finds highest-risk sex offenders are antisocial and have a sexual deviancy, such as an interest in children or strangers. Government data on sex offenders: most offenders are male, and most victims are female. Offenders are *less* likely to be rearrested after prison for any type of crime than other ex-inmates, but if rearrested, it is more likely due to another sex crime (Department of Justice Study—2003).

Group therapy decreases recidivism from 17 percent to 10 percent according to a 2002 study by Hanson of 9,454 sex offenders in 43 states. (Note the already-low 17 percent *without* therapy.)

A 1999 Department of Justice study found that those participating in relapse-prevention programs had a rearrest rate of 7.29 percent after five years, compared to 17.6 percent who had no treatment. The Department of Justice studied 11,000 offenders.

The problem with sex offender registries and residency requirements is that only *10 percent* of sex crimes occur by strangers. Ninety percent of perpetrators know their victims. The released sex offender living in the community is actually *less* of a danger than parents, friends, relatives, teachers, coaches, clergy, etc., who know the child.

The negative effect of laws like "Megan's Law" are that sex offenders are not registering and are going underground. One Midwestern sheriff said he used to know where all his sex offenders lived; now he knows the locations of approximately 60 percent. These laws are nothing but continued punishment after prison. They are emotional reactions to isolated incidents.

I know that Florida (and I think Iowa) had Christian-based prisons or pods. These actually worked. Recidivism rates from these setups were dramatically lower than for prisons in general. I believe they have closed due to lawsuits filed by prisoners over church/state relations. How stupid! You close what was actually working! These faith-based dorms or prisons work; they need support and the Supreme Court to back them, not close them down.

How families get punished by the prison system:

The first "tax" on families is the phone system. Our families pay outrageous rates because we have to call collect. Then the prison contracts with a vendor to supply phone and maintenance on it. The vendor claims the prison rules/restrictions make it difficult, so they charge extra. The kickback to the prison occurs from these rates to "support" prisoners' needs, like TV, recreation equipment, etc.

New York finally caught on and successfully sued MCI to reduce rates. Research shows that keeping in touch with family is the single most important thing for prisoners. Yet they do this to separate us from our families. Many cannot afford this and "block" their phones so the inmate cannot call. How sad.

Commissary is next. The prices are what you pay in grocery stores, or *more*. Many inmates' families send them money to shop at commissary and property. This is an added tax on them.

Our inmate accounts is another way to punish families. We cannot receive packages from our families. We are forced to buy from commissary or "approved" vendors. We must pay out of our account here. Our family or friends can't even pay for a magazine or newspaper subscription for us on their own. The have to send us the money first. Then we have to process it here and pay with a money order, which adds 32 cents to the bill, plus our postage.

If you owe Medical or the dentist any money, the money your family sends is taken to pay this off, and you may never see it. That is another "tax." Our families should not pay for our health care. Many inmates tell their families not to send money because of this. Some states have stopped this due to lawsuits, but many continue it.

These "policies" are nothing more than taxes on our families for trying to remain in contact with us and support us.

Medical Care:

Our medical care is horrible. The Department of Corrections is the ultimate HMO; they control all access points, the formulary and costs.

We pay $5 per physician visit, and $2 for each prescription that is not life-sustaining, which is basically almost all medications. Now, we make 23 to 55 cents an hour. A medical visit can cost you up to two weeks' pay or more.

If you need eye care or to see a specialist, you go on a medical "run." You get up at approximately 4:30, and are put in full restraints:

handcuffs with "the box," which restricts your movement and is connected to a waist chain and shackles. You go on a bus or van and drive about an hour to the facility. You stay in full restraints *all day* until you get back to the prison. Ever try going to the bathroom this way? Forget a bowel movement. Many go all over themselves.

There is dental care, but it is very basic and many things are not offered. They pull teeth, fill them, and clean them. That is about it. You can get dentures—about $180/set, at your cost. Waiting lists are long for dental care.

The physicians vary. Some prisons have very good ones. We do not. Our physician is an internist. He is not a specialist, yet he attempts to treat things he is not qualified to treat effectively. Since I have been at this facility, five deaths have occurred. Diabetics are mismanaged. Cancer diagnoses are missed because they are written off as other, non-life-threatening conditions. Blood-thinner patients are mismanaged. Orthopedic injuries requiring surgery are treated "conservatively." He told one of my cellys that if he wanted better medical care, he shouldn't have come to prison. You have to fight to see a specialist or get any decent care.

Preventive care, which proves it saves money, is nonexistent. This would be a terrific environment for it because so much *is* controlled. Yet the "same ol' thing" is done at higher costs.

Nursing care is also poor. Most are LPNS, not RNs. They are collecting paychecks. Most don't care about us. They are an embarrassment to what was my profession.

Inmates are afraid to go to Medical because of the physician. Others don't go because of the cost. This is not a medical system that works.

Food:

Along these lines is our food. It is full of carbohydrates and short on protein—diabetes waiting to happen. It is usually overcooked, not seasoned, processed, and at times, rotten. Our fruit is often at the rotten stage. Turkey meat is the "base" meat. Many inmates don't go to the mess hall when a turkey patty is on the menu. The registered dietician who approves these menus should be reprimanded or suspended from practice.

Getting Out:

I am a facilitator for a program that inmates must take to be released. It is a very basic program. It covers changes in society, banking and money management, healthy living, healthy sexuality, dealing with emotions, values and ethics, housing and transportation, employment, probation and parole, and resource and referral. It is a one-week, five hours/day class. Most sessions are forty-five minutes long. It is not enough time to do these topics justice. The information is good; it is just too short.

There are so many restrictions it is amazing anyone stays out. Jobs are difficult to find and keep. The system provides minimal help upon release. Your best bet is churches and faith-based programs. If you have nowhere to go, the state finds you *something*, but many places won't accept certain types of offenders. Some housing is off-limits. It is a situation almost designed to fail. This is why recidivism is so high.

Chuck, I don't have the answers. I trust God to help me, but I do have to participate in that help.

Tim [not his real name] has an idea for incarceration in general. You don't get a specific time for a sentence; instead, you earn points toward release. You participate in programs, go to school (GED or college), train in a trade or two, good behavior, etc. Then, upon earning enough points, you move to essentially a travel-trailer park of inmates, get a job, continue programs and school, go to therapy, etc. His idea is to "test" you by putting drugs, alcohol, porn, etc. in your trailer to test your will to stop addictions. You slip up, then it's back to prison and increased programs. Moving down and building points, you get more freedom. You are released when you have a job and can support yourself, secure living and transportation, have support systems, and manage your addiction(s), anger, etc.

This is not a bad idea. It needs work, but it's a radical redesign of criminal justice and prison systems.

One last thing I want to mention about politicians and the politicization of prisons, especially regarding sex offenders.

For example, our attorney general, a "good Catholic," is on a witch hunt against sex offenders that takes restrictions too far. Did he not learn compassion, charity, love of neighbor in his church? Jesus taught these things. Yet, there is no compassion. Sex offenders are modern-day lepers. Forced to the fringes of society. NBC's *Dateline* took it to the sensationalist level. The media misinforms. Our "religious" politicians seem to have forgotten their Bible lessons when it comes to prisoners.

Which brings me to accountability. The prison systems are accountable to no one. They are free-rein organizations with no outside or independent oversight. Abu Ghraib happened for a reason, and it was led by an ex-prison guard from *this* prison. An inmate who knew him said he was an asshole when he was here, and they were glad he went to prison. Abu Ghraib–type things go on every day in American prisons, yet we hear nothing about it in the media, and no one is outraged.

Until prison systems are held accountable for their actions—and this includes parole boards—nothing will change. Oversight is sorely needed.

Dear Chuck,

I have some things that I want to add to my last "book" to you. It was good to see you Tuesday, and I'm glad you solved the mail problem. That was quick thinking on your part, and it fixes the issue nicely. Well done!

Here are some more of my thoughts on crime, criminals, punishment, and rehabilitation.

Let's take drug abusers. These people do not necessarily belong in prison. Yes, they broke "the law"—but addictive behavior (and I mean *any* addictive behavior, be it drugs, alcohol, sex, gambling, eating, shopping, Internet, TV watching, etc.) needs treatment—*not* incarceration. Rehab centers abound, but these are "quick fixes." What is needed are more long-term residential centers where the addicts work to support the center and rehab classes are included in the day.

Drug courts, in conjunction with rehab, are proven to work (from my last letter). Of course it is not 100 percent effective, nothing ever is, but we can come close if we work at making these programs better and better.

Another issue regarding sex offenders is the language used to describe them. The media is big on using "predator," "monster," "convicted sex offender," etc., to sensationalize the story. It also dehumanizes the sexual offenders. As a society, it is easier to mistreat or look upon with disdain those that we feel are inhuman. To rationalize the "Megan's Laws" and residency requirements, monitoring, and inane restrictions in general that are placed on sex offenders, we label them to strip their humanity. It makes us feel better to say "predator" or "monster" than "that person."

It is my guess that what the media calls sexual "predators" or even some "pedophiles" are not truly either in the meaning of the word. They are sexual addicts who, looking for a fix, turned to children or teenagers. With proper counseling and treatment, as I wrote last time, 90 percent can be successfully rehabbed. [According to a report from the Justice Bureau of Statistics, of the 9,691 male sex offenders released from prisons in fifteen states in 1994, 5.3 percent were rearrested for a new sex crime within three years.] Would you invest in something with a 90 percent success rate? I would. It beats a 66 percent fail rate with prisoners in general.

Spirituality is alive and well in prison. I believe that God is closer to prisoners than anyone else today. We are scorned, put away, forgotten, and abused. Rarely can we fight back physically, so we fight spiritually. God hears our cries for help, justice, peace, and new beginnings. God has promised to raise the lowly. Jesus came for the sinners to face the captives. He hears us and works in his time to do good with us.

Dear Chuck,

How are you, my friend? I am honored to be a part of your literary endeavor. As for me, my book idea actually stems from Mr. H's response to your *Catholic Virginian* article. Frankly, I believe I have the answer to recidivism after years of studying the problem. Some of the ideas and thoughts I've shared with you will probably be repeated in the synthesis of a larger overall work. I'm thinking of calling it *Decriminalizing America*. Sadly, there are many law enforcement personnel who lack the real desire to do so, or else they'd be unemployed. Treatment is often so much more preferred to the cure. Drug companies have made a fortune on this philosophy. Consequently, I expect resistance. . . .

For starters, we need to stop dehumanizing the ones who commit crimes even when they make it easy to do so. The conflict inherent in humanity starts the process of resistance to rehabilitation the minute a criminal is sentenced. When the police and prosecutors vilify the defendant, even and especially when he or she is guilty (heaven help the innocent), they calcify his/her heart in a defiant stance. How many judges delight in scathing commentary when pronouncing a sentence? Thus, our "adversarial process" of jurisprudence begins the cycle of suffering through recidivism. Justice must be wedded to mercy—not contempt—for those who do evil. That does not imply that there ought to be no consequences to the actions we do when we sin; merely that those consequences allow and encourage redemptive yearning. Please use this in your publication. I have so much more to say for mine.

Please know that I always remember you guys in prayer and I am happy you are staying so busy with your ministry work. It's especially difficult when the correction center officials try to violate everyone's First Amendment rights by trying to restrict your letter writing. Please keep up the good work and try to maintain your health! Cold weather is on the way.

I'll try to write back soon. Please keep me in your prayers, too. There are so many Catholic brothers here who also need your prayers. Pray for them and that we get a priest here. May the Lord guide you in your every step. . . .

Chuck,

Greetings, my friend. I hope you all had a Happy Thanksgiving. Mine was okay. Seems to be just another day in here. I have gotten used to not being able to spend the holidays with family.

I really am tired of this place, though. I figured out why they don't want you writing the inmates, or so it may seem. By your writing it shows the inmates that you really care about them. You are not just going through the motions by showing up once a week (or however often you do) but thinking about them always. By doing this, you become inspirational and may even motivate someone to make something of their lives. *The prison does not want us to make something of our lives*; they want us to fall into the status quo of prison life: fighting, gambling, and doing the wrong thing. They plant, water, and fertilize this with giving us so much idle time. As you know, recently I wrote about prison programs, or rather the lack thereof. But what really brought that to light was a recent event that happened to me.

Several months ago, I carved a kayak and boater out of soap. Three weeks ago I tried to ship it home. Personal Property told me I could not. I put in an informal complaint about it to the head of Personal Property. Her response was that I would need the warden's approval. Well, I wrote the warden, telling him the situation and describing how I carved it and what every part was made of. Today I got his response back. "You are not allowed to send such home. We do not have an Arts and Crafts program currently in effect. Who authorized you to make the artwork?"

As you can see, they expect us to sit here with too much time on our hands and not do anything constructive in nature. I really am fed up with the situation, and something must change so that inmates can better themselves instead of leaving this place more bitter than when they entered!

My spirits were lifted last night at services. Here's the latest information on my release date problems. If you recall, three months were removed from my sentence but my release date remained the same. I have written two letters to Richmond stating that that is mathematically impossible. Today I spoke with my counselor stating there were still problems with my release date. She told me she had just gotten a letter back about that. She made a copy and gave it to me. Richmond still claims that the release date is accurate. Even my counselor states it doesn't work out, but either can't help or doesn't want to help. Even the Supreme Court who made the corrections to my sentence will not get involved with the corrections to the release date. I am quickly running out of ways to get justice because no one seems to want to see justice served. I just don't know where to turn! If I get it corrected I only have about fifteen months left here. If I don't I have eighteen months. I'm trying to get to see the Institutional Attorney and see what further options are available.

Greetings,

Thank you for such a nice Christmas card. It is my favorite of all that I have received. The stained glass was a nice touch (a signature touch).

Since my last letter, I continue to pray for Lee, you, and the boys.

The Monday before last my counselor did my annual review, making two important errors which raised my custody level from 14 points to 19 points: the difference between a level 2 facility and a level 3. I pointed out the errors at the time, but she insisted the policy had changed last January. I did my homework and found she was wrong. I wrote and briefly spoke with her, which was useless. I submitted a complaint with the specific errors Friday. Monday, she corrected the oversights and apologized (twice). Shocking—considering the attitude she carries. Still, it felt good.

I submitted a complaint regarding the confiscating of my incoming funds Monday. The housing unit manager stopped by my room to tell me that it was the most well-written complaint that he has ever seen. I couldn't understand what he was saying. I don't have the best of hearing. I could only make out bits and pieces of what he was saying and thought he was responding to my complaint—the best he has received. I sent him a short letter explaining the confusion. I thought he was trying to trick me into signing off on the complaint like he does to others to lessen his building's complaint log. Talking through my roommate and a door doesn't help my hearing either.

My room still doesn't have any heat coming through the vent.

Tuesday, my pod was placed on lockdown for two days after a knife was found. Probably one left behind by the former tenants when the building was switched to a nonsmoking building. Anyway, it was Tuesday and Wednesday that I saw 20-degree temperatures as the whole building's heating system failed. I felt colder than I was in Korea for cold-weather training. With four pairs of socks, long johns, sweatsuit, pants, hat, and four layers of blankets, I stayed toasty. Heating my toes in the toilet helped. Now that the building has heat, my room gets some coming in around the door openings, even though none is coming through the vent. I call this training for the day. I'll have to pay my own heating bills again.

Friday, the regional ombudsman came to talk to me about my money confiscation grievance which they have been fighting me tooth and nail from logging. I now have a response, but it was never officially logged.

As a result of this week's lockdown (my pod only), I worked today and will tomorrow. Christmas week, I work Thursday and Friday; New Year's week, I work Wednesday and Thursday, followed by a full week off until January 14. Plenty of hours to fill. Typical prison schedule. . . .

Have a great holiday.

Hey Chuck:

I hope this letter finds you well and not downtrodden by what is going on at some of the other correction centers. I know it is a headache. Our situation is really starting to affect people. One of our guys started upholstery class on Monday last. When he got there he told the instructor that Monday mornings he would not be there and he would have to leave early on Tuesdays for religious services. The class is a full-day class. The instructor suggested to him to either take the class or go to church, but he could not do both and would need to let him know his choice by the next day. The friend told him he knew his choice right now and told him he was going to services.

The next day he saw and spoke to the infamous warden who made the schedule change and stated that we could not be punished by schools or our jobs for attending services. The warden told him he just had to decide which is more important, an education or Jesus.

The warden also made a very off-the-cuff statement at a previous meeting on religious services that made one of the Catholic brothers storm out of the meeting. The inmates were complaining about the possibility of the above situation when the warden said something to the effect of "That's the problem with you Christians. Jesus Christ could be born in the middle of Yankee Stadium with a million stars and you would still find something to complain about." Our chaplain has been fighting them for us tooth and nail. It's been mostly a losing battle; the only thing gained is him getting closer to losing his job, but still he fights. He's the best chaplain I've seen here.

I had a real bad problem with one of the chaplains here half a year or so ago. I had written a letter to the dioceses soliciting help from them. After three months of not hearing from them, not even a "Sorry, we can't be of assistance," I wrote a second letter. In that letter, I admonished them for not having the decency, being my own church, to respond when Protestant churches had. In fact, the help was to get my pardon, and one Protestant ministry even took the time to have a legal team look into the situation. Well, in my letter, in an attempt to wake up the church to help prisoners, I included the following poem written by one of our brothers:

Modern-Day Matthew 25

For I was hungry and you gave me something to eat . . .
. . . unless I was just a bum on the street,
so I went hungry.
I was thirsty and you gave me something to drink . . .
. . . until I appeared threatening, and caused you to think,
so I went thirsty.
I was a stranger and you invited me in . . .
. . . except by your standards, I was living in sin,
so I slept on the street.

I needed clothes and you clothed me . . .
. . . It was the least I could do; you said,
and I'd have to agree.
I was sick and you looked after me . . .
. . . with the only condition that I pay a small fee,
but I had no money.
I was in prison and you came to visit me . . .
. . . until you found out it was for pornography,
so I was beneath your dignity.

Then the King will reply: Assuredly, whatever you neglected to do for the hungry or thirsty or stranger or naked, the sick of body or mind or the worst criminal among you—you neglected to do the same for me. I also added, "Be not like the Pharisees, for we are all sinners and have fallen short of the glory of God."

Well, as you can imagine, that woke them up. Shortly after receipt they called up here and spoke to one of the chaplains, asking what problem I was having as they had received a disturbing letter from me. She then called my chaplain and had him meet with him. The chaplain and I met and he told me she was upset at having received a call from the dioceses and wanted this straightened out. I told him my situation and about the letter. He agreed with me totally. Later that day before services, an inmate coordinator for our services, who usually greets me by my first name and a handshake, came up saying, "Mr. ——, we need to talk." He took me into another room, pulled out a chair, ordered me to sit, and then said he'd be right back.

When he came back he said, "Sorry, don't worry about it." By then I knew what the deal was and I told him no, and said, "What were you going to ask?" It was, "What's your problem, and why are you writing the dioceses? The chaplain wants to know." I told him it was none of his business, and since it had nothing to do with the prison, and since the chaplain is not part of our church, it is none of her business either.

The next day I wrote an informal complaint about her sending another inmate to get into my personal business and stated that she was lucky that my demeanor is such as it is because if most inmates had been approached in the way I was, there would have been a fight.

The response from her was basically arrogantly written, calling me a liar and telling me any correspondence I send to the Church must go through her. My mom has her response, and when she read it, my mom was even hot!

My cellmate just went to sleep, and the light is off, so not only will my spelling be bad tonight, but my handwriting might be worse.

Well, since we are speaking some about my pardon, it seems a good transition into my next subject: the pre-sentence report. From what I understand, you should have gotten it by now. My mom said she sent it. Mom said she also sent her own letter. I don't know what that was about. Knowing Mom, it was asking you or thanking you for trying to get me out. I have given up on that prospect. We've tried all we can to do that and been shot down. I only have a bit over a year left and believe justice in the form of an early release is not God's will or plan.

My finding indicates that according to case law, I was not guilty of any felony activity, as the crimes did not meet the statute language as defined by case law. I will be putting in for another pardon once released, and it is more possible to receive clemency. At that time I may ask your support in a character reference or something. As you know, pardons are more politics than anything. I figure the more people who support me and have legal knowledge, either from the courts or law enforcement, the better. I already have full support from a friend who was the lead investigator for the Massachusetts State Police and now works as a bailiff. He's looked over my transcripts and afterward wrote a letter about the injustice in my case for my last pardon. I just like to keep this injustice in the spotlight and not let it be swept under the rug.

If you are ever interested, I have almost all my transcripts, just lacking the transcripts from when I pled guilty, which is just the charges being called out and me saying "Guilty." At worst, it would be good for a laugh at just how sorry my $12,500-paid attorney was!

The lawyer was right about getting corrections. In my habeas, we showed how I was coerced by my attorney to plead guilty; how the facts of the case do not meet the language of the statute as defined by case law; and much more. The attorney general's office, in their response, didn't touch on any of these issues in their rebuttal. Yeah, the Supreme Court ignored all the issues and closed my case with basically "You pleaded guilty."

Tomorrow morning, I have a meeting with a man from Veterans Affairs to talk about options available to me when released. It feels good that all those pre-release things are starting to happen.

Well, I am extending an invitation for you and Lee to meet my family, or at least my mom and stepdad. They will be doing a craft show in the Richmond area somewhere around St. Patrick's Day. Might be an interesting show for the both of you, as there are all sorts of different crafts. Maybe even some beach carvings! Let me know if you are at all interested and I'll get you better information.

Well, like you, I've been fighting the flu. I'm about over it now but it's getting late and I'm probably boring you to death, so I'll close now. Please know you and all the oppressed are being prayed for. Please do the same for us.

Dear Chuck,

It was good to receive your letter the other day.

I was fortunate to have my mother visit me last week. She lives in Florida and her business requires her to work weekends. This is the normal time for visitation. She wrote the warden here over one month in advance requesting a special visit. Policy dictates that requests be made at least fourteen days in advance. Four weeks later she still had no response and it took her six phone calls for someone to find out the requests were buried on someone's desk. This was the week prior to when she wanted to visit. Even though she drove here from Florida, they only allowed her to visit me for one hour. The Department of Corrections states that they feel contact with family members is important to successful reintegration into society, yet they drastically hamper that contact. Guess they don't want us to successfully reintegrate. Even though short, it was a wonderful visit. Due to distances from family, she is the only one I see and that is only twice a year. All my family is either in Florida or Maine.

I'm still fighting to get all the errors in my sentencing order corrected. Just when I think I've got it, something new pops up. While Department of Corrections removed the extra three months I was given in error, my release date stayed exactly the same, yet they say there is no problem. It's beyond logic.

There is nothing else really going on. Just wanted to touch base with you and say hello. Blessings to you and the Mrs.

Dear Mr. Brown:

First, thank you for staying in contact with my son. Enclosed is a copy of his preliminary report that he has asked me to send you.

We sincerely appreciate your interest in inmates and what really is taking place in our prisons. Since my son's incarceration there has been *no* effort by the prison to help him in any way. He has received no counseling or aids to help in rehabilitation. In fact, he recently carved a kayak out of soap and on cell search the authorities found it and told him he would either have to send it to me or throw it away. When he went to mail it he was told that he could not. He wrote to the warden regarding the situation, and the response from the warden was that there were no arts and crafts, so who gave him the authority to do arts, and therefore, he must throw it away.

Why do prisons want the inmates to remain inmates? What I mean by this is that if they are stagnant for several years, then they will have no chance on the outside world when released. How is an inmate going to be any better when he is released if he is not allowed to do anything with his hands or mind while incarcerated? What is shown to the American people on television is a far cry from what actually takes place in the majority of prisons. You and I both know that a criminal according to society is not supposed to be treated like a human being, but there are individuals that made a grave mistake and sincerely have learned from it. They deserve a second chance, and this is where help from the facility while housed there comes into play.

My observation regarding my son's facility is that the people employed have little education, and those that have an education do not want to work. Take, for instance, in his case, when the court typed out the order; it incorrectly stated that he had four years and fifteen months. When I reviewed the transcript the judgment was four years and twelve months. It took several frustrating years of contacting numerous people to finally find someone in Probation who would care enough to help us get it corrected. Once corrected, however, the Department of Corrections told him that his release date was still the same as if he had fifteen months. When he spoke to his counselor regarding this matter, she said, "It doesn't make sense, but that is what they say so it must be so." There is no one in the facility that cares enough to go the extra mile for some of these inmates, and they become very frustrated. I have spent endless hours writing various people, but what about those poor inmates that have no one?

The prison system is all about MONEY and nothing more. They could care less if the inmates are rehabilitated when released. In fact, it's better for them because they are guaranteed that most likely he/she will return, generating what? More money!

What my son did was very wrong, but clearly, he did not deserve the sentence received. My husband and I viewed in the courtroom approximately 75 percent of the video before the judge realized we could see it and there was no nudity on what we witnessed, yet his attorney led us to believe that the Commonwealth Attorney had to charge him with the felony because of the nudity. Our family was so naive, and I have done a great deal of investigating since his incarceration. I feel from what information I discovered, he should have been charged with misdemeanors for the time his sixteen-year-old stepdaughter was unknowingly filmed in her bra and panties and charged with a felony. He has been classified as a Level II Sex Offender, yet he never touched her nor did he ever sell or distribute the video. Because he is a Level II he is not allowed to have a work release. Clearly he is no threat to society, and so he just sat, month after month, year after year, doing nothing with his time.

There are severe to mild situations, and yet the mild have to suffer as if they had done something severe. This is wrong not just for my son but for every inmate that is in prison.

I can't thank you enough for caring about inmates and rehabilitation. You have touched many people's hearts.

Dear Chuck,

Grace and peace to you and your wife, for whom I add a special prayer of health and healing through Christ the Lord. Amen.

I am grateful for the address. I have written the Virginia ACLU and the Rutherford Institute about the situation here. We have Catholic brothers either being dropped from vocational classes or refused from attending because they attend the only Catholic services available to them. I've also alerted them to the preferential treatment afforded to the Protestant program, the *only* faith group allowed to meet on Thursday nights and Sunday afternoons. No Protestant here has to choose between worship and work/school. I have *never* in my life (and this is no exaggeration!) experienced such blatant discrimination on the basis of faith. It is like I'm not even in the United States anymore. Of course, growing up a Southern Baptist in North Carolina as I did, one is not likely to find himself the subject of discrimination of a religious sort. I honestly believe that the institution is afraid of our Catholic group growing.

Catholics, as you undoubtedly know, can be more meddlesome, and an annoyance to power. Plus, church hierarchy—*where it exists*—has a way of leaning on prison systems that are recalcitrant or ill-disposed toward Catholic inmates. Speaking truth to power, in my humble opinion, is an obligation of any man who holds the mantle of bishop. I fear that the church hierarchy is too comfy with the politics of Americanism—something Pope Leo XIII railed about in one of his encyclicals. Would Benedict do something of the same to get the church's attention over here?

Our mutual friend shared with me some of the sentiments of your most recent letter to him. I am very pleased to learn that the bishop has instructed/encouraged the pastors to take an active role in prison ministry. I believe this is fortuitous. God has quickened the hearts and minds of many inmates toward the fullness of truth, which exists in his church. The spirit is moving in here. The problem is that we are so tenuous. We barely get by as it is. I truly believe that the next generation of Catholic religious deacons and priests may very well be sitting inside American prisons. The church is totally undervaluing this profound probability. It is missing an opportunity to cultivate a mission field right under its very own nose. The men in prison who come from Christian backgrounds (such as myself) discover that whatever it was that they may have believed about Christ, the church they attended, the Bible, the faith, etc., was obviously flawed by virtue of where they're at. So, like myself, they go very deeply into a search for the truth. Because they search so hard, they often find it. Unfortunately, *it's hard to find what's not there to look for*, and this is the problem for the Church.

I had the opportunity sometime back to communicate by letter to Fr. Bradley K. Arturi, prefect of Opus Dei in the United States. I had written him about the Prelature to find out more about it. In my initial letter, I made him aware of the same sentiment I've just shared with you, and I added that I felt it was too bad that Catholics in prison do not have the opportunity to associate themselves in a more meaningful way with a religious society. After all, prison is the closest thing to a monastery outside of one. He wrote me back a nice letter encouraging me to continue pursuing my interest in Opus Dei, but flatly dismissed my idea of a kind of tertiary association with the Order. I then read some of St. Escriva's writings (he founded Opus Dei), including *The Way*, *The Furrow*, and one other book I've now forgotten the title of. [Other books written by this saint include *The Forge*, *Christ Is Passing By*, *Holy Rosary*, *The Way of the Cross*, and *Love for the Church*.] St. Escriva had a couple of really touching things to say which I copied down.

Here's a sampling:

> **A man or a society that does not react to the suffering and injustice and makes no effort to alleviate them is still distant from the love of Christ's heart. While Christians enjoy the fullest freedom in finding and applying various solutions to these problems, they should be united in having one and the**

> **same desire to serve mankind. Otherwise their Christianity will not be the word and life of Jesus; it will be a fraud, a deception of God and man.**
> **—St. Josemaria Escriva de Balaguer,** ***Christ Is Passing By***

> **You don't have an ounce of supernatural vision and it is only their social standing that you notice. Souls mean nothing to you at all, nor do you serve them. That is why you are not generous but live far from God with your false piety, even though you may pray a lot. The Master has said very clearly: "Depart from me . . . into that eternal fire . . . for I was hungry . . . I was thirsty . . . I was in prison . . . and you did not care for me."**
> **—St. Josemaria Escriva de Balaguer**

That's right on target! That's the way a saint writes. And that's the way a Catholic ought to sound in the face of indifference, oppression, marginalization, or insincerity. And so when I responded again to Fr. Arturi, I reemphasized the great blessing it would be if Catholics such as him could think of a way to make some kind of religious association possible for inmates—for Catholics who want to go deeper in their faith-walk while still in prison. I never received a response to that letter. But, the good saint knows that I wrote it, and I sought his intercession for it. So, perhaps it is a seed that will take root some day. But, I don't know. Saints are not in great abundance on this side of heaven. There are too many Catholics concerned with pleasing men (or governments) rather than God. Taking the Gospel too seriously has always been the greatest flaw of our saints, hasn't it? Imagine a man acting as crazy as Christ. Why, he'd be crucified!

Well, Chuck, I just wanted to drop these few lines to your post. I think of you often and always hope the best. I pray you are well from your illness. May the God of all mercy be just and forgiving, in accordance with the measure of his faith given unto you. The blessing of God be with you now and forever.

Dear Chuck,

Hello, my friend. I pray all is well with you and Lee. Chuck, in the past we have had some discussion about how I got to where I am today, and I want you to know my situation in my own words as you have suggested. Wow! This can be complicated. Before I even begin to explain that familiar tangle of words again, let me start by saying how much I hope you and your better half are in good health and spirits.

Now then, how I got where I am . . . After a heartbreaking break off of my engagement to a lovely girl in '94, I landed in Manassas, Virginia, with thoughts of rebuilding my life in '95. I met a very nice women (substituting actual name with Susan) who was feeling lonely, vulnerable, and at a loss for purpose in life. It didn't help that she, shall we say, offered herself in the most intimate way possible on our first date. Not being the type to "love 'em and leave 'em," I cleaved on to her. . . . Any port in a storm? The fact that she had two kids didn't deter me, either. I love children.

Susan was very reserved at first. She basically tried to hide the depths of how troubled she was . . . at least, until she could forge a more meaningful bond with me. The fact is, I'd already become enamored of the idea of being a father to her kids. More fooled. Sadly, I wasn't in much of a position, financially, to provide for them. I did my best anyway.

It becomes important to note that she had managed to tap into my deep-seated need for affection, and yes, sexual congress, to skew my judgment of her behavior. Basically there came a point in my "bliss" where I couldn't see the truth about things because I was emotionally blinded. It's still a form of selfishness when a relationship provides an emotional "fix" such that all else becomes secondary. Addicts don't realize they're neglecting their kids because they don't really see them anymore through their own hazy desires. Denial of truths becomes a way of life.

Consequently, when suspicious bruises started appearing on the children, all I did was ask Peggy [not her real name], Susan's mother, for explanations. Oh, she assured me, everything was normal, and not to worry. Susan, however, was exhibiting plenty of questionable behavior. I simply didn't want to believe a mother could be a danger to her own children. Even the Gospel marks this as unlikely. As we've seen more recently, the list of mothers who care nothing for their own kids is growing exponentially. Even more fool was I . . .

Susan beat her son Keith [not his real name] while I wasn't looking, clearly inflicting the fatal blow without my realizing it. I tried to revive him, but I completely missed the problem. I thought he was choking on milk, but he was dying from a brain hemorrhage. His little blue eyes went glassy and far away as he spoke his last: "kisses." He wanted to kiss me good-bye. That kiss turned out to be full CPR. I failed, and I didn't do it correctly . . . It wouldn't have mattered, but it wasn't until after the autopsy that I realized this. For months leading up to the trial date, I believed I might've somehow been responsible for his death because I didn't properly regulate my breathing into his vastly smaller lungs. That alone almost drove me completely insane.

When it came to light that Keith died of a closed head injury and that Susan accused me, I finally knew the truth: She killed him and was dumping the blame on me. All the signs I had ignored or denied came rushing to the forefront of my consciousness like a blast wave. Moreover, there was no one to corroborate my observations. Her family knew, but they weren't talking . . . until after my conviction. I ended up handing them my own head, and frankly, I shouldn't have.

My attorneys actually convinced me that I was culpable because I failed to report my suspicions when I had the chance. Add to that, this tragedy occurred on my premises, and all responsibility suddenly falls on me. So between legal and moral responsibilities, how much was I truly to blame? I wrestle with that one even to this day. I provided the means by which a woman could kill her own child: a private place away from those who knew her propensity to act violently to do just that.

The irony is, I went to prison while she stayed free. In short, I wound up pleading out to the most convoluted misrepresentation of the law imaginable. It's like thinking you're admitting to negligence while you're being blamed for murder as the primary agent of the crime. I truly denied myself justice by trusting my attorneys to represent me. Nary a true fact was spoken in that courtroom when they put all the sins of that woman upon me.

Well, that's a long story made short. It's still difficult to root around in these memories, but I do so mainly for the edification of those young souls who may be tempted to make the same mistake by falling into the same trap. In truth, I admit I was attracted to Susan from a desire to fulfill my lust. However, I *stayed* in a terrible situation because I loved both Susan and Keith and Tim (substitution for actual name), her other son. Despite my honorable intentions, great evil came about because I attempted to compromise the ideals of our faith. The irony is, were I more pious or more evil (one or the other), I wouldn't be in this place, and perhaps Keith would be alive.

Well, Chuck, this is the "short form" of the details. Please take care of yourself and keep me in your prayers. I'll do the same for you, my friend. Please write back when you can.

PART V

INTROSPECTION

My Dear Brothers,

Introspection to me is about examining your own feelings, thoughts, and motives in order to cope with a given situation. The older I get, the more I realize how much introspection affects my behavior or attitude. Many of life's failures are due to not realizing how close you may have been to success before giving up. Once you are able to consider all the alternatives, it all boils down to determination that drives your initiative.

Each and every one of us has been faced with insurmountable difficulties in life, but the remarkable thing is, we have a choice every day regarding the approach or mind-set we embrace. We cannot change our past, nor can we change the fact that people will act a certain way. In short, we cannot change the inevitable.

No matter what has come against you or what is causing you to slip and fall, no matter who or what is trying to push you down, you need to keep getting up. When problems confront people and they allow their doubt to cloud their determination, their faith begins to weaken. If you take on a negative posture, it will dry up your energy and weaken your spirit.

Keep in mind that God is with you. You may not sense it or see it yet, and your circumstances may look as they did for the past ten or fifteen years, but then before you know it, everything will fall into place. It is important to remember, however, that it will only happen in God's time, so be patient. I am convinced that the way I cope with life's challenges will determine the quality of my life. And so it is with you . . . We must all be cognizant of our goals and in charge of our objectives.

God love ya and God bless ya too!

Chuck

Dear Chuck,

The influx has begun. As of now, there are no definite plans to double the area I am in, but that is *always* subject to change. I thank God for his providence each day and I hope to move into the honor pod sometime this year.

We do hope to reap more men into the group. One of the men in my pod came for a while, dropped out, and try as I might, I can't get him to come back. Oh well.

It is too bad you won't be able to help with the program dealing with parenting, but it is totally understandable. Space is an issue here.

I have read both of your letters. The one about the Rodis incident is very good. All too often we want to elevate clergy to "God" status and they are anything but. We are all human. So just as the sexual abuse scandal made the headlines, rogue priests who are money idolaters are making the headlines now. The Church is a fairly large target, so I expect more, but we are not alone in this. The evangelicals have their homosexual-oriented pastors, as well as their embezzlers. Your letter reminds us that our humanity is alive and well, even in the clergy.

Your prison ministry letter was my favorite for obvious reasons! One thing I have a "problem" with is that prisoners themselves were not part of the research. I am okay with the Church and the free laity as part of the polled, but the results may have been stronger by the inclusion of how those of us who *are* incarcerated feel we are being served by the Diocese and what we feel we need in support from the various parishes. Some things may not be feasible to do, but our input, in my humble opinion, would be valuable to the bishop and to the Prison Ministry Advisory Committee and the Office of Justice and Peace. I may write my own letter to the committee and suggest this. Of course, there is no list of Christians incarcerated in Virginia, but maybe this can be the start of one.

In fact, I think I will prepare and send a letter from me—not the community as a whole. It couldn't hurt.

I pray that your letter is printed, and if/when it is, I will send one to respond to it to the *Catholic Virginian* in support of prison ministry and what it means to inmates. Chuck—well done, my friend, on both letters. Your writings are very provocative, and may they help us as Christians to see how we can better serve our neighbors.

P.S. The bells are working out well. We are finding ways to use them in our lay services and during the Rosary. Thank you for your work in getting them for us.

Dear Chuck,

I very much enjoyed reading the article on my friend, Chuck Brown. Very impressive! You had told me before that you had gone to Fordham, but I didn't know you had been at Kentucky for a year. I know that back then (no offense with the "back then" comment!), freshmen were not eligible to play on the varsity squad, so I wonder if you were coached much by the great Adolf Rupp? After the Christmas/New Year rush is over, maybe you can tell me a bit about that experience.

Speaking of college basketball, I have been a Duke University fan since I was a young teenager. Even though I grew up only a few miles from the University of Maryland campus (Hyattsville/Bladensburg area) and earned my BA from there, I've remained a Duke fan. It began when I was in eighth grade and my basketball coach took me, my father, and two other players to the ACC tournament in Greensboro, North Carolina. I was a Terp fan, but then I saw the Duke team, which had four out of five starters being white players—and they were good! Even in 1977 most teams were for the majority, sometimes entirely, composed of black players. I don't think I have anything to apologize for in thinking that way—I just got a kick out of seeing players who looked like me playing very well in a sport that didn't seem to value players who looked like me! In the almost thirty years since, Duke has continued to field teams just like that, and their success speaks for itself—twelve Final Fours, three National Championships, and numerous ACC championships.

Things are being shaken up a bit here right now. The administration has announced that this place is slated for an additional ninety inmates, with possibly more to follow after that. To make room for this population increase, they are taking away most of our "single cells." So men who have merited their single cells by being model inmates (remaining charge-free for one year or more) are now having that taken from them. One pod, the "honor pod," will be spared for now, and possibly two others, but most guys with single cells will feel the pain. Terrible.

Probably connected to this restructuring, many old-timers who have been here for years and years are being transferred. It's only been a few guys so far, but word has it more will follow.

That reminds me of something else. For a while now, I've been planning on applying to the Franciscan University of Steubenville (Ohio), seeking a master of arts in theology. I believe I've mentioned this to you before. I will be sending my application in a couple weeks, and I'd like you to fill out a recommendation form if you would—if you believe me to be a worthy candidate. I have the forms; I'll send you one and, if you agree, you'll send it straight to the University. I won't see what you'll write, so you can bomb me and I'll never know it! All said and done, total tuition would be a bit over $10,000. Obviously, this is out of the reach of most inmates. I plan first on getting as much financial aid from the University as they'll give me, and I have several ideas for asking for money from different organizations. Perhaps you and Father might have some other ideas on organizations/groups that might grant scholarships to a worthy student in need? I'd appreciate any ideas you might come up with. Challenging problem, but exciting.

Too bad you can't swing by the room here. I have it all decorated for Christmas. I always cherished the Christmas season when I was out on the street, and I figure, why should that change just because I'm incarcerated? It's not about me or my situation at any given time; it's about the glorious incarnation: God made man. With the birth of Christ, God and his people were made one again. What does me being in prison have to do with that? I choose to make merry just as I would in any other circumstance!

Okay, Chuck, I've taken enough of your time. Get back to your stained-glass windows, you master craftsman!

Dear Chuck,

It was nice to get your letter and to see you this past Tuesday. I am really glad there was a glitch in the system for our regular Mass this month because it gave you the opportunity to see what one of our "lay" services looks like. It is quite a bit different from our Mass as you could see. I hope one Tuesday after the afternoon Mass you can stick around for the evening service that we do—the Rosary and an apologetic session. These are great sessions and compliment the Mass well.

I'm not so sure if one has to stretch the positives if being manipulated. My nursing and psychology backgrounds give me some insight into that. We choose to be in certain situations and we get some kind of positive payoff because of it. You are correct that we are new creations in Christ. St. Paul says this in Romans. So you were getting some payoff with the manipulations, but God has changed you and your thinking to where this is no longer acceptable to you—the payoff was no longer important—and now you are a new person in Christ and your family's old ways will not work. That is what is so awesome about God. You can be changed. It is also a pitfall when, like me, you are in therapy and the therapist is not big on religion. This man has given me some good insight into my criminal activity, but I don't agree with the personality disorder he says I have, and we will need to have a discussion on it in the future. I do not believe that I can be pigeonholed into this diagnosis because if my addictive behavior is what drove the criminal behavior, then the diagnosis collapses. If this makes sense.

I am working on both the spiritual and regular dimensions—trying to merge them, as they must be, for me to be changed. This is not easy, but as the Kairos brothers said, this is my opportunity to find and know God and take advantage of it, even if you have to do the twenty-two to twenty-six years you have left. And that is what keeps me going.

You have great insight into our plight, Chuck. I love to read your letters and prayers; they inspire me to try harder myself and not get bogged down in the bad stuff about being in prison.

I struggle with my prayer life, wondering if my prayers make any difference. I pray for many different people, but many of my prayers are petitions about me and my situation, and I wonder if God gets sick and tired of that from me.

I am exploring new avenues of prayer and will begin to experiment with them shortly to see if I get more out of it with them. I have tried the Rosary but find it hard to meditate on the mystery while saying the prayers at the same time. I'm a one-thought-at-a-time kind of guy.

Well, Chuck, let me get going. Thanks for your letter of encouragement.

Dear Chuck,

I thought I'd take the opportunity to ride along and say a quick hello to you from me.

It was nice to see you looking whole and hearty this Tuesday past. You have been and will continue to be in my prayers, as well as those of our other brothers.

I was glad to hear that you got some enjoyment out of our birthday card to you. It seems that our mail to you is easily lost or misplaced. I suspect this has been due to the church construction and, more recently, to change from a mailbox in the post office to the new sheet address.

I was surprised to see such warm weather last week, but I sure enjoyed it while it was here. A friend of mine here in the block and I like to get out and run some laps on our weekends and days off from work. We usually run twenty laps (which is about six miles) at each recreation period. Last weekend I ran in the morning (six miles), then exercised the dogs. Then in the afternoon, I walked four miles with a friend. Then, the next morning, I ran another six miles, but I was really stiff. It might have been noticeable in my movement at Mass. And, come this Sunday morning, I'll be out again at 8:30 running laps, only this time they're forecasting 27 degrees. I'll be dressed a bit warmer, which will slow my time down. It generally takes me between forty-eight and fifty-two minutes to run the six miles, depending on temperature, wind, how much sleep I got, and what I ate the night before. Carbs help fuel my run. So does adequate rest.

Chuck, thanks for your love and support. Take good care of yourself. God bless you, your wife, and your family.

Hi, Brother Chuck,

I got your monthly letter and it is good to hear from you. How are you doing? I am doing okay after a mild setback. My wife and my daughter stopped by to see me. I was filled with joy on their arrival. My wife came to tell me something which put my heart on hold. She had to tell me something before I would hear it from anyone else. Their drive took them three hours from Fairfax. My wife said if I love her I would let her go and "move on."

Of course I felt heartbroken. I also have faith in God to know this is her plan. I love her dearly, and I know He loves her very much. I always ask God to watch over them and now have to suffer for my mistake in life. Whatever God put in front of her, she is still happy and doing better. Well, I take it that my prayers have been answered. There is another person in her life, and I hope that whatever happens, he treats her well. She is in my heart always, and I thank God for all the blessings He has given me and my family.

Dear Chuck,

In your last letter you asked some questions, and I will answer them in this letter; do not worry, I have no problems answering. In the past four years I have come to terms with many things and learned to deal with them. I am too aware that some scars are too deep for time to completely heal. However, I am living proof that in time, we can learn to deal and coexist with our pain and the past.

My mother and I have a good relationship and we communicate regularly by letter or phone; she tries to visit every couple of years, but because of travel distances, as well as financial costs to travel from Washington State, it is difficult. Last time I received a visit was in October 2004. I don't know anyone in Virginia. I hate to impose on people, Chuck; consequently, I learned early to make it on my own. I do the best I can.

I have already turned my life around; I am not in prison due to a search for quick money or being an evil person. My crime was committed . . . I don't know how or why. Part of my problem is that I do not understand my actions at that period in my life. I do not have such a problem today. I am not or have never been such a person, so how the hell could it have happened?

It is inconceivable, Chuck—that person is not me! Anyone who has ever known me can tell you that. I have no reason to lie, Chuck. I am not telling you I am innocent, please know that; I am guilty of some of those crimes, but why I did it, I'll never know or accept it.

I am dealing with it and I know God has a plan. I don't know why I was given so much to deal with, especially since I honestly don't think I was a very bad person. I always did my best and sometimes more; it just was not enough, never has been.

With that said, I can tell you that I know I can lead a good life when I get out, but I could never fulfill my dream of getting married and raise a family of my own. I don't believe I will ever find a woman willing to give me that chance, Chuck, not with a past like mine, and definitely not now with the crime I committed. I know that, and I know I'll die alone some day. Yet as much as I fear such a fate, I have learned to accept it. I am not a naive person, and I've yet to meet a woman who would give me any hope of changing my belief. I have some very good qualities a woman would like in a man, but once my past surfaces, it will all fall down again, and I am honestly too tired to take any more falls.

As I've said before, my whole life has been a struggle to survive the emotional, spiritual, and physical battles in my path. For better or worse I've made it so far. In the words of Leo Tolstoy, "I stare back at my life in horror and bitterly regret."

I guess I will close for now. Thank you for listening, and God bless.

Your brother in Christ.

P.S. Included is a poem I wrote a while back. I think it summarizes my situation perfectly. Let me know what you think.

Twenty Years Is Not Enough

Twenty years is not enough, you say
For a crime I committed in younger days.
So I continue to pay and pay every day
Don't know what I can do or say.
If I were to depart this world today
Would that be enough? What do you say?

Twenty years is not enough, you say
I too suffer; do you care? At all?
My life is over, I will die alone
Is that not enough? Need to hear more?
Endlessly I am reminded of the pain
I've caused, how many people I've let down
Of sinners and screw-ups, I am king
I wear the crown.
With tears of shame I looked down,
I loathe myself for what I've done,
What I've become.

Twenty years is not enough, you say
Have you felt my pain, loneliness, and shame?
You detest and judge me
But would you be able to walk one yard in my shoes?
Did your father hate you? Called you a fag?
Were you used by him as a punching bag?
When you got home too late
Did he try to throw you off of a bridge?
At the young and tender age of eight?
Did you see your loved ones beaten into bloody pulp?
Did you have to drag them away from daddy's hands?
Begged him to stop?
Knowing too well you'd be next to drop?
Did you ever wish you were dead

When you were a kid?
Wish you were never born?
I did.

Twenty years is still not enough, you say
What I have done is wrong.
There is no forgiveness for me,
I will know no peace, no joy or love.
You want me to pay for my sins
For the rest of my days
Well, I began the day I was born!

Dear Chuck,

I got both of your letters this week. As you know, we were on lockdown this week. It is never fun having your cell rampaged by the COs. I had small stuff taken—nothing too crazy and no charges.

Thanks for your support of sex offenders. I have no problem being here, but we all need treatment, not just the ten men in our group here. And our sentence should be based on how serious we are in treatment and how we work to change our thinking. Until that happens, prison is where we need to be.

You are correct. We sex offenders, based on the latest published studies, have a 20 percent (high end of the studies) rearrest rate for the *same* crime. The studies show a 15 to 20 percent rate. If the offender is in treatment, that drops to 7 to 13 percent. If the offender is a college graduate, the rearrest rate is less than 1 percent. Lower rates than all criminals except murderers. Ain't that something? Oh well, in time this will be figured out.

I read in the paper today that the Vatican upheld the celibacy rules for religious. Oh well. It will happen sometime. Rome wasn't built in a day!

I hope we all get out of here soon. I can understand how parole-eligible men can get upset. Since I am not eligible for parole, I don't know what that is like. I was told that this is your release date and it won't be any sooner. So here I am.

So the bells are ready. Well, not this month—lockdown messed that up.

Chuck, we appreciate the support you give; hence, the card. You do a lot for us and we appreciate it. Thank you. Your letter may be all the mail a man or two gets a month.

Regarding my own annulment case, I recently found out, through a friend, that my ex is using a new last name, not her maiden name. So I deduce that she is remarried and the annulment book I have has helped me understand why she wanted an annulment because I know how she thinks. It *all* makes sense to me now. So I can put it behind me, and understand and participate in the process at the same time. I think about them daily, but I can't disagree with my ex's decision to do what she did. The annulment, for her, is a coping mechanism. I don't think it will work well in time, but I understand her motive. You and your wife will always love your sons, *and* their wives and grandchildren, but figuring it out, you may never do that. I keep praying for you.

Election Day was a total mess. I feel for you about the choices. The candidates were nasty. But it doesn't matter who you vote for, politics is politics and not much will change. I hope that this new Congress pressures King Bush to make some decisions about Iraq. If we get some plan, then it will be a major accomplishment.

Dear Chuck,

They are going back to the single-cell pods here starting next week—this week coming up. The population increase overwhelmed the mess hall, laundry, medical, and school, as well as the H_2O usage went up—so they will decrease the population by thirty-two, moving the men from A-2 out to the other areas of this side, eight at a time, and moving in, eight at a time, from the list of men who used to have single cells. Then, in the fall, the other two pods will go single-cell again. With all the transfers to the new prison and other transfers, it should be a smooth transition back. Fights also went up. So that is some good news.

They will no longer sell sewing kits to repair our clothing. The needles were being used in the construction of homemade tattoo guns, so once again, the sins of the few punish the many.

I am now in the Commercial Foods program. I will learn to cook for the jobs in a restaurant. This is a bonus, as we eat the food that is cooked, so I will be eating well in the class! The meals we had have all been excellent so far. It takes up my whole afternoon now, but I am exercising in the morning now so I don't gain weight.

Okay, Chuck, wanted to update you. Oh, my marriage has been annulled at the first stage. It has to go to Baltimore to be retried, which should not be an issue, and then it will be official. So another chapter closes. Take care, Chuck. God bless you and God love you.

Dear Chuck,

Thank you for your letters. Since I last wrote there have been some changes in my life here. Having a regular working schedule is the primary change. I am blessed to have this teacher's aide job in the Electrical class; jobs are scarce. However, I have less time now for my exercise program, my reading, and, of course, my letter writing. The change to daylight savings time has helped somewhat. Busy is good!

I think you'd mentioned having lived on the Eastern shore. One book read was James Michener's *Chesapeake*, which centered on the development of the Eastern shore from the early Indian settlements up through modern day. The Choptank River area was the primary locale. I learned so much in that book about the Bay area and the wonderful diversity and interdependence of the wildlife there. I gather you've probably read it, but if by some circumstance you haven't, I strongly recommend it. I think you'd really enjoy it.

Considering your busy lifestyle, finding time to read anything must be a challenge. Thank you for all the love, time, and attention you put into lifting our spirits and bringing smiles to our faces. I hope your efforts on our behalf are successful and bring you the joys of accomplishing something beautiful.

It does give me some sense of accomplishment working as an aide. Most of the guys here are a bit old to be learning a trade as a vocation, but this is a trade that can always be useful around the home or as a supplement to other preestablished vocations. Plus learning anything new and constructive gives a man a sense of self-worth and personal achievement.

All in all, I'm more relaxed now. Living down here in the new dorms with my friend has helped a lot. Plus, I've made a lot of new friends, including those who meet together on Monday nights right here in the dorm for a Scripture study. One good thing here also is that we are able to attend other religious programs. So I have been attending the Messianic Jewish group who are studying Hebrew after services (we get two hours for services here). Our Catholic group continues to grow as well. Father is great! Take care, my friend. God bless you! Please convey my love to my brothers!

Dear Chuck,

Man, it was good to see both of you Tuesday afternoon! I guess we did a good job pulling off a service since Father was indisposed. However, go figure, we went on lockdown at 6:00 P.M. So for the second month now, we couldn't recite the Rosary. Our Good Friday service, as you heard, really went well. Only a couple of minor glitches. I enhanced a wooden crucifix so it could be carried on a pole, i.e., broomstick handle. However, it wasn't placed on the "things–we're-allowed-to-have list," and so the commanding officers wouldn't let us have it—for security reasons. Anyway, without saying how I really feel about that, next year I'll be better prepared. I'll bring a couple of newspapers and roll them up into a small pole. Ha! There's more than one way to . . . well, you know!

I'm glad you and my aunt had a good talk. Many of the people she used to know aren't around anymore, and many times I'm sure she's quite lonely. She really misses the D.C. area and its social life. I was never much of a fan of all that, especially being enlisted. The officers' club was always very uncomfortable.

Anyway, at this point in my life, and for some time now, in fact, it's been my mission to try and be there for her when I get out. All the more reason why—as you can imagine—I need to be released as soon as possible.

I'm not optimistic about my uncle's health. Even as a child, my aunt was the only one ever really there for me—besides my grandmother—out of the whole family. More so than even my uncle in the way of love and affection. He is a man's man and can be cold quite often. I believe a more accurate term could be "exceptionally narcissistic." It's something I believe my wife was nervous about. So my aunt very well may be all alone if something happens to him. Thank you very much for calling her. I'm sure it made her day a little brighter.

On another note: I was going to attempt to answer some questions you had asked regarding the parole board and their objections/intentions. Specific with me at least is the fact that they really know nothing about me. They're not aware of my mental health issues with depression, stress management, and addiction to pornography and sex that existed back then. Nor how it is all connected and how it contributed to how and why everything back then happened. They are also fully unaware of how far I've progressed in overcoming the above illnesses to a very productive degree.

Instead, they rely on hidden information which they don't permit the public to see. They, in my case at least, rely on a pre-sentence report which is 30 percent or so filled with false testimony and tainted evidence. They're not aware of how the Commonwealth Attorney railroaded my case and produced the tainted evidence and fostered the false testimony by even enhancing the testimony's damning portrayal of what happened.

The parole board is unaware that the civic attorneys did this in part to bolster their careers. One went on to become a federal prosecutor and the other a general district court judge. The board is also unaware of how my attorney failed to represent me to the best of his ability because of the pressure put on him by the other side. How he lied and deceived me regarding his intent to help me.

It's common knowledge that compared to other cases worse than mine—but not necessarily as bizarre—I should have received no more than twenty years, instead of life plus eighty years. Just look now at how the men in the Duke Lacrosse case were being railroaded. They, however, got lucky. Very lucky!

I'm not innocent, of course, but the process of prosecution remains the same. And that's all the board really considers—what the prosecution has delivered to them on paper.

So, in effect, I'm being sentenced all over again because my attorney, and even the judge, believed I would do only fifteen or sixteen years and then be released. Instead, it's the board's intent, and it is now the norm, that I do twenty-three or so years.

There is no accountability here. The public and lawmakers are unaware of how and why the board does what they do. And, in part, a huge part at that, they make their decision based on their feelings about what one did twenty or thirty years ago. They give no feeling to the fact that we are now older, some more mature, and more and more, we're getting too old to even re-offend.

The large number of people who return to prison nowadays who were out on parole are doing so because of their inability to abide easily enough with the strict, and oftentimes, unreasonable parole guidelines, and the massive amount of fees they're required to pay just to be so-called "free."

Well, my friend, that's it in a nutshell. Of course, it's all much more complex and involved than explained, but you know me—I can go on and on! So I better close for now!

Oh! Before I forget, check out this joke, real quick!

> **Joe had always dreamed of flying helicopters, so he bought one and took lessons. During his first solo flight, the helicopter went up and up; and then it went down, down, and down—hard!**
>
> **"What happened?" asked the instructor. Joe, as he climbed out of the wreckage, said, "Well, it's like this. I took her up to 1,600 feet—no problem. So, I took her up to 2,000 feet—and no problem. Then I**

> **took her up to 3,000 feet, and I started to get a bit chilly, so I turned off the ceiling fan!**

Sorry Chuck, I gotta get some help!

Dear Chuck,

I had a counselor at another correctional facility tell me when I did my receiving interview that if it were up to her, because of crimes against my own child, she would never let me out of prison. I told her it was good that she was not my judge or my counselor. There is a lot of that mentality here with staff. You have people with a high school education and zero people skills watching us. Think Abu Ghraib.

You are correct in your questions about letting our fears control us, especially our feelings of unworthiness. Our only way to get out of the "rut" is to trust in God and live a life in God.

In my addiction studies, I see this pattern of unworthiness and shame, and it fits with an *overwhelming* number of us here. People who say they don't need God are fooling themselves.

The cooking class is awesome. We had pancakes, sausage, cheese omelets, and banana-nut muffins for one meal, and pizza, French fries, and Jell-O with pears for another. Man, was that good! First time in three and a half years I had French fries! I am exercising to make sure I don't "blow up" from the food.

Dear Chuck,

I received our bundle of the *Catholic Virginian* papers just this morning, and your letter came in this evening's mail. My response to H's letter was a bit of a knee-jerk reaction, in that when I read it, I felt it demanded a response, and real issues needed to be addressed rather than the ones Mr. H. perceived or wished to paint over in your very fine article. It rolled off my pen and was posted without reduction.

I appreciate your compliments. They give me encouragement to pursue a project I've been working on and I hope I'll survive to see through. I'm (slowly) collecting resources on restorative justice. My hope is to produce a monograph on the subject. I want to write a book for the common man that will explain restorative justice, describe current models, and encourage folks to apply the principles in their personal and public lives.

In the past eight months we have had two groups meet here to discuss restorative justice with Sylvia Clute, a retired attorney who is promoting it in Virginia. She has published a novel called *Destiny Unveiled* that is an interesting teaching tool, and has a website.

Regarding our mutual friend: I had missed him for a couple of weeks but saw him today. He's on crutches, fresh after having a knee replaced. I'll pass on your salutations in the morning.

I'll be glad to drop you a line now and again. It is good to be able to network on church matters—and restorative justice issues if you like.

Until next time, then, be assured of my thoughts and prayers for you and your ministry. God bless you!

Dear Chuck:

Greetings and salutations. Hope this finds you and yours well. Thank you for your letter; it is always a pleasure to hear from you. I really enjoyed your article on "What's in a Name." Good writing, it gets an "A." And I shall certainly keep you in prayer for your upcoming skin cancer procedure. Has Mr. Hopkins considered working two jobs? I did when I first got out, Monday–Saturday, going on four or five hours of sleep a day. I was doing hard physical work, and I remember being soooo tired. But I was willing to pay the price, and gained my independence. You know, I spent twelve years at Staunton Correctional Center. Good, good people up there. I'm still in touch with a few folks from up there.

I really liked the heart of your message in your letter to all the brothers. Self-worth, self-respect, and self-esteem are definitely traits lacking among the incarcerated. I guess that it's human nature that if we're told it enough, we start to believe it. Also, I think the subconscious realizes things the conscience can't quite put its finger on. Given those two things, the prison system seems to be designed to eat you down (mentally) and keep you down. We are subtly degraded many times every day. People just accept it after a while. I'm not surprised you hear plenty of negativity (I do too); this place is a breeding ground for it. And in all probability, what you see is the cream of the inmate crop. Not only are these places full of all sorts of criminal activity (drugs, violence, weapons, gambling, prostitution, etc.), the majority of the men in here have hardened hearts and criminal or downright evil intents once released. You probably see those with a good heart and good intents.

I think this is one of the dilemmas of our justice system: how to accurately identify which a person is. For the good of society and the sake of the innocent individuals, the former must be dealt with accordingly, keeping in mind that a heart can change. And the latter, for the sake of justice (can it even be called justice if fairness is absent?) should be dealt with accordingly, keeping in mind that people can, to varying degrees, backslide. Thus, I wholeheartedly agree with you that many have paid way more than what any reasonable debt assessment would require. I think I heard once that that's why Johnny Cash always wore black, for the man in prison who had long since paid for his crime.

I've got to tell you though, given that nothing is perfect, for the most part I agree with our "new" (1995) abolishment of parole law. I think for the most part judges try to be fair, and now a man does the time a judge gave him. That's one reason I believe a man should go back before a judge for parole consideration. Our parole board has clearly stated and demonstrated that they will not be fair, knowing that the laws are such that it's very difficult for anyone to do anything about it. I know just what you mean about being so busy. Been there, done that, hope to be doing it again soon.

Thank you for complimenting my attitude. I must confess, though, some days it's a battle to stay positive. And some days I lose that struggle so badly it's a slaughter! Then along comes an encouraging word (your letter, this time), and I get myself back into the right frame of mind again. Of course, you know what my battle is, and that's what the parole board has done to me, and the price I've already paid. I told my boss my situation. He has ruffled feathers that his tax dollars are paying for my incarceration, and asked me, "How in the world are you supposed to swallow that pill?" My answer was I haven't swallowed it, and some days I choke on it. I know very well that negativity is self-detrimental. I think my problem is I am not acclimated, and reality does not escape me. And though it would be easier, I don't think I want any of that stuff. You're right, what we think is so important. It's the foundation of Joyce Meyer's *Battlefield of the Mind.*

Here's my favorite: An old Indian told his grandson that inside every man is a great fight between a white wolf and a black wolf. The white wolf represents all that is good and noble, the black wolf all that is bad and evil. The young boy asked which wolf will win? The old Indian answered, the one that you feed, for it will be stronger. But neither wolf can ever die.

I must get ready for work, such as it is. Thank you for your letters. You are indeed a light that shines through the darkness. God bless, and peace be with you.

Dear Chuck,

Jambo. Thought I'd add some culture to my correspondence. Got your letter; good to hear from you. Hope this finds you and yours well. Not much new here, but I'm beginning to suspect it's that way by design. All your hobbies sound very interesting, things I would enjoy. I'm definitely not a couch potato. I don't watch any sports on TV, but I'll go participate in a pickup game. To a large extent, my work is my hobby. To me, repairing, renovating, and remodeling houses is fun. And I get much satisfaction from a job well done. I make it look "beautimous," as a customer's kid once said.

Since it doesn't appear that any of the politicians contacted on my behalf are taking any action, I'm beginning to explore legal avenues. After all, it was the politicians, as a whole, who created these laws that set up the parole board as a functioning tyranny. How did I violate parole when I was never granted parole? How can they now make me serve the good time I earned in prison for something that isn't even a misdemeanor conviction, that happened three years after

I got out of prison, when I completed my sentence? How can they give me eighteen years for the exact thing a judge had just released me for? What happened to Constitutional rights such as ex-post-facto, double jeopardy, and due process?

My biggest problem is I have no knowledge or experience in doing legal work. I am totally, 100 percent clueless. I do realize there's a reason lawyers go to college for four years to learn how to do this stuff. I had the money to hire a lawyer, from when I sold my house when the parole board violated me. A couple years ago my dad was in danger of losing his house, so I sent him my money to prevent that. No matter what my circumstances, I'm not gonna let my dad lose his house when it is within my means to prevent it. I don't regret it, and would do the same thing again. As of yet, he hasn't been able to repay that money, and may never be able to. So, since I can't hire an attorney, and I can't do it myself, the only other option I can see is to enlist the help of one of these jailhouse lawyers. To my way of thinking, this is like hiring a handyman to build the Taj Mahal, but it appears it's all I have available to me at the moment. And our law library here is about the size of a lawyer's bathroom, with one typewriter and no computer research assistance. How inadequate does that sound?

But I am college educated, so I'm gonna go fumble my way around and see what I can find. The theory being, even a blind squirrel finds a nut every now and then. I know I have several points in my favor, and my common sense tells me what I'm looking for is there. It's just a matter of knowing how to find it and how to use it. Two judges have already let me go on this, but that was with an attorney's help. I think it's a crying shame that anyone can even be in the position I'm in right now! My dad has been sending me pictures that I sent him while I was out. Pictures of my girlfriend and I before and after, of my house, the inside of the house all decorated at Christmastime, etc. . . . Sitting, looking at a shot of she and I in our den, I said out loud, "Damn, baby, we really blew it." I got some strange looks, which I ignored. I sure did lose a lot, Chuck, a whole lot!

The consequences of my drug usage wreaked total havoc in my life. Those consequences alone were a steep price to pay. Of course, many a drug user has paid those same prices. And I include the court's ruling in that price. But what the parole board has done, I feel like I've just been charged $300 for a Snickers bar! It just ain't right; it can't be! Chuck, I voluntarily admitted my substance abuse problem and asked for help getting into a treatment program. What I did, I did in the privacy of my own home. I paid my taxes, and matched others. I gave people good paying jobs. I bought houses and brand-new vans. I did volunteer work, I helped the needy and less fortunate. And now, once mine, my family's, and your tax dollars are paying to keep me locked up, in spite of what two judges have said. It just isn't right, and as Forrest Gump said, "That's all I've got to say about that" (for now).

So thanks for letting me vent. Take it from an HVAC technician: lack of ventilation will cause something somewhere to overload sooner or later. You may have just saved my compressor! Nothing else much going on here. I've figured my actual working hours are about four per week. About half of this 100-man dorm I'm in sleeps until ten or eleven every morning. I wonder how this is preparing someone to reenter society. Every day at 6:00 A.M. I was in the Lowe's parking lot waiting for the doors to open. Apparently the Department of Corrections thinks my work ethic needs to be corrected, but I ain't goin' for it! These people will ruin you if you let them.

Well, I'm gonna end on this mini-novel for now. Thank you for your friendship; it means a lot to me. As soon as my situation is rectified, lunch is on me. Take care and God bless you.

Dear Chuck,

Prayers for the health of your household. I am enjoying Ken Burns's series *The War* immensely. I trust you have heard about it, and I imagine you are watching it as well. He's done a marvelous job with it so far, and I am spellbound by the sublimity of its content. God forbid that our world should ever again find itself so given over to evil forces—yet, I cannot but doubt the collective memory of a nation. It seems an uncannily predictable fate, repeated over again throughout history, that the next great war follows soon after the residual dissipation of man's remembrance of the last one. I suppose this is why they come in 100- to 120-year intervals. Maybe the advent of television and other communications technology will prolong the residue this time around. Let us pray so.

I had to chuckle when you revealed the sentiments of your neighbor's friends. Yes, it would often appear that everyone in prison is innocent . . . at least to hear them talk. As a prisoner, however, I am struck often by the candor of most inmates. The vast preponderance of those with whom I've spoken about the events which led them to this place do not beg to be indulged. They are normally the first to proclaim their guilt. In fact, some of these guys are literally rhapsodic about the facts of the crimes they've committed, reveling in them with animated delight as they retell their escapades to anyone who will listen. It sickens me to watch. Like watching a pig that simply has no compunction about wallowing head-deep in his own excrement.

Nevertheless, it is worth pondering the reasonableness of a person who feels as though he is innocent, unfairly convicted, or disproportionately sentenced to take the time and effort necessary to let someone know about his grievance. After all, the many thousands of prisoners who do not write lengthy letters about such things are obviously satisfied that justice (or some form of it happily ensconced in their heads) was well served. So, I assume that what your friends would like to learn are the challenges of living in a prison environment. Truth be told—this is a kiddie camp with a lot of picayune rules and petty regulations. Modern penology, in my estimation, is the equivalent of a poorly run train depot designed for overnight guests. Taxpayers who imagine that prisoners are suffering from the inhumanity of yore will be sadly disappointed.

Well, this place is a laughingstock. It's a doggone joke! Which is precisely why I don't understand why the taxpayers enjoy spending so much dough to send rather low-level miscreants to a place where they merely graduate to become mid-level miscreants. That is plain idiocy. Stupendous ignorance. The state is not simply housing criminals; it's training criminals! That IS the real story of prison life in America. Anyone who says different is either profiting from it (in some way—even if only politically) or he's a bald-faced liar.

There is somewhere a wonderful quote taken from a U.S. Supreme Court opinion some years ago wherein something is said to the effect of "the petty thief has every right to protest that his right to due process and equal protection has been wrongly violated when he is convicted of grand larceny." I believe that this may in fact be part of the problem with present criminology. The deck is stacked against citizen defendants, and a great number of people are held to stand trial for charges that there is rarely enough substantial evidence to prosecute—yet, the prosecutions get convictions anyway because everyone knows (if he's wise enough to pay attention) that the rules of appellate procedure make it next to impossible to overturn a conviction. The prosecutors know this. The defense attorneys know this. Most important, the lowly (lower) court judge knows this.

Worse, still, is the fact that whenever a man's life is ended in an unfavorable verdict, should it ever turn out that he was actually innocent, or that he was convicted for a crime he didn't actually do, or that he was denied a fair process to face his accusers—if any of these things are ever discovered, it is nearly impossible to hold any of the irresponsible parties personally responsible for their negligence and tortuous harm. This is the greatest weakness in our criminal justice system. ANYONE who is so naive as to think that our law enforcement, our prosecutorial professionals, or our esteemed jurists are to be presumed honest, diligent, or irreproachably moral in the conduct of their public trusts is living in a castle in the highest sphere of the heavens. Mark me carefully. I did not say that there are no honest, diligent, or moral public servants. I am saying, instead, that they no longer deserve these presumptions. And, that's why it's important to change the law so that they can be held personally liable when they ruin a man's life in the courtroom.

It would also help to change some rules of appellate procedure so that an appeal is more favorable to a defendant. Most important of all, altering appellate rules to favor a defendant, and making law enforcement, prosecutors, and judges liable for their mistakes (by abolishing the last remaining vestige of Divine Right: absolute immunity) will make it much more likely that a citizen is given a fair trial the first time he stands trial. The American system of justice has always sought to secure the rights of the citizen against the insidious powers of government. *Civis Americanus Sum!* This should be a citizen's only necessary plea. Yet, in reality, the Roman citizen was far better protected from his government(s) than we are. What on earth has gone wrong?

It is my contention that the lynchpin to every single aspect of prison and criminal justice lies in the single issue of voting rights. And I believe that we face this "square-on" as the civil rights challenge of our epoch in history. Over 650,000 prisoners return to the streets each year, and every single one of them should receive the automatic restoration of his voting rights. Not everyone will register. Fewer will actually participate. But only a blind man cannot see that over a period of ten to twenty years, a substantial block of voters would gradually take form among ex-felons. (The only ones who aren't blind to this daunting reality are the people working overtime to prevent an automatic restoration of voting rights.) Imagine, if you will, a voting block consisting eventually of some 10 million ex-felons who are organized and who vote in solidarity on issues affecting prison living conditions and criminal justice. This would be a force with which to contend. By the time I am fifty, this one geopolitical constituency will be considerable in size. And it will still remember its own experiences. What I am describing is a nightmare reality for neoconservatives and right-wing fundamentalists. But it is writing on the wall, and is as good as accomplished already. Those who favor an ever-increasing criminalization of behavior and a steady growth in prison populations are unwittingly creating their own political doomsday.

Moreover, once organized felony begins to recognize its own political muscle—say ten to twenty years from now—it will work to let loose thousands more prisoners who are now doing time under the sentencing reforms of the early- to mid-'90s. This will serve to strengthen its posture even further. The phase which follows—twenty to thirty years out—will see the gradual dismantling of the entire behemoth of prisons built from 1985 to 2005. Prisons will then be reserved for the worst of the worst, and no longer used as instruments for social engineering and societal aggression against marginal behavior.

Will there still be crime? Of course! Will it be worse? Who knows? America's problem is a whole lot harder to diagnose than what meets the eye. Our problem is that our experiment in self-government has entered into a phase of torpor which will ultimately be followed by an age of "strong men" and eventually devolve into severe crisis. This is not shocking to people of historical acumen. Indeed, it's predictable. We are very much like a star that burns its very brightest before it implodes. Our implosion requires only two things: a crisis significant enough to compel the willful abandonment of first principles, and a paradigmatic shift in global markets such as we witnessed in the late 1700s. The first has already occurred and the second is taking shape (check out the status of the dollar as of late). Perhaps it is fair to say that we are primarily held together by the sheer force of faith most people have in their belief that everything is okay. Yet for centuries the Church has focused on *one*_chief indication of the health of a society: the status of its families. Little more need be said about how far along the path to destruction we likely already are. So I guess what I'm saying is that crime rates will be the least of our public concerns in thirty years. Holding our republic together will consume all that we have—and the very idea of locking millions of people up will be a waste of money and resources nobody will be enthusiastic about supporting.

I have not even allowed for the contemplation of nuclear meltdown in the Middle East, the continued depletion of oil resources, the destruction of a couple of major U.S. cities by renegade terrorists, the rise of an armed segment of anarchist Americans, etc. . . . All these possibilities are in play. And, oddly enough, it is the government's present nervousness about these unknown factors that is leading to the very causes which, in turn, perpetrate greater and greater danger to the foundational principles of American government. We are in a kind of self-destruction mode that I only occasionally hear an outcry against . . . and then often with calls for the worst possible solutions put forward (a new Constitutional Convention, a directly elected president, a greater reliance on international law, etc.).

What we need is a return to the original framework for government and a restoration of the virtues which made us a great people:

limited government (including, of course, massive overlays of law enforcement at every level), a firm commitment to the fundamental rights of men (chiefly to be left alone by government), and an economic system that is based upon the agrarian model (which is most aptly summarized in the writings of antebellum southerners and affirmed by Pope Leo XIII).

Politically, our system should be streamlined from top to bottom, with Congress taking on more responsibility for the machination of government; leaving the president to execute congressional mandates (the original concept). I also believe that the two-party system ought to be demolished and replaced by a multiparty system more reflective of the great diversity of American culture. Coupled with that (as almost a necessity) would be the repeal of re-apportionment so that Congress would swell to a size large enough to ensure that no single congressman represented more than 80,000 American citizens.

Well, I know you must be getting tired of hearing (reading) my gibberish, so let me dispense with further divagations. I appreciate your encouraging comments and unmerited compliments. You are a fine man with a golden heart and a glowing love for Christ our Savior. I thank you for your friendship and only look forward to the day when I can help you more effectively in the work of God. In the meantime, be blessed and well and let us join our prayers together for kingdom come.

Dear Chuck,

I am glad to hear that you have decided to proceed with your book. I hope to help you in any way possible. It is high time we all start looking out for our brothers and sisters. If we don't, it's unthinkable what this country and the world will be like in the next ten to twenty years.

Whether we realize it or not, the justice system and its errors affect every one of us, the incarcerated as well as the non-incarcerated. We are all touched by either having someone we know in prison or paying higher taxes in order to feed the monster.

Just recently it was announced that due to budget cuts, Virginia would have to restructure its budgets. The very first budgets to be cut in Virginia were funds for education. One who knows about the prison systems in Virginia knows that $2 billion prison projects were just completed and more are in the works. It also takes millions of dollars annually to run the prison systems. Even with the new prisons being built and two recently opened, our local jails are overcrowded because there is no room to send those already sentenced to prison. It's high time we start looking at avenues other than locking someone in a 7x12-foot cell with another person and reserve our prison cells for those who cannot possibly function in society or are an immediate threat to life or limb in local society.

You already know a small bit about me and my case, but this was given from my point of view. In order for you to come to know me best, I think it best to give you evidence ascertained by another person. Being that you were once in the FBI, I'm sure you are familiar with a pre-sentence report. If not, this is a report produced by a probation officer and details almost every aspect of a person's life. The probation officer basically profiles you and ascertains what the best course of punishment should be.

My main reason for having this sent to you is not because I believe you do not believe me, but more because it is factual evidence of my life and the thoughts the probation officer had of me. Unfortunately, this is the busy season for my mother's business and she will be on the road until December 1. When she returns I will have it sent.

As per your letter I received today, you will be focusing on rehabilitation (as if that actually happens), and reintegration into society, so I will try to keep my correspondence on that track, though I may stray a bit.

I hope what I have already written is readable, as it is 2:30 A.M. and I can't sleep, but my cellmate is so I am writing with the lights off by using the floodlights outside that seep into the cell through a 1½x2-foot window. Nevertheless, it is still quite dark. I have to work at 9:00 A.M. tomorrow (well, today), so I'm going to try and get some sleep.

It is my opinion from what I see here that 80 percent or more of the people in prison have at least one of the following as the cause for the commission of a crime: low or no education, financial stress, depression, and/or strong psychological problems, most of which can be controlled with proper counseling or drugs. Imprisonment only serves to enlarge the latter three problems, and if they were not existent prior to imprisonment, they will be there at least in minor form upon release. The financial stress is evident. Most times the released no longer have the properties previously owned. They get out without a job, without a car, and often without a driver's license. They more than likely have court fees that must be paid, and maybe even child support debt. Many of them don't have family support, and if they do, it is very limited because of their own financial woes.

I can count myself lucky for the most part, financially speaking. I have family support. They have paid all my fines, have bought much of the stuff I will need when released, and own their own business where I will be employed, if only temporarily. Even still, I will owe about $9,000 in child support, and that is only because I worked a deal with my ex-wife, stopping support on my daughter. If it had continued I would have owed $25,000, plus or minus.

It's my belief that many who are released have big problems financially and finally decide they need the fast cash to make it, thus turning to crime again. If they get away with it, their problems are over. If they get caught, the stress and problems are over because you go back to prison where you get three hots and a cot. For too many it is a hopeless cycle.

If you come in here depressed, unless you are able to focus yourself into a positive outlook (usually through religion), your depression will only increase. You are usually taken away from everything that brought a slight bit of happiness, i.e., hobbies, friends, and family. This is then doubled by the unknowns: How will I survive once released? How will this affect my life? What will I do for work—will anyone hire me? And the list goes on. The Department of Corrections does very little to help with any of this. A large amount of vocational programs here are basically nonessential jobs or training. How many inmates will get out and get a job where you will need to know Microsoft Office without additional training? I taught a small engine-repair course where you never touched a working engine or did any actual troubleshooting. No one will hire you with that training. What's more, if you get a certificate in one of these classes, you cannot take another vocational course for at least five years.

The psychological problems produced by prison are numerous. At the very least you lose some of your ability to interact properly with others. You spend twenty-four hours a day, seven days a week, surrounded by criminals with criminal minds. There are basically two types of people in here: those who don't care about making friends, only having a couple and living a semi-reclusive life (like myself), or those who want to have many friends. The latter, which is the majority, generally take on at least some of the traits of all their friends—usually negative traits.

The only psychological help available is given to the more severe cases. This usually consists of minimal counseling (usually a short monthly meeting to monitor), and a treatment of not getting to the root of the problem but a pill to keep you somewhat under control while in custody—and the pill line is huge!

Basically prison only benefits those without an education by providing the chance to get a GED if you don't have a high school education. But even this is limited by the overabundance of the non-educated and lack of enough classrooms and teachers. You can almost forget about a college education, at least in here. About 75 percent of correspondence courses have gone to Internet bases and they won't allow us Internet access. Then there is once again the financial aspect of those courses.

So what do we as a country do? The United States has the highest crime rate and incarceration numbers of any other country in the world per capita. I think it is also important to note that we are the least educated of all the first- and second-world countries. It should be obvious that prison does not work to stop or lessen crime. We have tougher sentences with longer prison terms, yet the crime rate still goes up. We should be studying these other countries in order to see why their crime rate is so much lower and implement a system such as theirs.

We need to get away from prisons, except for those who are the most violent or those who pose an immediate threat to the community. We need to stop labeling people as violent when there was no act of violence associated with their crime. In my case, I am perceived as violent, yet there was no physical violence or contact with the victim, nor was there a threat of violence. They look at it as though I did this, so I have the potential to do much worse, and therefore we better get him off the street. It's no different than saying that during an argument with your wife you raised your voice, so next time you might hit her, and therefore we better put you in prison in order to protect her from this possibly happening.

We at least need to move to a second-chance type system for everyone not involved in a medium to violent crime, this being either physical or an actual threat of physical violence, i.e., armed robbery. With today's technology we have the ability to monitor people better, so the lesser crimes with no actual violence or threat thereof get probation, and the threat that if that probation is violated they go to prison. I realize that this is somewhat what we already have, but right now we think prison above all. Instead, we need to focus on probation first. With that probation, some of your freedoms are taken away, sort of like house arrest, but instead of a curfew-type deal where unless working you can't be out past 10:00 P.M. unless otherwise cleared by the probation officer. A full-time job must be held and state-run counseling programs pertaining to the crime attended.

It's my belief that at least 50 percent of those given that chance would not recommit a crime because most of the four factors given for commission above would not be multiplied by the prison experience.

By doing this you reduce the number of prisons and amount of money spent to house and feed people. That money can be shifted to employing the people needed to oversee the second-chancers and the equipment to do so. The criminal remains in the community and is of economical benefit to the community, as he/she would have to buy his own stuff to live on and would be paying taxes to the government through property, sales, and income tax. That money could be used to better our education system, and the more educated someone is, the less likely that they will be dealing drugs or committing robbery. The majority of crimes in prison stem from this. The majority of murders are related to gangs and drugs.

The nation as a whole is about entertainment. We just want to have fun. It is unreasonable to think that our children are not the same. Because education seems to be one of the first budgets cut in all matters, our teachers are underpaid. Because the teachers are underpaid, they are not energetic about their jobs. They go to work with a humdrum attitude and that is passed on to the children. Learning, then, is no longer fun. As they get older the child may find something more entertaining (hanging out with friends) and skip school to do so, or even quit.

If a teacher is energetic and tries to make learning fun, the child also becomes energetic and wants to stay in school and learn. In order for this to happen, our teachers must be better paid.

The most important thing that we as a nation and even as a world need to get into our heads is that this is not a "me" world—it is a "we" world. Everything I do either directly or indirectly affects everyone else in the world. Recently the talk of the news has been the MRSA outbreaks. In one interview I heard a CDC representative mention that in England, there has not been an outbreak outside of the hospitals. This made me think about the possible reasons. What I came up with was this: Hospitals have a large number of people in various health conditions, but they are dedicated to the diagnosis and cure of these conditions. The symptoms can be spotted there and treated prior to release back into the community. Prison numbers are low there. Here the prison numbers are high. People of various health conditions are in close contact all of the time. Disease is easily spread. Those people are then pushed back into the community carrying whatever they have. Health care in prison is a joke, and they are released without any physical screening. It's then passed unknowingly to our family and friends, and then our children bring it into the schools, another place with close contact and high numbers, and all of the sudden it appears. In a way prisons are detrimental to our children in many different ways. Thus, as I said, everyone directly or indirectly affects everyone else.

Well, Chuck, please keep up the good fight for the dignity of man, and may God bless you, your family, and all of your endeavors.

Dear Chuck,

Well, my friend, enclosed you will find my response to Mr. H. I put it in an addressed, stamped envelope for you to forward to the *Catholic Virginian*. I thought you might wish to read it first. I sat down and started to write as soon as I could. I figure it may not be published because it is too long, but who knows. The *Catholic Virginian* can use all or part—anything that will help. I might have taken this in a different direction, but right now, I am too tired to rewrite it. Hey, I'm a high school dropout, diagnosed at age twelve as being dyslexic when they discovered I could not read. Of course, that was a few years after I got out of a wheelchair—and six or so years after I was raped. Life can be a little unfair.

I spent most of two days on the enclosed response letter, so I must get to bed now. Tomorrow, Sunday, will be makeup time for the other five letters I must write this weekend. Yes, Mr. H. took up nearly twenty-four hours of my time.

I wish I could write better . . . You are right, Chuck—Mr. H. doesn't have a clue.

> *Letter written by this inmate to a local Virginia newspaper, in response to a "Letter to the Editor":*
>
> **Dear Sir:**
>
> **As I read B.H.'s recent letter, "Criminals Need Change of Heart," I couldn't agree more with him. Criminals need a change of heart and more. So how can we Virginians help to facilitate a change of heart for the nearly 40,000 Virginia prisoners? His suggestion is to lock criminals up and throw away the key—claiming the state cannot change the hearts of individuals (evidently, he hasn't visited any of the forty-eight prison facilities in Virginia).**

Wanting to give Mr. H. the benefit of the doubt, I reread Chuck Brown's April 23rd letter, "Whatever Happened to Rehabilitation and Restoration?" I was shocked by Mr. H's harsh criticism of Mr. Brown's letter, without providing any substance of his own. I, like Mr. Brown, see the danger of poorly thought-out laws and ordinances that put more people in harm's way in the name of prevention. Mr. Brown "advocates policies that help reduce violence, protect the innocent, and offer real alternatives to crime, and resists policies that simply call for more prisons and harsher sentences." After the prison expansion program I saw in the '90s, whereby the number of Virginia prison beds was increased by 138 percent, I don't believe Virginia needs or wants to bear the cost of policies like I have seen that only advocate more prisons. It took nearly ten years to completely fill the new beds with Virginia prisoners at the cost of retaining thousands of rehabilitated prisoners to keep the extra beds full. In the process, the expansion made the Department of Corrections the largest employer in the state, and made Virginia the state with the largest number of prisons per square mile in the nation.

I was shocked that Mr. H thinks "treatment programs" cost millions in tax dollars. Treatment doesn't have to cost the taxpayers, but if and when it does, the cost is far less than building new prisons to warehouse more inmates. Some correctional centers in Virginia hold Alcoholics Anonymous meetings. I know of one that is run by three outside volunteers who do more to change the hearts and minds of the men there with their weekly meetings than any sixteen-week AA program a prison counselor can provide. And it's free! Bon Air Baptist Church Prison Ministry and the Northstar

Community offer a twelve-step recovery program that takes over a year to complete, a reflection of those prisoners with hearts going through change. And it's free! Yet this program isn't accepted by prison counselors.

I have spoken with Catholic volunteers who want to bring the word of God to the prisoners weekly, as a few other prisons allow, but were discouraged by the prison administration (it was only within the past year that they were allowed to visit . . . progress without a mind-set for rehabilitation is slow). Ironically, Mr. H. calls for a change of heart, yet these free human resources are being squandered.

At one correctional center I am aware that a doctor—an eighteen-year veteran and chief psychologist—runs an intensive therapy group of ten hand-selected men out of a thousand to deal with the underlying issues of why the offenders committed their specific crimes. He does not have to facilitate this program. He goes out of his way to provide real rehabilitation, yet he lacks the support from Central Classification in Richmond, Virginia, to retain a full group of men long enough to complete his program. Shortly after I spoke with him about the lack of support, I contacted my congressman on behalf of one of his patients that was recently transferred with no regard to the importance of the program to the prisoner, the community, or his doctor to keep the group together. This particular prisoner has been tormented by the crime he committed. I wonder if politicians would change if people started demanding accountability. I can't see change coming unless it starts from the top. This one doctor doesn't need more money for his program—just more support!

It costs more than just money to neglect prevention of crime. Any political system that neglects rehabilitation and restoration of errants is not working for the people but for their own interests. I think of the extra years and extra money wasted on Jack. Jack was convicted of grabbing a shiny necklace from between a woman's breasts (I am not trying to minimize Jack's actions or the impact he had) at a public pool in Virginia. His first felony. Jack became a sex offender shortly before the doctor I am referring to went to work for the Virginia Department of Corrections. Yes, you can locate Jack on the Virginia Sex Offenders Registry—that is why I'm not using his real name. What makes Jack unique is that the prison system diagnosed Jack with schizophrenia and put him on medication where he became the nicest guy I have met. When Jack was sentenced, most judges understood that a prisoner would serve 65 percent of the total sentence if they were a model prisoner; but Jack was forced to serve the full twelve-year sentence (even though he was a model prisoner) in order to keep prison beds full during the '90s, and because of the parole board's fear of paroling sex offenders.

In December 2006, the doctor shared with me that he has never seen Virginia parole a sex offender in the eighteen years that he has worked and treated sex offenders for the Virginia Department of Corrections. Fear keeps people in a box and makes for bad policy. Jack became eligible for parole after seven years. Had he been paroled then, there would have been $150,000 extra to be used on youth projects. Jack has been a productive, tax-paying member of society at the same job for the last ten years in northern Virginia. I just think of the wasted capital that

could have been better spent. There are plenty of Jacks in the Virginia prison system that made mistakes, whether as a result of mental illness or being under the influence. Most are not career criminals in need of a lifetime of incarceration.

Mr. H thinks that "there needs to be a continuing dialogue on crime and punishment, responsibility, and rehabilitation." I disagree! That should have been done *before* fear-based laws were enacted. Now, all we can do is clean it up. Mr. Brown is right. The time is ripe for some changes that promote prevention from all angles. Our prisons are only a small portion of the problem, but they need to be more than an expanding human warehouse.

Dear Chuck,

Greetings from the Big House. I received your letter with your monthly update letter to all the brothers. It is always great to hear from you.

Over the long Labor Day weekend, I was able to relax and finish up my portion (questions, essays, and term papers) of both my ICBT courses and get them in the mail this morning. I still have the proctored exams to do, but they are given to me. At this point, I feel I'm done and released.

Wow—seventy-one! You don't look a day over forty-six. Yes, I know . . . I'm going straight to hell for being so truthful. Have you ever read the book *Tuesdays with Morrie*? It's a story about a professor dying of amyotrophic lateral sclerosis (Lou Gehrig's disease) and a reflection of the aging process. A longtime friend recommended it for my reading—a great story.

Well, my friend, persistence helps. I found a book—not only on St. Theresa—but by her. It's *Story of a Soul*, the autobiography of Saint Theresa of Lisieux. Last night, I added it to my nightly routine before saying the Rosary. Or, to be more truthful, what part of the Rosary I get done before falling asleep. Some nights I make it through; others, I wake up with my Rosary in hand.

Yes, I'm my boss's sucker. The guy he goes to when he wants the job done right. Why did God make me so meticulous?

The day has progressed and I'm waiting on a shower so I can call it a night from the jungle. With pen in hand (pencil), I can pass the evening hours.

This week church services were canceled for both Monday and Tuesday. A bit of a surprise. Here the Brothers meet twice a week from 6:30 P.M. to 8:00 P.M.

My boss goes much further than "pour me a cup of coffee . . . man, you are good . . . how did you do that?" He tells me to give him a cup of my personal coffee (instant coffee) and expects me to prepare it and add one of my personal sweeteners to it. There is something about personal servitude that rubs me wrong. I think, Get off your butt, your lazy butt. My friend, I'm counting the weeks until I am transferred. Hey, if I did make the deposits for him after church collection, the church would probably see an increase in deposits. He's the type of guy God has blessed because God knows he needs all the help he can get.

I've been looking forward all day long to curling up with St. Theresa's book tonight. I have barely gotten started, but I know where I want to be. Unfortunately, I have about four hours of writing to do before I reach that point in my day.

I am so sorry to hear about your wife's recent scare. I had no idea your better half struggles with MS. Consider her in my prayers. Something I don't take lightly.

If you are joining the Diocesan Prison Ministry, I don't know how you are going to fit it all in.

Your first question to the board could be, "Why does the largest prison Catholic community in Virginia lack missals?" A few weeks ago when we had trouble getting the full Catholic community together (we have three separate units—like three separate prisons that coordinate one large church service), only my section could meet, and not a missal among us.

Not only does medical science tell us that "people with a determined, feisty spirit get well quicker than people who are prone to be negative and discouraged," but those who are able to forgive others easily are happier, healthier people.

My longtime friend's home was recently burglarized. The police suspect their home was staked out for some time. I feel the pain they must have been feeling. He says many of the pieces were one of a kind. His wife lost all of her jewelry. So much of the stuff was family heirlooms.

Well, my friend, I need to wrap it up. Thought I would go out for pizza . . . Oh, I keep forgetting they have medication for such delusion. I'm waiting on God. I just wish we were using the same watch.

Chuck,

Hi! How are you? Sounds like you're busy from your letters. Sorry I have not responded sooner, but I was very sick last week. The beginning of the holiday season since I have been incarcerated always seems to make me ill. I know it is just depression, and every year I say I am not going to let it get to me, but it does. I get so depressed about not being with my family, and I think about all the people I have hurt, disappointed, and let down, including our Lord. But through the grace of our Lord I am better now, a new creature in Christ!

Thank you for your letters. I shared them with the men and the volunteers. All of us are very excited to meet our new priest. As a matter of fact, our volunteer stated that he spoke about his coming to us last week at their parish council meeting; apparently he will start after the New Year. Last night we met and had a little Advent service, and then I led discussions on Advent and Immaculate Conception. I think it is important to clarify the Immaculate Conception, especially with many people in our congregation who are converts. These discussions are sometimes difficult for converts to grasp, and are new to the faith, and I don't like to get too in-depth so as to confuse anyone. It is easier for me to give these lectures, as I am the chaplain's assistant here.

I guess I can tell you a little bit about myself. I am forty-five; I was born and raised Catholic in Long Island, New York. I am retired from the U.S. Navy after twenty years. I was a sonar tech, and after I retired I worked for Lockheed Martin on sonar systems. I have been married twice. I have two stepchildren who have my last name: a boy of fifteen and a girl of twenty-two. I was found guilty of the rape of my stepdaughter in a trial that lasted two hours and that she didn't testify in. The night before, my lawyer had said, Don't worry—the case is going to be nil-processed.

I know you began your career with the FBI, and I am sure you have heard it all; I may be guilty of a lot of things in this life, but rape is not one of them. But apparently the Lord had a plan for me, and has me just where he wants me. I have spent enough money on lawyers and appeals to feed the children in Darfur for a long time, and I have not gotten any relief, but I digress.

My stepdaughter has recanted her story, from "No, he didn't do it," to "Yes, he did"—too many times to too many people. So I just leave it alone now. My stepson and I are very close. I don't consider him my stepson—he is just my son, and I am his dad, and he has no other dad but me. His mother (my ex) and I are still pretty close. She doesn't believe I am guilty of what they charged me with, either. She says they could have given me a thousand different charges, but I wouldn't accept a plea, so that is what they stuck with.

Enough for now about me. I just pray for all our futures. I consider myself lucky to have a retirement check coming, plus I have been investing for a number of years, so when I get out, I won't be destitute. I do worry about finding employment. Who would want to hire a fifty-year-old felon sex offender. So I may have to open my own business. I am into fishing, or perhaps I'll see if they will give me an ABC license so I could open up a little pub/restaurant. I am going to be taking the HVAC course so I will have something to rely on.

Thank you for all the hard work you do for us. Our prayers are constantly with you. May you and yours have a blessed Christmas and the happiest of new years. May the peace and blessings of our Lord Jesus Christ be with you always.

Dear Chuck,

I received your last letter with your tales of Department of Corrections rules and regulations. Victory can often be snatched from the demon's jaws if you have an effective toothpick. Anyway, I am still praying for you and your wife, and I still desire great comfort from your letters, so keep 'em coming.

Yesterday, I got all my books and software for my computer degree program. So, I'm riding a pretty good high at being able to work toward restoring my future. My biological mother in Michigan sent me a letter a while back, which explains much. My real parents in Florida are doing very well after feeling sick from their northern exposure. All is truly well for me. I pray that your personal affairs are doing well, too.

Life here continues to be quite challenging, but with the Lord's help, I'm making it through. These folks here keep making up stupid new rules as they go along. As duly elected inmate representative, I'm being shut out from meetings. The administration doesn't even have the temerity to provide us a forum in which to air grievances. If things keep going the way they've been, these guys are liable to throw a "tea party" like the one in Boston over two hundred years back. I've gotta get outta this place.

Well, I'll close for now in order to get this into the mail and on its way to ya. May the Lord continue to bless and keep you all the days of your life.

Dear Dr. Chuck,

Always nice to hear from ya! Received your January 20 letter just in time for me to answer over the weekend.

Sick is not the way to begin another year. Not the way I would want to do it. Do hope both of you are feeling better.

Regarding a recent *Richmond Times-Dispatch* article, I haven't seen it. You mentioned we should be spending money on rehabilitation and preventative programs. I agree. Apparently the parole board does too. The parole interviewer this year told me, "It [parole] is all about whether you will remain out." In the absence of rehabilitation is an absence of parole. In fact, I wasn't asked anything about how I might succeed if I were released. I was asked only two questions. The first: "How long have you been in prison?" The second: "Why were you transferred from the previous corrections center to this one?" Doesn't sound like much of an interview.

Since the Catholic community here has been divided into three autonomous groups, I don't receive regular copies of the *Catholic Virginian*. The December issue was the last one made available to us. So if your article is published, please send a copy. I am delighted that my example of dealing with the cold was helpful.

Over the years, I have completed every possible course, program, or therapeutic group I have been allowed to attend and complete. Most no longer exist within the system. Here's the funny part: In seventeen years, the only program I was specifically instructed to complete is one I don't qualify to enroll in. Go figure! Today, I see the Department of Corrections as a human warehouse. Every year at my annual review, I'm told to remain employed and infraction-free in order to fulfill my treatment plan obligations.

Limiting access to volunteers is just another way of removing the obstacles to warehousing. Clearly the Department of Corrections is a warehousing operation. Any pretense to the contrary is a smoke screen. It has been that way for over fifteen years. Parole was abolished, then they overexpanded the prison system from 13,000 beds to 31,000 beds in the '90s. Then it took over ten years to finally fill those extra beds with Virginia prisoners—all along, keeping men years and years longer just to keep those beds full. In the process, program after program disappeared. Educational courses were limited. I must say I saw a lot more programs before in other facilities than I see here. I could go on and on. I only pray my next transfer will be a prelude to parole. I think it will be. That is the hope that keeps me looking ahead.

Time to move on to something on the bright side. I know God has paroled me—I just wished he would get with my schedule.

My celly had charges brought against him by his twenty-seven-year-old nephew who claimed something happened ten years previously. He was in the ministry for forty-one years. Afterward, he started his own business. In fear of his nephew trying to sue him for his assets, he put everything in his daughter's name, with her having power of attorney. His thirty-three-year-old daughter had lived with him for the previous ten years after the remarried mother of the children threw both out of the stepfather's home.

Recently his house sold. Then he received a letter promising a visit for Christmas and some money. Christmas came and went without a word. No Christmas cards. Last week his daughter wrote claiming she is so hurt by what had happened (him going to prison and the impact it had on her) that she wants nothing to do with him. In the letter she refers to his money, and included the $305,000 from the sale of the house as her money . . . looks to me as if Satan is at work.

I would have missed church for the first time in many years had not the volunteers showed up. I don't like being hassled about church. I'm also sick of doing my boss's job for him, so I have decided to seek employment elsewhere. I'll lose about ten cents per hour, but I'll work a fraction of the hours and get paid for the full 120 hours each month. I'll also be able to go to church and Bible study unabated. Plus, I'll be able to get some much-needed exercising going again. I should have done this long ago. I figure I still have four to six more months to go before I see the inside of the next correctional center.

Dear Mr. Brown,

I am currently working with one of the men you visit at our correction center. He informed me that you often correspond with Virginia inmates, and that you thought it would be a good idea if I introduced myself.

I have been incarcerated for the past twenty years of my life. I was introduced to the Virginia prison system at the age of twenty-two. Because I am what is considered an "old-law" prisoner; I am eligible for parole. Although, despite my best efforts, and they are extensive, I have been unable to convince the parole board that I am worthy of a second chance at life.

When I committed my crimes, I was married, had a seven-month-old daughter, and worked as a heavy equipment operator. Once I was convicted and sentenced, my wife divorced me. I saw my daughter once after my first three years of incarceration. I waited fifteen years to see her a second time, but I am so glad I have a second chance with her. She will be twenty-one in May. There is so much I need to do for her, but it seems as though there is so little I can do from in here.

I haven't wasted the years I've spent as a guest of the Virginia Department of Corrections. I earned my GED while in jail. I used the Pell Grant in '92 and '93 to take several college classes, but was not able to earn my associate's degree until 2005. Classes were offered under the Youth Offender Grants, and I was permitted to take the classes if I paid for them myself. It was not an easy endeavor, but well worth the time and sacrifice.

I also earned certification as an electrician's helper through a vocational program at Keen Mountain. Then, after being transferred here, I earned certification as a personal computer operator. I work in the shoe shop, which is part of Virginia Correctional Enterprises. I'm currently using a computer to write an instruction manual for the entire shoe shop, and once the book is complete in Word, I'll be creating a PowerPoint presentation. I like being able to use the skills I learned in computer class. Without the shop allowing me to do this, I would probably forget most of what I learned from the seven months of instruction.

I've written a few articles related to prison issues. More specifically, a detailed article on the effects of federal mandates for the current "85 percent laws." Many believe it was a state-initiated response to crime, and a "tough on vrime" policy by Virginia lawmakers. However, it was an initiative by the federal government that was tied to hundreds of millions of dollars in federal grants to the state which motivated lawmakers to enact the "85 percent laws."

If you are interested in corresponding, I would be glad to answer your letters. I don't usually type the letters I send because I believe my handwriting is legible. I'll answer any questions you have. I participate in a program called "Educationally Straight." It is a program that allows college groups, juveniles, and executives from the Federal Institute to speak directly to small groups of prisoners, when those groups schedule tours of the institution.

I thank you for taking the time to read my letter. I look forward to hearing from you.

Dear Chuck,

Thanks so much for your March 6 and April 28 letters. It is always a pleasure to hear from you. I am looking at your March 6 letter, and wondering how you found the Prison Ministry Board meeting. I expect it was like sitting at a table with dilettantes spinning their wheels. Prisons aren't a priority. We lost our advocate when Bishop Sullivan retired. Bishop Francis DiLorenzo, I'll bet, has never set foot in a prison.

All the aftercare and mentoring that I've seen done by the church in the last thirty-two years was done by the network of volunteers going into the prisons. Things I've never seen are an institution, like a Catholic-sponsored halfway house, or an offer of services from Catholic Family and Children Services. The Protestants are way ahead of us in this area.

Your comments on the Holy Spirit in your April letter took me back to the night of my confirmation in June 1978 at the Virginia State Penitentiary. I'd like to tell you *all* about it sometime, but not today. I really just wanted to let you know I enjoy your letters and I remember you at prayers.

I can't often write as much as I'd like to. I'm glad your wife Lee enjoyed seeing the broad-pen lettering on the envelope. Wish I could do more of that, too.

If you come across a text of the Second Chance Act as it was passed into law, would you mind sharing it? Thanks.

I'll sign off for now. Thanks for all you do in the prisons. *Dio ti benedica!*

Dear Chuck,

Sorry for the delay in getting back to you! I could offer a short list of excuses, but that would be in bad taste. So to be outright honest about it, I've just gotten very lazy about writing anymore—to anyone. In recent years, it seems that letters to me have dwindled down to practically none, and when the warnings about letter writing to inmates went out to volunteers, well, that really took the wind out of my sails.

Well, as usual we didn't get much of a chance to talk the last time you visited, and believe me, you are one person that I think I could spend a few hours with and walk away with a great deal of peace and understanding and clarity. I regret deeply that I don't have that opportunity.

I'm doing well, and I really can't complain, although it's so easy to find something in here to be disturbed about. But because I'm so blessed with comforts in here that I know others don't have, and because I do have people on the outside that do care about me, I have no right to be upset . . . about much at all! And besides, even though I'm not happy about the "amount" of time I'm comparatively doing, I have to remember a very valid point someone made to me a while ago: "If I don't like the ride, I shouldn't have bought the ticket." That is why I am resolved to get back what I gave away a long time ago—to live the life that I want to live, with the good and the bad, the rough and the smooth, all marked by my own choices and not someone else's. My incarceration *was* by my own choice, and not someone else's, but I gave my power away and was influenced very strongly by lies and deception, by jealousy and fear. I was so trusting and naive that I got sucked into a way of thinking that was self-destructive.

So now I guess my personality could be considered as a shy, quiet, loner type, but I'm not antisocial. I'm very protective of myself and what I believe in because I can at all times be so easily influenced, even when I know better. I regularly try and find some sort of middle ground with people, and it amazes me how many people are willing to compromise their own self-worth by not requiring more of themselves. I gotta tell you, Chuck, the truth has gotten me in trouble more times in my life than I can remember. It seems people would prefer that you go along with their lies, or play along with their social masks, just so they'll feel better about themselves. That's part of my social dilemma: I don't dance that dance! That could make for a very lonely lifestyle.

I believe it is going to be tough for me to make it out there financially, so I'm considering a number of different possibilities for earning extra income in my spare time. Greeting cards from my own photography work is another possibility. Currently, I haven't started any new projects because art supplies have gotten so expensive. We're only permitted to order from one supplier, and the minimum shipping can be as much as $8.00. There are still several projects I'd like to work on: another sailing ship, lighthouse, and a jewelry box. So maybe by July I'll be able to start again.

I've really been amazed at how far our faith-based church group has come over the last couple of years. I believe we've vastly and steadily improved in how we do things, and that we still have room to do more. At some point I'd like to see us get together a donation in some form to a worthy cause once in a year. I would also like to see us move to another room, one that's larger. If we want to expand in membership, moving will be necessary. Also, it would, of course, be more comfortable for everyone to move around. I'm not sure that we necessarily need to have tables. But wherever we go, there will be tables there anyway.

I realize that you've felt very restricted about writing, and that it's been very discouraging for you as well because of the new volunteer writing restriction. At least for myself (and I know of others as well), I miss hearing from you. Also on a personal level, I feel a little uneasy that you were taking on the writing to so many of us each month, and that no other volunteers were sharing the burden. I think one volunteer's idea of seeking out pen pals from the parish is a good one, and maybe could still be pursued.

Well, till later, big guy, please take care. As always, thank you for being you! And, also, for being such a good friend.

EPILOGUE

The population of incarcerated people of all ages is growing around the world. The United States has the largest prison population, followed by Russia and China. It is alarming that the United States has 5% of the world's population and 25% of its prisoners.

For centuries, societies have dealt with people who hurt others or cause harm to a community through ostracization or pain. Today, the term "warehousing" is frequently used when referring to the incarceration of human beings. There are combinations of reasons that cause the growth of the population behind bars. When those reasons are discussed, it's often to let the (voter eligible) public know our political leaders are "tough on crime" and working to keep us safe. But is it safety they seek or is their purpose really to control a population of poor and desperate people? The inability of those people to afford a proper defense in our so-called criminal justice system, and a growing opportunity for big business to profit on human misery may also be factors in the prison population explosion. Changes in laws in the late twentieth century related to drug offenses, and the lower tolerance for repeat offenders (the three strikes rule) likewise contribute. Parole boards are growing increasingly tougher about granting parole. The consequence of denied paroles and harsher sentencing is growth in the prison. As prison populations grow, governments have given the management of the prisons to private enterprise. More prisons are built, but even these cannot keep up with the population growth. And in all parts of the world, the shift of population from rural to urban areas for economic reasons and the growing populations of refugees who try to escape violence and insecure living conditions, cause economic and family disruption, leading to more criminal activity. Finally, inmates are not always provided proper and adequate rehabilitative treatment while incarcerated and so are not prepared for the life that awaits them after they re-enter society. The lack of treatment often results in recidivism.

And, let's not overlook for a moment the business of running a prison today. It is a huge and profitable enterprise. The for-profit side of running a prison began to explode in the 1980s when incarceration rates began increasing dramatically. As the need for additional prisons grew, a large group of private businesses saw opportunities for their own growth and sought a piece of the action. These include architectural and construction companies; food service contractors; all sorts of equipment, hardware and other suppliers of steel doors, razor wire, communications systems, and health care and medical supplies. And of course, we don't want to overlook the vast need for uniforms and assorted weapons including products for restraint, such as chemical sprays and taser electro-shock guns that emit 50,000 volts of electricity that can kill. And there's much more. The care and feeding of a couple of million humans takes a lot of supplies. When you total it up, it equals big business, and it gets bigger with every new prison. Unlike our oil supply today, there is no need to worry about running out of prisoners.

The big players in this growing industry are the private companies that run the prisons. And the ones they run are even more gruesome than the public ones. Private, publicly owned corporations with shareholders always need a growing revenue and profit stream and strict cost control to maximize the bottom line. That means understaffing, low pay for poorly trained staff, and poor and unsafe conditions. Also, private contractors are not obliged to pay wages or benefits and can take full advantage of all those bodies free of charge. Why would they ever pass that up. It's one more revenue and profit stream.

The private side of running prisons is still a small part of the total, but it's growing. This growth does not bode well for the country. How we treat our disenfranchised and underprivileged speaks volumes about our strength and integrity as a country.

There is positive news and hope for our justice system. On March 11, 2008, the United States Senate passed legislation that will reduce recidivism rates and give ex-offenders a second chance at life. (The Reducing Recidivism and Second Chance Act of 2007 H.R. 1593). The President signed the Bill into law on April 9, 2008. The legislation is designed to reduce the number of convicted felons who became repeat offenders, help make communities safer and ensure that former offenders successfully transition back into society by providing states and non profit prisoner-reentry organizations funding for job training, substance abuse treatment, mental health assistance and other support services to help ex-offenders reintegrate into the community.

Specifically, the new legislation authorizes a total of $324 million to

- Improve existing state and local government offender reentry programs by authorizing $50 million annually for the Department of Justice's state and local grant program, incorporating best practices from the reentry field, and requiring the measuring and reporting of performance outcomes.

- Create new competitive grants for innovative programs to reduce recidivism. The bill authorizes $110 million each year in new grants for state and local governments and private entities to develop and implement comprehensive substance abuse treatment programs, academic and vocational education programs, housing and job counseling programs, and mentoring for offenders who are approaching release or those who have been recently released. The bill requires grantees to establish performance goals and benchmarks and report performance outcomes to Congress.

- Strengthen the Bureau of Prison's ability to provide reentry services to federal prisoners and establish an elderly non-violent offender pilot program; and

- Authorize $ 2million for grants for research and best practices relating to innovative drug treatment methods, causes of recidivism, and methods to improve education and vocational training during incarceration.

It is perceived that the legislation could eventually save American taxpayers hundreds of millions of dollars, given that, on average, the annual cost of incarcerating a prisoner exceeds $20,000—a number that increased six-fold between 1982 and 2002.

The Second Chance Act has tremendous support from over 200 local and national organizations, including a wide cross-section of civil rights, justice, faith–based and community organizations. The American Bar Association, the Justice Fellowship, the Leadership Conference on Civil Rights and the NAACP, among others, have been instrumental partners in ensuring that this legislation offers ex-offenders hope for the future.

One of the most effective means for aiding in the rehabilitation process during incarceration is the introduction of faith-based programs. Many of our concepts about the criminal justice system come from the media. Popular television shows about detectives and the criminal justice system include scenes of courts and prisons. Movies help form our thoughts about criminals, about innocent people who are wrongly accused, and the efforts of former inmates to re-enter normal life. News stories show us details of crime and violence both outside and inside prisons. We hear about prison abuses, overcrowding of prisons, and we keep death row watches. More and more often, individuals know of a person who is accused of a crime, incarcerated, or who has suffered from violence. As our experience with the criminal justice system becomes personal, individuals will have a variety of responses. One response might be a desire to bring healing to the brokenness of the situation. This is one way God calls us into ministry. For others, some incident or happening occurs in one's life that brings about an awareness of pain and suffering of others. God has many ways of getting the message delivered and He is the one who calls each of us into ministry action. We are challenged by the grace of God to forgive, to judge not, and to restore right relationships with other people.

Because faith–based programs are so effective in bringing about change in behavior and attitude, churches, synagogues and faiths of all denominations, are encouraged to raise awareness of the benefits of prison ministry. There are numerous ways to bring awareness and connect human need with biblical principles. For example:

- Invite a prison chaplain to your place of worship to preach and teach about their work.
- Provide a newsletter that informs parishioners on the issues of the criminal justice system.
- Invite volunteers and ex-inmates to share their stories and how the ministry has affected their lives.
- Hold a Sunday school class that might be a bible study, current events study, or an introduction to restorative justice and peace making techniques.
- Mentor a child whose father or mother is incarcerated and who may be struggling in school.

For those who come forward to ask questions about the ministry, tell them to pray about the ministry and encourage them to solicit prayers from others in the congregation asking them for God's direction and to guide your discernment of ministry.

Once an individual has been called to serve in this ministry they will soon learn that many of the men and women they minister too are searching for God's love and forgiveness. They have nothing to gain from a volunteer, except what we can offer in the way of friendship, understanding and compassion.

We do not ask about their crimes or ask about the length of their sentence. Many are embarrassed to discuss their crimes. If they wish to volunteer that information, we do not share it with others. What is most important to these men and women is to know that we are sincere in our compassion for them.

I want to share a few comments from a few inmates I have visited in prison. I believe their words of gratitude for volunteer's offers a compelling reason to answer God's calling to this ministry.

"Among its many benefits, prison ministry provides spiritual care-and who can doubt the close relationship of spiritual development to rehabilitation in general? This, for many is every bit as important as other areas more commonly associated with rehabilitation, such as education, vocational training and therapy."

"By introducing aspects of "real-life" into a prisoner's existence, a humanizing affect occurs. Generally speaking, exposure to what lies beyond the walls helps prepare us for what lies beyond these walls! It lessens the culture –shock, this interaction with "real people."

"Many of us in prison, for various reasons, have been abandoned by our families, friends and other important people in our lives. We may have infrequent contact with people on the outside. Some of us have visits and some of us have never had a visit. The importance for us to have contact with people in the free-world in a spiritual context cannot be underestimated. Volunteers give us hope, love and faith."

"The volunteers need support from more caring people to help them in Christ's mission. They need more volunteers to offer the "light" to us in here who are lost, confused, abandoned, hopeless, and saddened with the outlook of life. Most of the time, it's only volunteers who can make a difference to those of us in prison."

People have often asked me, "Why do you visit the prisons Chuck?" My answer, "What better reward can I ask than for the gratitude of another human being?

God love and bless all of you.
Chuck Brown

Chuck began his career with the Federal Bureau of Investigation while attending Fordham University in N.Y. After serving a number of years with the Bureau, he joined Coopers and Lybrand Management Consulting practice, now known as PricewaterhouseCooper's. His career ended in retirement from PwC after serving many loyal years in senior management positions including assignments from the Secretary of Navy to lead and perform industrial operational improvement programs for the U.S. Navy's shipyard and aviation depots across the nation. Chuck and his wife reside in the Blue Ridge Mountain region of Virginia. Today as a retiree, Chuck is actively involved in Prison Ministry and is a member of the Catholic Diocese of Richmond Prison Ministry Advisory Committee. Additionally, he is a newcomer to the art of stained glass who has already created numerous stained glass projects, nearly all of which have been donated to charity fundraisers.

Chuck is also a licensed pilot, certified NAUI Scuba Instructor, licensed U.S.C.G. charter boat captain and sport parachutist.